Monday
Morning
Cooking
Club

It's Always
About
the Food

Monday Morning Cooking Club

It's Always About the Food

Lisa Goldberg

Merelyn Chalmers

Natanya Eskin

Jacqui Israel

Lynn Niselow

Photography by Alan Benson
Styling by David Morgan
Design by Daniel New

HarperCollins*Publishers*

Contents

Foreword

By Joan McNamara

Food should be fun, simple and shared. There's nothing I love more than feeding people with both food and love. That's the philosophy that is brought to life at Joan's on Third, my gourmet marketplace/cafés in Los Angeles. It's also what the Monday Morning Cooking Club celebrates: creating a space to bring together family, friends and community around food.

Many Australians drop in to Joan's, perhaps lured by the vibrant gathering place we've created, the rustic communal tables and the irresistible food. One day a visitor from Sydney, Lisa Rosen, started chatting with me about the Monday Morning Cooking Club and their stunning first book. Lisa's mother, a Hungarian Holocaust survivor, is featured in the book, and she was touched by how her recipes were now preserved in print. When she explained that the book is an anthology of wonderful home cooks and family recipes, and that the Monday Morning Cooking Club meets and cooks every week, my curiosity was piqued. I love any mention of 'family recipes' and adored that it was a group of women cooking together. I am part of my own cooking club (of sorts), with an eclectic group of creative, inspiring women. 'The Spoons' meet and cook every month, sharing great food, friendship and stories in total abundance.

The grapevine works well, and only days later, Monday Morning Cooking Club's Lisa Goldberg was visiting the United States, had a book in her suitcase and dropped by Joan's on Third with a copy. I was enchanted by how beautiful it was, but, more than anything, it reminded me of my mother's comfort cooking. As the daughter of hard-working Czech immigrants, where life revolved around the kitchen, I learnt at my mother's apron strings and absorbed her countless secret recipes. There was a connection I felt through the book's stories of Jewish women cooking across generations.

Since those early days, the Monday Morning Cooking Club women have become great (and delicious) friends. I was honoured to host their first Los Angeles cookbook launch in 2013 at Joan's on Third and, since then, both their books have always been sold in our stores because they are in synergy with my philosophy. I'm thrilled we are only one plane trip away, and over the years all the women have dropped by to say hello during their travels. There's nothing like a warm hug, an omelette and, of course, a chocolate brownie, to cure their jet lag.

So that the Monday Morning Cooking Club – and you, the readers – can have a bit of me at home, my chocolate brownie recipe is on page 304. Hope to see you all in Los Angeles very soon!

The MMCC Story

In the Beginning

For the last ten years, people have asked us, 'What do you do?' We pause, take a deep breath, and try to explain the Monday Morning Cooking Club. We started as six passionate and unstoppable Jewish Sydney women who just wanted to create a beautiful cookbook. A book that would sit alongside the best cookbooks in the world and tell the story of our food-obsessed community. We would operate as a not-for-profit group and hoped to raise some money for charity along the way.

Over many cups of tea, and of course the odd piece of cake, our project slowly evolved into what it is today – a commitment to collecting the very best recipes from our community, and an intention to honour and share stories of immigration, survival, joy, family and connection.

Time really does fly when you're having fun. Little did we know that in just ten years we would have produced and published two bestselling cookbooks. For our first book, *Monday Morning Cooking Club – the food, the Stories, the Sisterhood* (2011), we drew on the best-loved, most precious family recipes and stories from our local Sydney Jewish community. Encouraged by its success, we then broadened our scope to collect recipes from the Jewish community right across Australia with our second book, *The Feast Goes On* (2014).

It's been ten years of meeting the girls every single Monday morning. Ten years of collecting, selecting and curating recipes from our community's kitchens. Ten years of testing – prepping, cooking and tasting dishes from around the world. Ten years of sharing (many things), laughing (often hysterically) and arguing (in the best possible way). Our sisterhood has endured and enjoyed a roller coaster of challenges and successes – from the low of our first rejection by a major publisher, to the sense of achievement when holding a copy of our first published book in our hands, through to the joy of the likes of Nigella Lawson, Nicole Kidman and Yotam Ottolenghi telling the world how they love our books.

So here we are, ten years on, still meeting every Monday, and now Tuesday, often Thursday and electronically on all the days in between. We are continually inspired by our community's love of family, friends and celebrations, which always seem to revolve around food. And we love nothing more than talking about food – especially when we are eating at the same time.

Heirloom Recipes

Our passion is finding those precious family recipes passed down from the older generations, which have never been written down and would otherwise be lost – those recipes without weights and volumes, with a 'handful of this' and 'a pinch' of that. Our joy is to modernise and accurately document these heirloom recipes and make them easy for any cook to follow, no matter where they live. It's not just the recipes from the older generations that matter – we also need to document and preserve the dishes that feed and nurture our generation, our communities, and our families.

What a thrill when a handwritten recipe on yellowing paper lands on our kitchen table. So many seem foreign – dishes that we've never even heard of, let alone tasted. We've worked hand-in-glove with cooks – or families of cooks – to learn, understand and master these new dishes. The result is a collection of fail-proof recipes that we hope will find a new life in kitchens and on tables around the world. Our motto is 'contemporise traditional recipes and traditionalise contemporary ones'.

We are Curators

We are not merely idle collectors, pasting together other people's recipes. We are wholeheartedly committed and involved curators. For each book, we receive hundreds and hundreds of recipes. Every single one is a gift to us and so special. We take the time to review, consider, test and taste them all. We wish we could include them all. We thank each and every person who took the time to share their food memories with us. Even though many were not included, without all of them this book would not be possible.

Our books are a partnership between us and our adored cooks. We have so many conversations back and forth by email, phone, Skype and standing together in the kitchen, where possible. We learn something new almost every day and the final, often collaborative, version of a recipe becomes a legacy to treasure. Sometimes, the recipes you see here are our version of the original, converted for home cooks all around the world to enjoy. Thank you to all our wonderful cooks – without you, there would be no Monday Morning Cooking Club. We are privileged to be the trusted gatekeeper of precious heirloom recipes.

The Sisterhood

It's hard to believe our sisterhood has been together for so long. We're asked all the time if we still get on. The answer to that question is a definitive yes: we actually have an amazing bond. Monday has become the best day of the week for each of us. At the same time, we have become great friends, confidantes, advisors, therapists, parenting experts and fashion consultants to each other. If only there was a hidden camera to capture the never-ending banter, the hysterical laughter, the circuitous debates and the regular eye rolling. What's the best way to seed a pomegranate? How can you not remember where the rolling pin is after ten years? How much salt should we add, a measure or a pinch?

Since our last book, Lauren and Paula have taken a step back out of the test kitchen, and we now welcome the delightful Lynn; we are thrilled to have her on the team.

The Global Search

In 2013 we decided to hit the US food scene with gusto. We ran around from early to late, from the hallowed halls of Martha Stewart and NPR radio, to cooking demonstrations at Williams Sonoma and Eataly, to book signings and media interviews – all while *fressing* at every café and restaurant we could squeeze in. We did private charity events, public book signings and scoured every store for our books, delightedly introducing ourselves to the shelf stacker at Barnes and Noble.

As our first two books made their way to kitchens across the world, we realised that the community created by the Monday Morning Cooking Club had actually stretched further than we had ever imagined. We realised we just had to document the food of the global Jewish diaspora for our next book. We reached out to friends old and new, and to home cooks around the world, and spent the next two years searching for recipes that come from the heart, much-loved dishes that have been feeding family and friends for years.

Through emails, Instagram, Twitter, Facebook and even the old-fashioned postman, we heard stories of people's love for food and cooking, and the importance of the family table. All over the world, the ritual of cooking grounds us, connects and nurtures us.

And so this, our third book, came to life. *Monday Morning Cooking Club – It's Always About the Food* is a delicious and rich, story-filled snapshot of cooking in the global diaspora. It is a wonderful collection of recipes on its own and the perfect complement to our earlier volumes. We have found some of the very best cooking from our global community. This book holds the most delicious family recipes – not from a restaurant or a test kitchen, but from the heart of our homes.

May these stories and recipes inspire us all to take the time to cook, to share, to eat, to talk and to sit at the table, together.

~ The MMCC girls, 2017

Visit us at www.mondaymorningcookingclub.com.au

The Sisterhood

Lisa Goldberg

I am now happily entrenched in the Monday Morning Cooking Club as Chief Pot Stirrer, a delicious change from starting professional life as a solicitor. It has been such a joy since 2006 to be with this truly amazing bunch of gorgeous women to produce and publish three extraordinary cookbooks. I am a *fresser* with enormous (and sometimes unbridled!) passion for food and cooking. I hang on to the part of Jewish culture that embodies the saying 'it's always about the food'. This project has changed my life and pushed my obsession with food to a whole new level.

Any time I have a spare minute, my first question is, 'What shall I bake?' I adore shortbreads and butter cakes and pretty much anything related to bread. But what I really enjoy is creating salads from scratch, whether it be the salad bar lunch where everything is on the table, or our family favourite, quinoa, fresh herbs and walnuts with a tahini–yoghurt dressing and barbecued salmon (page 118).

Merelyn Chalmers

Monday mornings are the best time of the week for me. I love spending time with the MMCC girls and bringing my food PR experience to the team. What I love about this project is sharing cooking tips and techniques, teaching unconfident cooks that cooking can be fun, and talking about food till forever.

I have a pedantic respect for well-measured ingredients and classic pairings and I just love the precision of my digital scales and a freshly sharpened cook's knife. The challenge of baking pastry and desserts really appeals, though my everyday cooking focuses on filling our plates with delicious salads and vegetables accompanied by a well-spiced roast, whether meat, chicken or fish. My go-to dessert is fruity, healthy and sweet, like baked apples stuffed with sultanas (golden raisins) and brown sugar (page 218). I have inherited my mother's passion for searching out elusive ingredients, believing I can cure any of my family's ills with food and endless cups of tea.

Natanya Eskin

Working with MMCC for the last ten years has meant that my three children have basically grown up asking me every time I cook something new, 'Is this a tester for the next book?'

I have always been happiest in my kitchen, cooking for my family. I have also developed a strong passion for uncovering and preserving recipes, especially from the older generations. My guacamole (page 40), just a simple avocado dip, is now a regular on all the MMCC girls' tables, and their friends' and families' too. And so, a tradition begins ...

This amazing project has given me so many opportunities. I love talking about all aspects of food on the radio, and I now even enjoy standing in front of a crowd at food markets and cooking schools sharing what I have learnt.

The best part is standing in the MMCC kitchen with the girls – our sisterhood – discussing and debating what to cook, laughing and sometimes crying together, working as a team to create something special for generations to come.

Jacqui Israel

I joined MMCC for a 'one-year project' and ten years later, I'm still here. I brought with me my schoolteacher-perfect handwriting, my need to colour code, and an organisational determination that I still try to insist on. When I think back to how I felt in those early years, with little cooking confidence, it was unfathomable that I would be part of such a beautiful series of cookbooks that would sit in bookstores across the world. Being part of this project has unearthed a cooking heritage I had never taken the time to explore. My nana's date nut loaf (page 278), generously *shmeared* with butter, reminds me of those afternoons with my whole family, sipping tea, chatting, eating and then taking home silver-foil packages of leftovers for the coming week. I love how much my cooking repertoire has improved since the MMCC has been in my life – it has actually been transformative, and I now consider myself to be a cook.

Lynn Niselow

Inspired by my mother and grandmother, food is the way we share and express love in our family, and it became a passion for me. My working life has been diverse, ranging from fashion buyer to running a successful catering business and being a community organisation executive. What I love about catering is that every function is a celebration. Being able to share in my clients' special moments with food I've prepared is pure joy. I have now come full circle as I find myself back pursuing my true passion – food. When the opportunity presented itself in 2014 to join the girls in the MMCC kitchen, I embraced it. I am both excited and privileged to be part of a sisterhood that cooks together and is inspired by heirloom recipes and their stories.

I just love food, in all its forms, and now also run private cooking classes from home. Baking and desserts have always been top of the list; however, over the years, fresh ingredients prepared simply – like a gazpacho (page 68) – have become a big part of my everyday cooking.

Dip & Bread

A little bit of Ireland in Sydney. I love that you can make a rustic loaf of fresh, hot bread that tastes so good – in half an hour. There are never any leftovers. ~ *Natanya, MMCC*

See Myrna's story on page 18

Myrna Calmonson

Irish Soda Bread

450 g (3 cups/1 lb) plain (all-purpose) flour, plus extra
1 teaspoon bicarbonate of soda (baking soda)
1 teaspoon caster (superfine) sugar
1 teaspoon salt
350 ml (12 fl oz) buttermilk

Preheat the oven to 220°C (425°F/Gas 7). Grease a baking tray.

Sift the flour, bicarbonate of soda, sugar and salt into a large bowl. Gradually stir in the buttermilk until the mixture becomes a moist dough.

With lightly floured hands, divide the dough in half, shape into 2 round loaves and place them on the prepared tray. Using a sharp knife, mark a deep cross on the top of each loaf.

Bake for 25 minutes or until the loaves are golden and sound hollow when tapped underneath. Cool on a wire rack.

Makes 2 small loaves

MYRNA CALMONSON

I grew up in an orthodox home, part of a small Jewish community in Dublin, Ireland, which had over 5000 people at its peak. We moved to Melbourne more than ten years ago as our family and many friends had emigrated to other parts of the world. I have wonderful memories of Jewish life in Dublin; the traditional dishes mixed well with Irish culture. Potatoes were a must with every meal, so *latkes* were not just for Chanukah. Colcannon, creamy mashed potatoes with fried onions and finely chopped steamed cabbage, went very well with pickled brisket or fried *gefilte* fish. Clanbrassil Street, where the kosher deli and butcher shops were located, was known as 'Little Jerusalem'. At the end of the week the fishmongers from the markets came to the street, wheeling their prams (minus the babies) loaded with fish to sell to the Jewish women who were standing kerbside, shouting and haggling.

When we were expecting our first child I craved fish every day, so we used to drive to Dún Laoghaire to buy straight from the fishing boats. The fishermen's wives would sell fish so fresh they were still hopping. One of them, with that wonderful Irish sense of humour, said to me: 'To be sure, ye will have a mermaid with all the fish ye are eating!' Well, that mermaid turned out to be a merman who is so fascinated with fish he keeps a giant tropical fish tank in his home!

My mother was a traditional Jewish cook, but sadly she passed away at a young age. I became an adventurous self-taught cook, always inquisitive of new ingredients. My daughter Mish always joked that while her friends were eating chopped liver and chicken soup, our family was chomping down on wontons and curries. She was inspired to become a chef and now has her own cooking school here. My great joy is that the tables have turned: where I was once the teacher, I am now happily her offsider and sous chef.

Now, living in Australia, I continue to love entertaining, and the combination of being Jewish and Irish means a great party with the most delicious food *and* drink.

MYRNA'S RECIPE

Irish Soda Bread: page 16

With parents who survived the Holocaust, food was never taken for granted in our family. Eating meals together were loud and cherished moments that are still vivid in my memory. Having leftovers on my plate was never an option; luckily for me our dog, Carnie, was always sitting under my chair waiting for my discreet discards. It was a win for both of us: he became happily overweight and, as I had 'finished' my main course, I qualified for dessert.

The use of paprika in my cooking was handed down to me through my Hungarian lineage, by my mother and her mother, Onyu. As a little girl I would climb onto my wooden stepstool in the kitchen, balance on my tiptoes so I could reach into the pot and stir whatever Mama was cooking. I loved being sous chef, tasting and suggesting what needed to be added to the pot to make the dish taste just right. Thanks to the apprenticeship in Mama's kitchen I don't need a recipe for my family dishes, as continental cooking is in my blood.

Growing up there was always a tub of *liptauer* dip in the fridge, ready to be spread on fresh *challah*, rye bread or the iconic Australian cracker, Vita-Weat. When I had my own family, my children would eat *liptauer* after school with veggie sticks, which they still love today, as adults. And so, the tradition carries on. Making and eating these foods will always be a sweet reminder of my beautiful mama.

ANNIE'S RECIPES

Liptauer Dip (Körözött): page 34
Beef Goulash Soup: page 71

All our family celebrations in Sydney involved my Aunty Fela's legendary *borekas*.

Fela lovingly devoted her life to her family, and our lives were greatly enriched by an extraordinary aunt. Her early life was filled with sadness. Born in Poland, she was orphaned at age 14 when she tragically lost her entire family in the Holocaust. It's impossible to imagine how hard it must have been for Fela to rebuild her life, but she did. After the war, Fela moved to Israel, where good fortune finally came her way. She met my father's oldest brother, they fell in love and married.

Fela and Yehoshua moved from Israel to beachside Bondi and spent 60 happy years together. They raised two beautiful daughters, seven grandchildren and many great-grandchildren. Fela was always in the kitchen, creating sumptuous meals. Her specialty was *borekas*, our favourites, and we could never have enough. Her handmade puff pastry was extraordinary and tasted equally as good *parev* as when it was made with butter. They hosted Shabbat dinner almost every Friday night, and the moment we walked in the door, the aromas wafting from the oven drew us into their home to be embraced in their warmth and unconditional love.

Auntie Fela was never bitter about her terrible early years and embraced her very close-knit family and friends. Now residing in a nursing home and unable to communicate, her strength and determination is truly inspirational and one of the reasons why I love her so much.

– *Sara Karpin, niece*

FELA'S RECIPE

Safta Fela's Borekas: page 43

SISSEL ROSENGREN

My mother could never fathom where and how I developed an interest in cooking. She is one of Norway's pioneering female engineers who studied at the same university as Einstein. She had a very successful career, including running her own company until she retired at the age of 78. Even though she delegated cooking so she could focus on work, she still taught me about good food and wine.

My family can trace our aristocratic Norwegian roots back to 1451, when my mother's ancestors owned farmland and a forest near Oslo. The other side of my mother's family dates back to 1750 to the East Coast of Sweden, and prior to that the Rosengrens were German Jews from White Russia. I am very proud of my Jewish heritage alongside my Norwegian and Swedish foundations.

I was born in Oslo, Norway, but have spent much of my life travelling and living in many cities. My husband is Australian so we are back in Sydney, where I love my work in food industry research and forecasting.

After high school, friends and I formed a cooking club to cook and exchange recipes. Years later I formed the Sydney Cooking Club with four close friends. Every other month we get together to cook a three-course dinner. We taste wine, critique the food and exchange opinions, often passionately. And the best part? Husbands and children are not allowed in the kitchen or at the dining table that night!

SISSEL'S RECIPE

Norwegian Herring Salad: opposite page

SHEREE STONE

In New Zealand we are blessed with incredible produce. Farmers' markets, recipe blogs and chefs, especially Yotam Ottolenghi, inspire me. I extract parts of recipes, and apply these to other recipes, in the same way I construct images in my fine art practice of collage. I love to experiment with textures and flavours and have obsessions with particular foods and spices, like pomegranate molasses, limes and nigella seeds, plus almost anything grown from my garden.

Although I am a second-generation New Zealander, when I was young the food we ate was mostly continental cuisine; my grandparents all originated from Eastern Europe. I live in Auckland but this rich heritage still underpins everything that is related to food.

As a child, I loved hanging around the kitchen with my mother and grandmother. Dad, a capable cook as well, used to make each of us a special birthday breakfast – before the days of café culture.

I particularly spent a lot of time in my grandmother Esther's kitchen. On one occasion she had a dinner party planned that night and there was an overwhelming amount to be done, so I stepped in. At 14 years old I spent the entire day preparing the dinner and decorating the table with her family silver and crystal, in the formal dining style of those days. That memorable occasion marked the beginning of my passion for food and entertaining.

SHEREE'S RECIPES

Smoked Fish Pâté: page 24
Lavosh: page 25
Poached Chicken with Lentils: page 123

We were so proud to contribute to *The Great Australian Cookbook* (2015). At a launch event in Sydney where we made baby honey cakes for 100 people, Sissel introduced herself and the girls from her cooking club to us. They had been following the MMCC project and we were as excited to meet them as they were to meet us. Chatting to Sissel, we were curious to hear about her Scandinavian and Jewish heritage and her traditional Norwegian recipes. ∼ *MMCC*

Sissel Rosengren

Norwegian Herring Salad

3 fillets pickled herring

160 g (about 6) tinned baby beetroot (beets)

1 granny smith apple, unpeeled and cored

2 hard-boiled eggs, chopped

½ brown onion, finely chopped

2 large pickled gherkins, thinly sliced

sea salt and ground black pepper

rye bread or pumpernickel and butter, to serve

Dressing

100 ml (3½ fl oz) thickened (whipping) cream

2 tablespoons whole-egg mayonnaise

½ teaspoon sugar

Rinse the herring fillets in cold water, then dry well with paper towel. Slice into 1 cm (½ inch) thick pieces. Put into a large bowl. Cut the beetroot and apple into 1 cm (½ inch) cubes. Add to the bowl along with the egg, onion and gherkin.

To make the dressing, whisk the cream until firm peaks form. Add the mayonnaise and sugar and whisk to combine. Pour over the salad and stir gently to combine. Season to taste with salt and pepper and serve with rye bread or pumpernickel and butter.

Serves 8

Photo overleaf

Sheree, being from New Zealand, has access to wonderful smoked white fish – Manuka Smoked Trevally, Kingfish or Kahawai. It's not so readily available where we are, so we opted for hot-smoked salmon and still loved the result. The original recipe calls for lemon-infused olive oil, which is not always in everyone's pantry. A good alternative is to include the zest of the lime, which will impart a similar flavour. ~ *MMCC*

See Sheree's story on page 20

Sheree Stone

Smoked Fish Pâté

65 g (¼ cup) cream cheese
2 tablespoons sour cream
finely grated zest and juice of 1 lime
1 teaspoon extra virgin olive oil
1 tablespoon prepared horseradish
400 g (14 oz) smoked fish fillets,
    skin removed
1 tablespoon dill sprigs
sea salt and ground black pepper
lime wedges, to serve

Place the cream cheese, sour cream, lime zest and juice, olive oil and horseradish in a food processor. Blend until smooth and creamy.

Gently break up the fish fillets, flaking them into small pieces, and add them to the mixture in the food processor. Add the dill and process until the mixture forms a thick paste. Add salt, pepper and extra lime juice, to taste.

Cover with plastic wrap and place in the fridge for at least 2 hours. Serve chilled with lime wedges and lavosh (opposite page).

Serves 8

Photo on previous page

Who would've thought something we've always bought in packets is so easy to make at home with ingredients from your pantry? ~ *MMCC*

See Sheree's story on page 20

Sheree Stone

Lavosh

150 g (1 cup/5½ oz) plain (all-purpose)
    flour, plus extra
50 g (⅓ cup/1¾ oz) wholemeal
    (whole-wheat) plain flour
2 tablespoons black sesame seeds
2 tablespoons white sesame seeds
1 tablespoon fresh or dried oregano
1 teaspoon sea salt
1 teaspoon sesame oil
60 ml (¼ cup) extra virgin olive oil
125 ml (½ cup) water
1 clove garlic, crushed
60 ml (¼ cup) olive oil, for brushing
sea salt flakes, for sprinkling

Preheat the oven to 160°C (325°F/Gas 3). You will need 2 large baking trays.

In a large mixing bowl, stir together the plain and wholemeal flours. Add the sesame seeds, oregano and salt. In a separate bowl, combine the oils and water together, then add to the flour mixture, stirring to form a soft, flexible dough.

Divide the dough into 4. Place a large piece of baking paper on the benchtop and lightly dust with plain flour. With a floured rolling pin, roll one piece as thinly as possible into a large rectangle, about 34 × 16 cm (13 × 6 inches). Cut into 10–12 long shards. Carefully transfer the lavosh shards, together with the baking paper underneath, to a prepared tray. Mix the garlic with the olive oil, lightly brush over the lavosh and sprinkle with the salt flakes. Repeat with remaining pieces of dough.

Bake for 15 minutes or until the lavosh are crisp and golden. Allow to cool on wire racks. Once cool, store in an airtight container for up to 1 week.

Serves 8

Photo on pages 22–23

I'm excited that this recipe comes from Bialystok, Poland, as it's the very same place that my mum's parents lived before they moved to Melbourne in the late 1920s. A *bialy* may look like a bagel but actually it is not. It is a flattish bread roll, baked not boiled, with an indent in the middle for a little pile of salty roasted onion bits and loads of poppy seeds. Best eaten fresh from the oven, with a big *shmear* of butter. ~ *Lisa, MMCC*

See Marcia's story on page 29

Marcia Friedman

Bialys

900 g (6 cups/2 lb) bread (strong) flour, plus extra
1 tablespoon sea salt
500 ml (2 cups) warm water
2 sachets (14 g/4½ teaspoons) active dried yeast
1 teaspoon sugar
olive oil
1 egg yolk mixed with 1 tablespoon cold water, to glaze
1 tablespoon poppy seeds
½ teaspoon sea salt flakes, for sprinkling

Onion topping

3 tablespoons dried onion flakes
125 ml (½ cup) hot water
2 teaspoons olive oil
½ teaspoon sea salt

Set aside 1 cup of the flour. Put the remaining 5 cups into a large bowl and mix in the salt. Make a large well in the flour and add the warm water. Add the yeast and sugar to the water, stirring until combined. Set aside for 10 minutes or until the yeast mixture is foamy. With a wooden spoon, gradually incorporate the flour into the yeast mixture in the well. Once combined, tip onto a floured benchtop and knead for about 10 minutes or until smooth, adding as much of the reserved flour as needed; the dough will be dense. Coat a large bowl with olive oil. Shape the dough into a ball and place in the bowl, turning it over to coat all sides in the olive oil. Cover with plastic wrap and set aside to rise in a warm place for 2 hours or until doubled in size.

After the dough has risen, tip it onto a lightly floured benchtop and punch it down by pressing in the middle to deflate. Divide the dough into 16 equal pieces and, with your hands, gently shape each piece into a ball. Place on a baking paper-lined tray, cover with oiled plastic wrap and set aside to rise in a warm place for 2 hours or until almost doubled in size.

To prepare the onion topping, place the dried onion flakes in a small bowl and cover with the hot water. Allow to stand for at least 15 minutes. When ready to use, drain off any excess water and toss the onions with the olive oil and salt.

Place an oven rack in the second top oven shelf position and place a baking tray (or a large baking stone) on the rack. Cut a piece of baking paper roughly the size of the baking tray (or baking stone) and set aside on a light tray or board to make it easier to transfer the baking paper together with the bialys to the oven.

Preheat the oven to 240°C (475°F/Gas 9).

Take 1 ball of dough, keeping the rest covered. Flatten and stretch it with your fingers until it is around 10 cm (4 inches) in diameter. Gently pull the edges outwards and, at the same time, press firmly with your thumbs until the dough holds a thin 4 cm (1½ inch) wide indent in the centre; the thinner the indent, the more the dough will keep its shape during baking. The bialy will look somewhat flat, but the edges will puff up in the oven.

Place on the prepared baking paper, brush with the egg glaze, fill the indent with ¾ teaspoon of the onion mixture and sprinkle all over with poppy seeds. Sprinkle lightly with the salt flakes. Repeat with enough of the remaining dough balls to fill the prepared baking paper, leaving a space between the bialys for spreading.

When the baking paper is full, lift the tray or board and slide the baking paper with the bialys on it directly onto the hot stone or hot baking tray. Bake for 9 minutes or until the bialys are golden and cooked through. Remove from the oven and allow to cool on a wire rack. Repeat with the remaining balls. Best eaten hot from the oven or reheated to serve later.

Makes 16

Photo overleaf

MARCIA FRIEDMAN

My Italian heritage comes from my father's grand-parents, who immigrated to the United States from Sicily. I converted to Judaism as a young adult, and now live in Arlington, Virginia. My cookbook, *Meatballs and Matzah Balls: Recipes and Reflections from a Jewish and Italian Life*, explores and celebrates the connection between these two heritages and culinary traditions.

I learnt the love of cooking in Mom's kitchen. As young children, we were always encouraged to help – knead dough, drop cookies, cut candy, stir and taste along the way. We would be sent out into the garden to pick fresh vegetables and create meals that I still remember to this day. She inspired us to bring all the senses to our creations and to be curious about flavour and texture. Best of all, she graciously allowed us to experiment with our own ideas, some much better than others – but that's how we learnt.

I am always mindful of the memories, connections and traditions that have shaped my love of food. I love re-creating the recipes for my father's meatballs and my husband's grandfather's *latkes* – right down to the hand grating. It's been an inspiring journey exploring the possibilities of bringing two great food cultures together.

MICHELE ELBAZ

I have lived in Paris, the most beautiful city in the world, all my life. I am a pharmacist, in charge of regulatory affairs for fragrances with the iconic French company Chanel.

My father's mother grew up in Tunisia where the Jewish community was very connected to French culture. Their children went to French schools, families spoke French among themselves and they felt much closer to the French community than to the Arabic. My mother's family also lived in Tunisia. They were originally from Livorno, Italy, where despite the Jewish community being highly educated and part of the bourgeoisie, anti-Semitism forced them to leave.

My parents left for France in 1959 before I was born; Tunisia was no longer a French protectorate and the future became uncertain for the Jewish community. At first, it was hard to get used to living in an unfriendly and cold country where immigrants lived cloistered in new developments. Luckily, all our extended family lived in the same area and we could share Shabbat and feast together. After several years we moved into the heart of Paris where life was much better.

My mother is, at 93, the most adorable romantic in the world. She is a wonderful cook, thanks to her obsession with healthy food, her own mother's Italian cooking and her Tunisian heritage. She has taught me all her secrets and I always serve Tunisian food for Shabbat, carrying on the family tradition.

MARCIA'S RECIPE

Bialys: page 26

MICHELE'S RECIPE

Gougère Crown: page 30

Michele's Shabbat cooking is traditional Tunisian fare but, day to day, she makes food inspired by local French recipes like this gougère. I love to serve this baked savoury choux pastry crown when I have friends for drinks or as a light starter with a simple green salad. Don't worry if it deflates a little. It can also be made into smaller cheesy profiteroles. ~ *Merelyn, MMCC*

See Michele's story on page 29

Michele Elbaz

Gougère Crown

250 ml (1 cup) water
100 g (3½ oz) unsalted butter
1 teaspoon sea salt
170 g (2⅓ cup/6 oz) plain
   (all-purpose) flour
4 eggs
150 g (5½ oz) comté or gruyère cheese,
   very finely chopped or grated

Preheat the oven to 190°C (375°F/Gas 5). Trace a 22 cm (8½ inch) circle on baking paper, turn upside-down and place on a baking tray.

Place the water, butter and salt in a heavy-based saucepan and bring to a rolling boil. Take the saucepan off the heat, add the flour all at once and mix quickly with a wooden spoon until it comes together. Return the saucepan to the heat and mix for about 1 minute until it is a smooth dough that comes away from the side and base of the pan. Tip the dough into a mixing bowl or the bowl of an electric mixer and allow to cool for 10 minutes.

By hand or in an electric mixer, add the eggs one at a time, beating very well after each addition until the dough is smooth. Add the cheese and mix well.

Spoon high mounds of the mixture about 1 cm (½ inch) apart on the baking paper around the marked circle, like a crown. If there is any leftover dough, place more on each mound.

Bake for 15 minutes, then reduce the heat to 180°C (350°F/Gas 4) for an additional 25 minutes without opening the oven door, then turn the oven off and leave for 10 minutes. Serve immediately.

Serves 8

We're so happy to ensure the legacy of this heirloom recipe by including it here. It was given to us by Hayley's friend in Sydney, Jacqui Blank, who always has a freshly baked loaf in her kitchen. Hayley found this 'health bread' (as she calls it) in the 1990s in a school cookbook and it is now her signature dish. It had come from Ilana Chester who had, in turn, found the recipe 25 years earlier. In addition to the seeds, Hayley often adds fresh or dried herbs or herbed salts. ~ *MMCC*

See Hayley's story on page 36

Hayley Goldberg

Oat and Seed Bread

600 g (4 cup/1 lb 5 oz) strong wholemeal (whole-wheat) flour

100 g (1 cup) rolled (porridge) oats or muesli

150 g (1 cup) mixed seeds, including linseed (flaxseed), sunflower, pepita (pumpkin), sesame, poppy

1 teaspoon sea salt

375 ml (1½ cups) warm milk, plus 60 ml (¼ cup) extra

1 teaspoon bicarbonate of soda (baking soda)

500 ml (2 cups) plain yoghurt or buttermilk

1 tablespoon golden syrup (light treacle) or honey

40 g (⅓ cup) seeds and rolled (porridge) oats, extra

Preheat the oven to 180°C (350°F/Gas 4). Grease or line 2 loaf tins.

In a large bowl, combine the flour, oats (or muesli), seeds and salt.

Pour the milk into a large jug or bowl, add the bicarbonate of soda and allow to stand for a few minutes or until small bubbles appear around the edge. Add the yoghurt (or buttermilk) and the syrup (or honey) to the milk mixture and wait for another few minutes until it begins to bubble further.

Pour the wet ingredients over the dry ingredients and stir to just combine. The mixture should be quite wet, so add the extra milk if it appears dry.

Sprinkle the base of the tins with half the extra oats and seeds, then spoon half of the dough evenly into each tin. Sprinkle the top of each loaf with the remaining extra seeds and oats.

Bake for 1¼ hours or until golden and cooked through. If you prefer a crisp crust all around, remove the loaves from the tins after 1 hour and place directly on the oven rack for the remaining 15 minutes. Allow to cool. Slice thinly to serve, fresh or toasted.

Store in the fridge.

Makes 2 loaves

Having eaten this dip at my friend Annie's home so many times, I am happy that she is finally sharing it with the world. What a delectable legacy.

~ *Jacqui, MMCC*

See Annie's story on page 19

Annie Rabin

Liptauer Dip (Körözött)

250 g (9 oz) cream cheese,
    at room temperature
⅓ white onion, finely chopped
1 teaspoon Hungarian sweet paprika
    or paprika cream
½ teaspoon dijon mustard
1 clove garlic, crushed
½ teaspoon caraway seeds (optional)
pinch of sea salt
vegetable sticks or rye bread, to serve

In a food processor, process the cream cheese, onion, paprika, mustard, garlic, caraway seed and salt for a few minutes or until creamy.
Taste for seasoning.

Transfer to a bowl, cover with plastic wrap and refrigerate.
Serve with vegetable sticks or rye bread.

Serves 6

Photo on previous page

This recipe, handed down from Amos's grandmother who spent her childhood in India, was dubbed 'super ketchup' by the family. It was made by Amos's father every summer with ripe tomatoes from the garden, and bottled for use throughout the year. For us in the MMCC kitchen, it was thanks to a few videos and email updates from Amos, as well as a bottle of sauce sent from Auckland to Sydney via Melbourne, that we finally perfected our technique. You can substitute 5 × 400 g (14 oz) tins Italian diced tomatoes for the fresh tomatoes. ∼ *MMCC*

See Amos's story on page 234

Amos Cohen

Grandma's Super Ketchup

2 kg (4½ lb) ripe tomatoes
500 g (2½ cups, tightly packed) brown sugar
375 ml (1½ cups) apple cider vinegar
3 cloves garlic, peeled, left whole
4 cm (1½ inch) knob ginger, peeled, left whole
1 teaspoon chilli flakes
3 teaspoons sea salt

Preheat the oven to 200°C (400°F/Gas 6).

Leaving the tomatoes whole, prick with a fork all over and place in a large roasting tin. Roast for 1 hour, then reduce the temperature to 180°C (350°F/Gas 4) and roast for a further 30 minutes or until the tomatoes have collapsed and a clear liquid has accumulated in the dish. Remove the tomatoes and place in a colander over the sink to drain and cool, discarding the liquid. When cool, remove the skins, then pass the tomatoes through a food mill (mouli) 3 times. Put the milled tomato into a large heavy-based saucepan along with the sugar, vinegar, garlic, ginger, chilli and salt. Simmer over low heat, stirring regularly, for 1 hour or until pulpy and thick.

Fill bottles or jars, seal and allow to cool. Store in the fridge for up to 1 month.

Makes about 2½ cups

My signature recipe is like a chain letter. It's almost 50 years old now, and I have made it for many friends who then ask me for the recipe. They then share it with their friends, and so it has spread all over the world. It gives me the greatest pleasure knowing that my recipe is baked in homes from South Africa to Australia to Hong Kong and beyond.

I grew up in Johannesburg, South Africa. Thanks to the kindness of a Hungarian man who sponsored us, my husband and I made our way to Sydney as newlyweds. After a little while we moved to Melbourne, where we could just afford to rent a small apartment – somewhat larger than what we could afford in Sydney. And in Melbourne, there appeared to be more *yiddishkeit*. In 1998 we moved to Hong Kong for my husband's work. It was meant to be a two-year stint, but we are still here and it is now our 'home away from home'.

Jewish life in Hong Kong is different from what we have experienced in South Africa and Australia. We are a warm and close-knit community, despite being somewhat transient and international. The JCC (Jewish Community Centre) and Chabad are in close proximity to where most Jewish people live, and our lives are constantly enriched with speakers, activities of all types, incredibly social and delicious *kiddush* (after the prayer service) lunches, and excellent schools.

Originally inspired by time spent on a kibbutz in my gap year, I am now a teacher at Li Po Chun United World College, a wonderful boarding college about forty minutes out of town. My family lives on campus, along with all the students and teachers (and their families) from around the world. The facilities there are world class and we love being part of an intercultural community. We decided to immerse our children in the local culture and language by sending them to a local kindergarten and primary school, immersing them in Cantonese and Mandarin, in which they are now proficient.

We are connected to being Jewish in many ways. At home, we keep what I call a traditional South African home with Friday night dinners and not mixing meat and milk. Food plays a major role in our lives and is very much linked with our traditions and heritage. The kids go to Chabad classes every Wednesday and often go to Jewish day camp in the holidays. I am on the board of the Hong Kong Holocaust and Tolerance Centre, which also keeps me connected. Being part of Jewish life in Hong Kong has made me realise how important it is to be a part of a community, especially one as remarkably philanthropic, generous and inclusive as ours.

HAYLEY'S RECIPE

Oat and Seed Bread: page 32

PATI JINICH

I was born and raised in Mexico City, one of four girls in a Mexican–Jewish family. We were taught to work hard, study hard and, above all, appreciate good food. At home, the conversation always revolved around food and it was always on our minds. This started with my grandparents, whose families immigrated to Mexico from different parts of Europe.

Our heritage and home was reflected on the plate. We ate many traditional Jewish foods for the holidays, like *gefilte* fish *à la Veracruzana* – Mexican style, simmered in a spicy tomato sauce and dressed with pickled chillies, olives and capers. Being Mexican and Jewish were one; I grew up eating *pan de muerto* and sucking on sweet sugar skulls on the Day of the Dead and sipping *matzo* ball soup on Fridays. We celebrated Passover and went to mass on Sundays with our nana, continuously treading between the two worlds.

When I moved to Texas I embarked on an academic career. My husband was travelling for work and I was writing my thesis on Mexican democratic institutions, but I was missing everything that had made me feel at home: Mexican food.

In hindsight, I think my interest in food built up as I tried to deny it. As a political analyst, I left things related to food for my spare time. Years later, living in Washington, DC, with degrees under my arm and a job in a prestigious think tank, I switched direction and went headfirst into the culinary abyss. My obsession became my calling, and since then I've made sharing Mexican food my mission as a cooking show host and cookbook author. I test every recipe until it becomes a magic potion, for my classes, episodes or family meals. One of my proudest moments was being invited to cook for President Obama at the White House for the Cinco de Mayo celebrations.

Mexican, Mexican–Jewish, Mexican–American: now, 18 years after moving to the US and raising a family, I feel confident sharing what it means to be Mexican. Because words cannot express how deeply I feel for my culture and identity, I prefer to let the food do the talking. Heavy with the flavours, scents and colours of Mexico, it shows what it means to be Latino and Mexican. After all, when you stir, blend and season contradictions into one pot, they taste absolutely delicious.

PATI'S RECIPE

Corn Torte: page 38

We often try new recipes on the weekend and bring a sample along to share with the girls on Monday. I made this corn torte at home and watched my kids' reaction to the unfamiliar American sweet taste. In the MMCC kitchen, we decided it was time for corn breads to become better known in Australia. We found this recipe on the all-encompassing *Jewish Food Experience* website and then got in touch with Pati. Delicious served savoury or sweet. ~ *Natanya, MMCC*

See Pati's story on page 37

Pati Jinich

Corn Torte

600 g (4 cups) fresh or thawed frozen corn kernels (about 4 cobs)

250 ml (1 cup) milk

230 g (8 oz/2 sticks) unsalted butter, at room temperature

165 g (¾ cup) sugar

8 eggs, separated, at room temperature

140 g (¾ cup/5 oz) rice flour

1 tablespoon baking powder

125 ml (½ cup/4½ fl oz) thickened (whipping) cream

1 teaspoon sea salt

icing (confectioners') sugar, for sprinkling (optional)

Preheat the oven to 180°C (350°F/Gas 4). Butter a 30 × 23 cm (12 × 9 inch) baking dish.

In a blender or food processor, pulse the corn kernels with the milk until roughly puréed. Set aside.

With an electric mixer, beat the butter on high speed until creamy. Add the sugar and beat until light and fluffy. Reduce the speed to low and add the egg yolks one by one, beating after each addition until they are well incorporated.

In a small bowl, combine the rice flour and baking powder. Add a little at a time to the butter mixture, alternating with the cream until you've added them all, beating until well mixed.

Add the corn mixture and beat until well combined, scraping down the side of the bowl as needed; the mixture may look curdled.

In a separate bowl, whisk the egg whites with the salt until stiff peaks form Fold a little of the egg white into the butter–corn mixture until blended. Gently fold in the remaining egg white until just combined – the batter should look streaky.

Pour the batter into the prepared dish. Bake in the centre of the oven for 45 minutes or until the torte is springy to the touch and lightly browned. Allow to cool in the dish.

The torte can be served warm, at room temperature or cold. Cut into squares to serve, with guacamole (page 40) or sprinkled with icing sugar as a sweet option.

Serves 12

Some of you may think you don't need a recipe for 'another avocado dip' – think again! This is a wonderful version that will become a permanent part of your repertoire, particularly when avocados are at their best. The most important part is the seasoning; be sure to taste and add more salt, pepper, lemon or Tabasco, so that your taste buds really sing. ∼ *Natanya, MMCC*

Natanya Eskin

Guacamole

3 ripe avocados

¼ red onion, finely chopped

1 roma (plum) tomato, seeded and finely chopped

1 good splash Tabasco sauce (or hot chilli sauce)

1 lemon, juiced

1 teaspoon sea salt

¼ teaspoon ground black pepper

2 fresh green jalapeno chillies (peppers), thinly sliced

Peel and mash the avocados with a potato masher or a fork, trying not to make it too smooth. Add the onion, tomato, Tabasco, lemon juice, salt and pepper. Mix well and taste, then season generously. Transfer to a serving bowl and scatter the jalapeno chillies on top.

Serve with corn torte (page 38), fresh challah or lavosh (page 25).

Serves 8

Photo on previous page

This eggplant salad, which I first tasted when I bought Dov's Yalla-brand dips some years ago, was the one that made me fall in love with baba ganoush. The mild smokiness that comes from charring the eggplant on a barbecue is simply wonderful. The more charred the skin, the smokier wthe flavour. ~ *Lisa, MMCC*

See Dov's story on page 93

Dov Sokoni

Baba Ganoush

2 large eggplants (aubergines)
100 g (3½ oz) tahini (raw sesame paste)
juice of ½ lemon, or to taste
50 ml (2½ tablespoons) water
1 clove garlic, crushed
½ teaspoon sea salt
⅛ teaspoon ground black pepper
⅛ teaspoon ground cumin
small handful flat-leaf (Italian) parsley, chopped
1 tablespoon extra virgin olive oil

Preheat a barbecue grill-plate to high. Pierce the eggplants all over with the tip of a sharp knife. Place directly on the barbecue and cook, turning regularly, for 1 hour (about 15 minutes per side) or until the skin is charred and the flesh is very soft. Set aside until cool enough to handle. (This can also be done on a chargrill pan over high heat or directly on a gas cooktop flame.)

In the meantime, make the tahini sauce. Place the tahini and lemon juice in a bowl and stir to combine; the mixture will become very thick. Slowly add the water, stirring until a thick sauce forms, then add the garlic, salt and pepper.

Peel and discard the burnt skin of the eggplants. Place the flesh and any juices in a food processor with the tahini sauce and cumin. Pulse until a thick paste forms and season to taste with salt, pepper and lemon juice.

To serve, place in a bowl, sprinkle with the parsley and drizzle with the extra virgin olive oil.

Serves 6

In Fela's original recipe, she rolled long strips of dough, and folded them several times to form a triangle completely enclosing the filling. We find it easier to cut the pastry into squares, fill and then fold into a triangle. For a pareve pastry, use margarine instead of butter. ~ MMCC

See Fela's story on page 19

Fela Levy

Safta Fela's Borekas

Pastry

225 g (1½ cups/8 oz) plain (all-purpose) flour, plus extra
75 g (½ cup/2¾ oz) self-raising (self-rising) flour
½ teaspoon salt
30 ml (1½ tablespoons) vegetable oil
30 ml (1½ tablespoons) white vinegar
125 ml (½ cup) water
150 g (5½ oz) unsalted butter, softened

Filling

1 eggplant (aubergine)
200 g (7 oz) feta cheese, crumbled
½ teaspoon dried oregano
1 teaspoon chopped flat-leaf (Italian) parsley
1 teaspoon lemon juice
sea salt and ground black pepper
1 egg, lightly beaten, for the eggwash
sesame seeds, for sprinkling

Start this recipe a day ahead of serving.

To make the pastry, in the bowl of an electric mixer fitted with the dough hook, combine the flours, salt, oil and vinegar. With the motor running, gradually add the water and mix until it comes together.

Shape into a ball, wrap with plastic wrap and refrigerate for 2 hours.

On a lightly floured benchtop, roll out the dough into a rectangle, about the size of an A4 page, with the short edge facing you. With a table knife, spread about one-third of the butter over the dough and fold into three like a letter – fold the top third down to the centre, then the bottom third up and over that. Spread a little more butter on the top and fold it in half. Cover with plastic wrap and refrigerate for 2 hours.

Repeat the above process once more, rolling out the dough into a rectangle and spreading the butter, folding into three, spreading the butter and folding in half. Wrap and refrigerate for at least 2 hours or overnight before using.

To make the filling, chargrill the eggplant over an open flame or on a hot barbecue grill-plate for 1 hour or until the skin is charred and the flesh is soft. (Alternatively, roast it whole in a 250°C oven (500°F/Gas 10) for 45 minutes.) When cool enough to handle, cut the eggplant in half and scoop out the pulp. Using paper towel, squeeze the moisture out of the eggplant pulp and tip the pulp into a bowl. Add the feta, oregano, parsley, lemon juice, salt and pepper and mix to combine. Taste for seasoning.

Preheat the oven to 180°C (350°F/Gas 4). Line a large baking tray.

Roll out the dough to a 50 × 30 cm (20 × 12 inch) rectangle on a well-floured benchtop. Using a sharp knife, cut into 10 cm (4 inch) squares. Place a tablespoonful of filling in the centre of each square. Brush the perimeter with a little water, fold the dough over to form a triangle and press down the edges to seal. With a sharp knife, trim the edges, then, using the flat side of the blade, press down, leaving an indent.

Brush each triangle with a little beaten eggwash and sprinkle with sesame seeds. Place on the prepared tray and bake for 30 minutes or until golden.

Makes 15

This is one of those recipes that came to us with a pinch of this, a handful of that and very little method so, working with the Fischers, we created our version of Mama Fischer's original recipe. ~*MMCC*

See George's story on page 208

George Fischer

Paprika Chicken Livers

500 g (1 lb 2 oz) trimmed chicken livers
4 onions, cut into thin wedges
60 ml (¼ cup) olive oil
sea salt and ground black pepper
1½ teaspoons Hungarian sweet or
   smoked paprika

In a large heavy-based frying pan over medium heat, sauté the onion in the oil for 20 minutes or until soft and golden brown.

While the onion is cooking, rinse the chicken livers under cold water and dry well with paper towel.

Remove the onion from the frying pan, leaving any remaining oil in the pan. Increase the heat to medium–high and toss in the chicken livers. Season well with salt and pepper and cook for a few minutes until dark golden. Turn the chicken livers over to cook the other side for a few more minutes until golden and just cooked through and season again. Add 1 teaspoon of the paprika and toss through for a minute. Return the onion to the pan, give it a quick toss and sprinkle with the remaining paprika.

Serve immediately, or at room temperature.

Serves 6 as a starter

Flavour, texture and colour: an extraordinary dip. To make it dairy-free, replace the yoghurt with 160 g (1 cup) soaked raw cashews. Soak them in plenty of water for at least three hours, then drain before adding to the food processor. ~ *MMCC*

See Ronit's story on page 106

Ronit Robbaz

Roasted Beetroot Dip

600 g (about 4 medium) beetroot (beets)
2 tablespoons extra virgin olive oil, plus extra for drizzling
3 teaspoons coconut sugar
250 g (1 cup) plain Greek-style yoghurt
1 tablespoon lemon juice
1 tablespoon pomegranate molasses
1 teaspoon ground cumin
1 teaspoon sea salt
½ teaspoon ground black pepper
grated zest of ½ lemon, to garnish

Preheat the oven to 220°C (425°F/Gas 7). Line a baking tray.

Peel the beetroot and cut into large dice. Place on the lined tray and toss with 1 tablespoon of the olive oil and coconut sugar. Roast for 40 minutes or until tender, then allow to cool.

Place the roasted beetroot, yoghurt, remaining olive oil, lemon juice, pomegranate molasses, cumin, salt and pepper in a food processor or high-speed blender and purée until smooth. Season to taste with salt and pepper.

Spoon the dip onto a serving plate, drizzle with extra olive oil and sprinkle with lemon zest. Serve with crackers or lavosh (page 25) on the side.

Serves 8

Photo on page 49

Meeting 'Tante Huguette' in our kitchen was such a lovely treat for me. She was so generous with her knowledge, taking me by the hand and showing me how to roll the pita dough with an empty small glass bottle. Once baked, the pocket inside appears like magic. And I even got to practise my rusty French. ~ *Merelyn, MMCC*

See Huguette's story on page 291

Huguette Ades

Syrian Pita Bread (Pain Shami)

1½ sachets (10 g/3 teaspoons) active dried yeast
½ teaspoon sugar
375 ml (1½ cups) warm water, plus 1 tablespoon
525 g (3½ cups/1 lb 2 oz) plain (all-purpose) flour, plus ½ cup (4½ oz) extra
1 teaspoon sea salt

In a small bowl, mix the yeast with the sugar and the 1 tablespoon of warm water and stir well until combined.

Pour the yeast mixture and remaining water into the bowl of an electric mixer and stir to combine. Add the flour and salt and stir into the water mixture. Beat lightly until a slightly sticky dough is formed. If the dough is too sticky, add a little more of the extra flour.

With floured hands, pinch off small pieces of the dough (about 35 g/1 oz each) and gently shape into a ball. On a floured benchtop, with a floured rolling pin, roll each one out flat into a 9 cm (3½ inch) circle.

Spread a clean blanket on the benchtop leaving half the blanket hanging down the side of the bench. Place a clean tablecloth or tea towels (dish cloths) on top of the blanket to create a work area. Sprinkle with the extra flour. Place the dough circles on the floured area and cover with more tea towels to prevent them from drying out. Cover with the blanket and allow to rise for 30 minutes (longer in cold weather) or until the dough circles have almost doubled in size.

Preheat the oven to 200°C (400°F/Gas 6). You will need a baking tray.

Carefully place dough circles on the tray, with space in between. Bake for 5 minutes or until puffed but still pale and cooked through. Repeat with the remaining dough circles.

Eat on the day of baking or store in an airtight container and reheat (in the microwave or oven) to serve.

Makes 25

Photo on page 49

On our global search to find the best Jewish cooks, we learnt that it's a small world after all. Four different people introduced us to Michael! He's a very busy man with a lot on his plate and we jumped up and down and waved our arms in the air until we got his attention. In his food, Michael brings together Jewish flavours with 'soul cooking', creating his own unique blend while honouring his identity. ~ *MMCC*

See Michael's story on page 178

Michael W. Twitty

Black-Eyed Bean Hummus

425 g (15 oz) tin black-eyed beans
   (peas), rinsed and drained
60 ml (¼ cup) extra virgin olive oil,
   plus extra for drizzling
80 ml (⅓ cup) tahini (raw sesame paste)
125 ml (½ cup) lemon juice
4 cloves garlic, crushed
1 tablespoon preserved lemon brine
   or 1½ teaspoons sea salt
1 teaspoon brown or raw sugar
1 teaspoon hot chilli sauce, such as
   Sriracha
1 teaspoon sweet or smoked paprika,
   plus extra to garnish
½ teaspoon ground cumin
½ teaspoon ground coriander
½ teaspoon chilli powder
2 tablespoons chopped flat-leaf (Italian)
   parsley, to garnish
1 tablespoon sesame seeds, to garnish

In a food processor, process the black-eyed beans, pulsing for about 15 seconds at a time until the peas are broken down, scraping down the side of the bowl in between. This can also be done by hand with a masher.

In a small bowl, whisk the olive oil and tahini together, then drizzle into the black-eyed beans, pulsing until incorporated. Add the lemon juice, garlic, brine or salt, sugar, chilli sauce, paprika, cumin, coriander and chilli powder and pulse again, adding more lemon juice or spices to taste if necessary.

Spoon the hummus into a serving bowl. Sprinkle with the paprika, parsley and sesame seeds and drizzle with olive oil.

Serves 8

It was so special for me to spend the morning with Nava, in her Bondi Beach kitchen, learning the disappearing art of making *malawach* from scratch. Back in our kitchen the next Monday, we were beside ourselves when our dough stretched to translucent. We rolled and folded it over with buttered hands – as she did – and then burnt our tongues eating the hot, flaky bread straight from the frying pan. ∼ *Lisa, MMCC*

See Nava's story on page 54

Nava Levy

Malawach

1 kg (6⅔ cups/2 lb 4 oz) plain (all-purpose) flour, plus extra
2 teaspoons baking powder
2 teaspoons sea salt
180 g (½ cup) honey or 110 g (½ cup) sugar
625 ml (2½ cups) water
2 tablespoons vegetable oil
375 g (13 oz) unsalted butter, softened or melted

In a large bowl, mix together the flour, baking powder and salt. Make a well in the centre and add the honey (or sugar) and water and gradually incorporate the flour with a wooden spoon until a dough is formed. Tip the dough onto a lightly floured benchtop or into an electric mixer fitted with a dough hook and knead for 10–15 minutes or until a smooth elastic dough is formed, adding a little extra flour every so often, if needed. Cover the benchtop with a little of the vegetable oil and give the dough a few extra minutes of kneading on the film of oil, until it is very smooth and soft and bounces back a little when you indent it with your finger. It should be a little sticky but not stick to your hands.

Spread 3 teaspoons of the oil over a baking tray. Divide the dough into 12 equal pieces. Knead each piece for a minute or two on the lightly oiled benchtop, adding a little extra oil to the benchtop if necessary, then shape it into a ball. Place the ball on the tray and slide it around to coat with oil. Repeat with the remaining balls. With your hands, spread the remaining oil over the tops of the balls, flattening each one slightly as you do so, so they are all covered with oil.

Cover the tray with plastic wrap so it is airtight and allow to rest for at least 1 hour.

To make the *malawach*, prepare the benchtop by spreading some of the softened butter over a large work area (or brushing with melted butter). Take 1 piece of the dough and place it on the buttered benchtop. Slowly and carefully flatten and stretch the piece, lifting, pulling and stretching the outer edges away from the centre, to form a very large, wide, almost-translucent rectangular shape, about 75 × 60 cm (30 × 24 inches).

50 ▪ **DIP & BREAD**

Take a knob of the softened butter in your hands and smear all over your fingers and palms. Gently dab your hands flat onto the dough, covering the entire surface with a thin film of butter. (Alternatively, brush the dough with the melted butter.) Fold the left side of the dough across to cover the centre one-third of the rectangle, then fold the right side on top of it, so you now have a smaller rectangle. Dab more butter across the surface of the rectangle. Fold the top edge down and keep folding over and over, pressing slightly to flatten after each fold. Once the folding is finished, flatten and stretch the rolled dough slightly, then roll it up tightly, like a snail, starting at one of the short sides. Cover with plastic wrap. Repeat with all the pieces, then allow the rolls to rest for about 30 minutes.

When ready to cook the *malawach*, use a 20 cm (8 inch) non-stick frying pan. Remove a roll, place it on the buttered benchtop and stretch the dough gently with your hands, pulling and pushing until flat and just slightly bigger than the pan. Heat the frying pan over medium–high heat and add 1 teaspoon of the butter. When sizzling, fry the *malawach* for about 5 minutes on each side or until golden brown and cooked through. You may need to reduce the heat if the *malawach* is browning too fast before cooking in the middle.

Repeat with the remaining rolls of dough.

The finished *malawach* can be reheated by wrapping in foil and placing in a 200°C (400°F/Gas 6) oven for 15 minutes. Serve either sweet or savoury – drizzled with honey and cinnamon ricotta or with hard-boiled eggs, finely diced tomatoes and *zhoug* (see below).

Makes 12

Zhoug

1½ bunches coriander (cilantro) or flat-leaf (Italian) parsley
10 cloves garlic, peeled
8 fresh bird's eye chillies (small hot red chillies), seeds removed
3 cardamom pods
2 tablespoons extra virgin olive oil
½ teaspoon each sea salt and ground black pepper

This condiment is super spicy – particularly on the day you make it – so if you prefer less heat, either make it a couple of days ahead or substitute long red chillies (seeded) for the bird's eye.

In a food processor, place the coriander (or parsley), garlic, chilli, cardamom, olive oil, salt and pepper and process until it forms a spreadable paste. Store in the fridge.

Makes ⅔ cup

Photo on page 53

NAVA LEVY

What would Jewish life be like without food? It would be neither Jewish nor life, really. Growing up in Israel in the early 1960s, with a Lebanese mother and Egyptian father, it was a place of hope, a vibrant home to pioneers building a new society together. We loved our traditions, the singing and dancing in the street, the food everywhere in abundance.

Being Sephardic, a lot of our food was stuffed. Chicken, zucchini, potatoes, eggplant – if it had a hollow in it or you could make one, you filled it with something delicious. My favourite was Mum's chicken, stuffed with mincemeat, pine nuts and sultanas. I loved to help her in the kitchen, shelling the peas or peeling the artichokes. Not that I had a lot of time to help. I had other important things to do, like chasing rabbits in the fields surrounding Holon or dragging a stray goat up four flights of stairs to show my mum.

These adventures were left behind as my family made the tough decision to leave Israel and start afresh in Sydney. To ten-year-old me everything was different, not just what people ate but the culture, the language, the energy. Mum maintained her traditional cooking, with spicy aromas often filling our building, much to the horror of our neighbours.

I met and married my now ex-husband during his travels to Australia after he'd finished his time in the Israeli army. His background was Yemenite and I set about learning his favourite dishes by watching his mother in the kitchen for many hours. I have so many fond memories of our small home overflowing with friends and family eating, chatting and laughing as we got together to feast on *malawach* and *jachnun* (a slow-baked version of *malawach*) – a traditional Yemenite breakfast – on a Saturday morning; they are still a favourite of my four boys and many of their friends. My cooking has now overflowed into the family day care I run. I love cooking with the children and even hold occasional cooking classes for the parents.

Much of my cooking has been prepared, over many years, in the most ill-equipped of kitchens, with an oven that can't make up its mind how hot it wants to be. This inspired me to start a blog called 'Cook you Bastard', from all the times I stood in front of the oven door urging it to cook my food on the inside before the outside was burnt.

NAVA'S RECIPES

Malawach: page 50
Olive and Pistachio Chicken: page 132

ELIZABETH SCHWARTZ

When I make or eat foods from my childhood and youth, I yearn for my mother, grandmother, father and all the people I have lost who handed me my first bites – seasoned with love. It's a very Jewish thing that the salt that flavours our food comes from our tears.

Some people learn to cook from their mothers and some learn to cook in spite of them. My mother was a professional so she didn't have time to linger in the kitchen, but she made a brilliant stuffed cabbage and my brother and I would live for those moments. When I was developing the recipes for *A Wandering Feast: A Journey Through the Jewish Culture of Eastern Europe*, I spent a wonderful afternoon in the kitchen with her, learning the art of this heirloom.

I grew up in a very assimilated household and really only delved into my heritage as an adult. It was that yearning for connection that led to every aspect of my life, including my art, my cooking, my music, my beautiful husband, Yale Strom, and my family. I realise now the food I loved as a child was always traditional Jewish style. I would visit my grandmother's

apartment every week and snack on sweet milky tea and egg *matzos* slathered with sour cream. My great-aunt Yetta took me to lunch at New York delis where I would have endless bowls of sour pickles and coleslaw. Every bite of my coleslaw salad reminds me of visits to my grandma. I experimented with many versions over the years, but this tangy recipe was my eureka moment.

My husband and I are both *klezmer* musicians and I can trace this passion back to my Romanian roots, the birthplace of my father's family. I have a very mixed European heritage, but both my parents were born in New York. I was a Hollywood executive for eight years, and now live in the San Diego area. I love to visit New York as often as possible; it's still the best place to go for a good kosher pickle.

There is a direct line from our history to our culture, and for me, as someone passionately devoted to *yiddishkeit* and a proponent of Jewish art, this is at the heart of everything I do, as a writer, as a musician and as a cook.

ELIZABETH'S RECIPES

Mufleta: page 56
New York Deli Coleslaw: page 90

We had all heard whisperings about this incredible thing called *mufleta*, a secret recipe made by Moroccan Jews to mark the end of Passover. So when Elizabeth shared her recipe with us, we were excited. *Mufletas* are yeast pancakes, made of soft dough and fried on one side only; the second side of each pancake cooks as it lies on top of a growing stack right in the pan. We literally tore them to bits, not being able to stuff the soft crumpet-like pancakes, dripping in butter and honey, into our mouths fast enough. Elizabeth's recipe first appeared on *The Weiser Kitchen*. ~ *MMCC*

See Elizabeth's story on page 55

Elizabeth Schwartz

Mufleta

1 sachet (7 g/2¼ teaspoons) active dried yeast
375 ml (1½ cups) warm water
500 g (3⅓ cups/1 lb 2 oz) plain (all-purpose) flour
2 heaped tablespoons sugar
2 teaspoons sea salt
125 ml (½ cup) light olive oil
butter and honey, to serve

In the bowl of an electric mixer fitted with a dough hook (or in a mixing bowl), combine the yeast, water and ¼ cup of the flour and allow to stand for 5 minutes or until the mixture foams. Add the remaining flour, sugar and salt. Knead the dough for 5 minutes in the electric mixer or 8–10 minutes by hand; it will be a very sticky dough. Cover the bowl with a damp tea towel (dish cloth) and allow to rise for 1 hour or until double in size.

Pour three-quarters of the olive oil into a bowl. Spread the remaining oil on a large rimmed baking tray. With a knife, divide the dough into 12 equal pieces. Lightly dip your hands in the bowl of oil and, with greased hands, shape each piece into a ball. Dip each ball quickly into the bowl of oil and place the balls on the oiled tray. Cover again with the towel and allow to rise for 30 minutes.

Grease a heavy-based frying pan and your benchtop with oil. Set the pan over medium–high heat. With oiled hands, take a ball of dough, place it on the oiled benchtop and flatten it with a stroking, outward motion to form a thin, nearly translucent disc about 20 cm (8 inch) diameter.

Place the circle of dough in the hot pan and cook for about 3 minutes or until it browns slightly. Meanwhile, make another disc with the next ball of dough. After this point, you won't need to oil the pan, since the dough will provide enough oil.

Flip the first pancake over and place the second one on top of it, on the just-cooked side. Let it cook for a minute or until the underside is golden, then turn over both the pancakes together (now the new pancake will be facing down, and the first one facing up). Place a new circle of dough on top of the stack, and flip the whole thing. Repeat with the remaining dough so that you have a stack of 12 pancakes in the pan by the end. Once you remove the mufletas from the pan, cover them quickly with a tea towel, so they stay hot and moist. Serve with butter and honey.

Makes 12

Ronnie's husband said this was the best dish he had ever eaten.
Best DISH, not just best soup! It has very quickly become one of my
favourites – glamorous enough for a dinner party and fast enough for
a midweek meal. Having made this soup too many times to count, I now
put the cloves in a little muslin spice bag. It makes it much easier to
find and retrieve them before blending. ~ *Merelyn, MMCC*

See Ronnie's story on page 62

Ronnie Fein

Carrot Soup with Harissa and Coconut

2 tablespoons coconut oil or
     vegetable oil
1 onion, finely chopped
2 cloves garlic, crushed
700 g (1½ lb) carrots, peeled and sliced
1 litre (4 cups) vegetable stock (broth)
6 cloves
1½–2 teaspoons harissa
250 ml (1 cup) coconut milk, plus extra
sea salt
toasted shaved coconut, to garnish

Heat the oil in a large heavy-based saucepan over medium heat. Add the onion and cook for 10 minutes or until it is soft and translucent. Add the garlic and cook for a minute. Add the carrot and toss through, then add the stock and cloves and bring to the boil. Reduce the heat to low, partially cover the pan and cook for 25 minutes or until the carrot is tender. Remove and discard the cloves. Purée the soup with a stick blender (or in a blender). Return the soup to the pan and whisk in the harissa, then the coconut milk. Bring the soup to a simmer over medium heat and cook for 10 minutes. Season to taste with salt and harissa.

Swirl in a little extra coconut milk and sprinkle with toasted coconut to serve.

Serves 6

RONNIE FEIN

I can't remember a time when I didn't love cooking. As a five-year-old, I volunteered to degut a chicken (my mother was about to throw it out because it still had its insides) because I wanted fried chicken for dinner. When I was nine years old, my mother taught my brother and me how to season a roast, prepare the potatoes and carrots, and put everything in the oven so it would be ready when they arrived home from work. For my own Bat Mitzvah, I even made a chocolate cake – complete with frosting – which we devoured at the small party at our home in Long Island, back in the days when Long Island was mostly potato fields and cabbage patches. The most important lesson my mother gave me was confidence in my own cooking, something I am proudly teaching my five grandchildren.

My mother lived by the philosophy that cooking should be enjoyed and never a chore, right to the end of her life; she had just finished making a delicious batch of salmon croquettes on the day she died. My parents were New Yorkers, with my grandparents from Romania and the Ukraine. I very much feel the pull of my mother's Romanian side in terms of the food I love to cook; I have so many fond memories of the *turte*, an almond phyllo cake, stuffed grape leaves and *mamaliga* (cornmeal porridge) from my childhood.

I make a dozen apple pies every October. I go to a local orchard near my home in Connecticut to buy Rhode Island Greening apples, which my mother always said were the best pie apples, and I prepare pies three or four at a time over the course of several days. I then freeze them and we eat one per month, so by the time the pies are all eaten I am ready to bake a new batch! Of course, my mother was the apple pie baker before me. She showed me how to prepare a flaky crust and to roll the dough. I can still hear her say, 'Don't kill the dough!'

Food has gone on to define my life. Through my cooking schools, cookbooks, newspaper columns and blog, my goal is to help people gain confidence in the kitchen, enjoy cooking rather than fear it and build all the skills they need. My passion is to bring the world of kosher food into the 21st century, reflecting on and celebrating the abundance of food and the glorious blend of cultures that bring so much to our modern cuisine.

I love giving my family the ultimate gift – the food they love – but I also love the activity of cooking. One of my favourite photos is of two of my granddaughters, one licking the spatula, the other looking at it longingly, both with splattered batter in their hair.

RONNIE'S RECIPES

Carrot Soup with Harissa and Coconut: page 60
Chermoula-Spiced Carrots and Parsnips: page 204

LAUREN CARMICHAEL

Our home is nestled in rose and lavender gardens in a vineyard just outside Christchurch, New Zealand – a beautiful corner of the world. Since 2004, my husband and I have run the Langdale Vineyard and Restaurant, where my lifelong love of cooking and sharing food has become a career. I am blessed to be able to cook and experiment with recipes not only from a wide array of gorgeous local markets but using fresh vegetables and herbs directly from my own garden.

As a third-generation New Zealander, I learnt to cook at a young age thanks to my mother. My grandmother and aunt were both great bakers but it was only when I moved to Israel that I became truly inspired. I travelled the world after university and ended up living in Israel for 14 years, converting to Judaism and then experiencing the ultimate joy in having my daughter born there.

Israel's melting pot inspired my love of Middle Eastern and Jewish food. As the Jewish faith was so new to me after converting, I created my own unique customs, but when we had our daughter I thought it was important to learn and understand the food stories and traditions of her father's Yemenite family. His family has prompted and encouraged me to embark on a new journey as I learn to cook traditional Yemenite dishes and make their dishes part of my own family's journey.

LAUREN'S RECIPES

Yemenite Bean Soup: page 65
Yemenite Rosh Hashanah Lamb: page 150

This warming, simple white bean soup is enhanced with an aromatic spice mix originating in Yemen called *hawaij*. Lauren has given us her family's recipe to make your own, but you can also find it in specialist spice stores. ~ *MMCC*

See Lauren's story on page 63

Lauren Carmichael

Yemenite Bean Soup

400 g (2 cups) dried cannellini
(or other white) beans
2 tablespoons olive oil
2 onions, finely chopped
3 cloves garlic, crushed
2 teaspoons hawaij spice mix (see below)
2 tablespoons tomato paste
(concentrated purée)
2 litres (8 cups) vegetable stock (broth)
sea salt
chopped coriander (cilantro), to serve

Hawaij Spice Mix

2 tablespoons ground coriander
2 tablespoons ground cumin
1½ tablespoons ground black pepper
1 tablespoon ground cardamom
1 teaspoon ground turmeric
½ teaspoon ground cloves

Start this recipe a day before serving.

Place the cannellini beans in a bowl and cover with plenty of water. Leave to soak overnight.

The next day, drain the beans, rinse under cold water and drain again. In a saucepan over high heat, place the beans and cover with water. Bring to the boil, reduce the heat medium and simmer for 1 hour or until just tender. Drain and set aside.

In a large heavy-based saucepan over low–medium heat, heat the oil and fry the onion and garlic for 20 minutes or until lightly browned and soft. Add the hawaij spice mix and cook for 1–2 minutes or until fragrant. Add the tomato paste and cook for 1 minute, then add the beans and stock.

Simmer for 1 hour, stirring occasionally.

When the beans are soft, mash slightly to thicken. Season with salt to taste. Sprinkle with coriander to serve.

Serves 6

Hawaij Spice Mix

This makes more than you will need for this recipe. Store the remainder in an airtight container in a dark, cool place for up to 6 months.

Combine all the ingredients together in a small bowl and mix to combine.

Makes about ½ cup

This is a lovely puréed and super-smooth cauliflower soup spruced up with golden roasted cauliflower florets and crisp *pangrattato*, a spicy rustic breadcrumb topping. The different textures make this simple soup really interesting. ~ *MMCC*

See Candy's story on page 235

Candy Gold

Cauliflower Soup with Pangrattato

115 g (4 oz/1 stick) butter
80 ml (⅓ cup) extra virgin olive oil
3 onions, roughly chopped
6 cloves garlic, crushed
2 tablespoons ground coriander
1½ heads cauliflower (about 1.5 kg/3 lb 5 oz in total), chopped
1.5 litres (6 cups) vegetable stock (broth)
2 teaspoons mustard powder
½ teaspoon Tabasco sauce
250 g (1 cup) plain Greek-style yoghurt, to serve

Roasted cauliflower

½ head cauliflower, cut into small florets
1 tablespoon olive oil
½ teaspoon sea salt
3 sprigs thyme, leaves only

Pangrattato

4 slices (250 g/9 oz) sourdough bread, crusts removed
3 sprigs thyme, leaves only
½ teaspoon sea salt
2 teaspoons chilli flakes
60 ml (¼ cup) extra virgin olive oil
50 g (1¾ oz) butter, melted

In a stockpot, melt the butter with the olive oil over medium heat, then sauté the onion for about 15 minutes or until it starts to brown. Add the garlic and coriander and stir for another minute.

Add the chopped cauliflower, half of the stock, the mustard powder and Tabasco to the pan, stir and cover. Simmer for 15 minutes. Add the remaining stock and simmer for a further 20 minutes or until the cauliflower is tender. Remove the soup from the heat, allow to cool slightly, then purée with a stick blender (or in a blender).

To make the roasted cauliflower, preheat the oven to 180°C (350°F/Gas 4).

Place the cauliflower florets on a baking tray and drizzle with the olive oil. Sprinkle with the salt and thyme and toss to coat. Bake for 15 minutes or until crisp around the edges and golden.

To make the *pangrattato*, in a food processor, place the sourdough, thyme leaves, salt and chilli flakes and pulse until roughly chopped. Transfer to a baking tray and drizzle with the olive oil and melted butter. Toss to coat. Bake for 10 minutes or until golden brown.

Serve the soup topped with the roasted cauliflower florets, *pangrattato* and a spoonful of Greek yoghurt.

Serves 8

Having grown up in South Africa, I am aware of Sharon Glass's impact on an entire generation of home cooks. Her real food recipes that encourage cooking from scratch have inspired me. One of my favourites is the refreshing gazpacho, a perfect antidote to hot Sydney summers. What I love is making the soup the day before and serving it straight from the fridge as is, or with olive oil-fried cubes of sourdough bread and chopped chives to take it to the next level. It is a regular part of my summertime repertoire.

~*Lynn, MMCC*

Lynn Niselow

Gazpacho

2 telegraph (long) cucumbers, peeled, seeds removed, roughly chopped

8 ripe tomatoes, roughly chopped

1 red capsicum (pepper), seeds removed, roughly chopped

½ red onion, roughly chopped

1 clove garlic

2 tablespoons red wine vinegar

1 large fresh red chilli, seeds removed

¼ teaspoon Tabasco sauce, or to taste

1 litre (4 cups) tomato juice

1 teaspoon sea salt

½ teaspoon ground black pepper

Start this recipe a day before serving.

In a food processor or blender, place the cucumber, tomato, capsicum, onion, garlic, vinegar, chilli and Tabasco. Process until roughly puréed, then add the tomato juice, salt and pepper. Process again until it is smooth. Season to taste and process again.

Transfer to a large bowl, cover with plastic wrap and refrigerate until serving. The gazpacho may separate in the fridge so give it a good mix before serving.

Serve chilled.

Serves 8–10

Despite growing up on goulash soup, I haven't made it since my mother passed away. It was one of those recipes that I never quite got around to writing down – tasting Annie's soup for the first time made me quite teary, and transported me back to Mum's kitchen. ~ *Merelyn, MMCC*

See Annie's story on page 19

Annie Rabin

Beef Goulash Soup

60 ml (¼ cup) vegetable oil, plus extra
1 kg (2 lb 4 oz) stewing beef, such as beef
    shin, cut into 3 cm (1 inch) pieces
2 onions, finely chopped
1 clove garlic, crushed
1 tomato, finely chopped
1 small red capsicum (pepper),
    finely chopped
2 tablespoons Hungarian sweet paprika
¼ teaspoon hot paprika (optional)
1 tablespoon tomato paste
    (concentrated purée)
750 ml (3 cups) best-quality beef stock
    (broth)
500 ml (2 cups) water, plus extra
    if needed
2 carrots, peeled and roughly chopped
2 potatoes, peeled and roughly chopped
sea salt and ground black pepper
dark rye bread, to serve

In a stockpot, heat the oil over medium heat and fry the beef in batches until browned. Remove from the pan. Add the onion and fry over low–medium heat for about 20 minutes or until well browned, adding more oil if necessary. Add the garlic, tomato and capsicum and fry for about 5 minutes or until soft. Add the sweet paprika, hot paprika (if using) and tomato paste and stir for a minute.

Return the meat to the pan, add the stock and water and bring to the boil. Reduce the heat to low and simmer for 30 minutes. Add the carrot and cook for a further 30 minutes. Add the potato, season with salt and pepper, and simmer for 1 hour or until the meat is fork-tender and the potato is soft and cooked; add water as needed to maintain a thick soup consistency.

Serve with dark rye bread on the side.

Serves 6

So why do we need another chicken soup, you may ask? This Persian version of the iconic Jewish staple is so different from anything we've come across. It tells a story of how Jewish people in the diaspora cook – often fusing the local ingredients with traditional recipes and methods. ~ *MMCC*

See Lainie's story on page 179

4 litres (16 cups) water
6 chicken marylands (leg quarters)
2 chicken frames
500 g (1 lb 2 oz) chicken giblets
6 chicken necks
8 carrots, peeled
1 small bunch celery, quartered
3 onions, halved
1 parsnip, peeled
1 leek, white part only, halved lengthways
1 turnip, peeled and halved lengthways
2 bunches dill
1 bunch flat-leaf (Italian) parsley
10 cm (4 inch) knob ginger, chopped
60 ml (¼ cup) apple cider vinegar
2 teaspoons ground turmeric
2 teaspoons sea salt
1 teaspoon ground cumin
1 teaspoon ground cinnamon
1 teaspoon ground white pepper
½ teaspoon Tabasco sauce
½ teaspoon ground cardamom
¼ teaspoon chilli powder (or to taste)
5 dried bay leaves
3 dried limes, each pierced with a fork
pinch of saffron, ground with 2 heaped
  tablespoons sugar

Gondi

5 onions, quartered
1½ teaspoons ground turmeric,
  plus 1 teaspoon extra
½ teaspoon ground cinnamon
¼ teaspoon ground cardamom
¼ teaspoon ground white pepper
1 teaspoon sea salt, plus extra
500 g (1 lb 2 oz) minced chicken thighs
2 teaspoons baking powder
250 g (1⅔ cups/8¾ oz) chickpea flour
  (besan)

Lainie Cadry

Persian Chicken Soup with Gondi

Start this recipe a day before serving.

Put the water into a large stockpot (at least 10 litres/10 quarts) and bring to the boil over high heat. When it comes to the boil, add the chicken pieces, frames, giblets and necks. If necessary, add more water to just cover the chicken. Return to the boil, reduce the heat to low and simmer for 15 minutes, skimming often. Add the carrot, celery, onion, parsnip, leek, turnip, dill, parsley, ginger, vinegar, turmeric, salt, cumin, cinnamon, pepper, Tabasco, cardamom, chilli, bay leaves, limes and saffron mixture and cook for 2½ hours, partially covered, skimming from time to time. Season with salt, pepper and extra spices to taste.

Allow to cool, then strain into a large bowl, discarding everything except the carrot. Cover with plastic wrap and refrigerate overnight.

To make the gondi, puree the onion in a food processor. Add the turmeric, cinnamon, cardamom, pepper and salt and process until well combined.

Tip the onion and spice mixture into a bowl. Add the chicken mince and baking powder, stir to combine, then add the chickpea flour and mix again.

Cover with plastic wrap and refrigerate for 30 minutes.

Bring a large saucepan of well-salted water to the boil and add the extra turmeric.

With wet hands, take some of the mixture and shape into a golf ball-sized dumpling. Place the dumpling onto a dessertspoon and lower the spoon, submerging the gondi in the boiling water for 5 seconds before pushing it off with another dessertspoon into the water. Repeat with the remaining mixture. Once all the dumplings rise to the top, simmer for 15 minutes or until cooked through.

To serve, skim the fat off the soup and discard. Reheat the soup and carrot in a stockpot. Serve with the gondi.

Makes 4 litres (16 cups) soup and 30 gondi.

Serves 10–12

On our search for recipes from the global diaspora I really began to understand that, much as we'd like to, we just can't reach every great cook in the world. It helped so much when we were introduced or recommended to someone. London journalist Alex Galbinski, who wrote a great piece about MMCC for Britain's *Jewish News* (2014), very kindly put me in touch with Silvia. This opened our doors to a world of Italian–Jewish cuisine that made us so excited. ～ *Lisa, MMCC*

See Silvia's story on page 198

Silvia Nacamulli

Pasta e Patate Soup

4 small waxy potatoes
   (about 500 g/1 lb 2 oz)
80 ml (⅓ cup) extra virgin olive oil
1 onion, finely chopped
1 celery stalk, finely chopped
1 carrot, peeled and finely chopped
60 ml (¼ cup) water
3 cloves garlic, crushed
2 anchovy fillets
pinch of chilli flakes
1 tablespoon sea salt
½ teaspoon ground black pepper
1 × 400 g (14 oz) tin Italian diced
   tomatoes
1.5 litres (6 cups) boiling water
200 g (7 oz) macaroni
5 leaves basil
grated parmesan cheese, to serve

Peel and cut the potatoes into 2 cm (¾ inch) cubes and rinse under running water. Set aside. In a large heavy-based saucepan, heat the olive oil over medium heat and add the onion, celery and carrot and toss through. Add the ¼ cup water, stirring, and bring to the boil. Cook until the water has evaporated and then add the garlic, anchovy, chilli, 1 teaspoon of the salt and the pepper. Cook for 5 minutes or until softened.

Add the tomatoes and cook over low heat for 8 minutes, then add the potato. Stir well and add the boiling water and the remaining salt and cover almost completely with a lid. Cook over low–medium heat, stirring occasionally, for 30 minutes or until the potato is cooked. Add the pasta and cook for about 10 minutes or until the pasta is firm to the bite (al dente). Season to taste with salt and pepper. Tear the basil and toss through the soup. Serve immediately with grated parmesan on the side.

If not serving immediately, the soup will thicken and you will need to add some water when reheating.

Serves 6–8

This hearty and filling soup should really be known as 'Pea and Lam' soup, as it is a kosher version of a very non-kosher idea. A meal in a bowl so thick your spoon could stand up in it. ~ *Natanya, MMCC*

See Libby's story on page 220

Libby Skurnik

Pea and Lamb Soup

500 g (1 lb 2 oz) green split peas
2 large smoked bones or 500 g
    (1 lb 2 oz) smoked beef brisket
3 lamb shanks
1.5 litres (6 cups) water or vegetable
    stock (broth)
1 onion, roughly chopped
1 carrot, peeled and roughly chopped
1 teaspoon ground black pepper
sea salt

Rinse the split peas under running water and drain well. In a large stockpot, place the split peas, smoked bones (or brisket), lamb shanks and water (or stock) and bring to the boil.

Skim well, removing any scum that rises to the top. Add the onion, carrot and pepper.

Cover and simmer, stirring occasionally, for 2 hours or until the meat is fork-tender. Remove from the heat and allow to cool slightly. Take out the smoked bones (or brisket) and lamb shanks and chop the meat roughly; discard the bones. Return the meat to the stockpot and season to taste. Serve hot.

Serves 8

I tested this recipe on family and friends for a Friday night dinner and they insisted it had to be included in this book. The MMCC girls and I wholeheartedly agreed. ～ *Natanya, MMCC*

See Susan's story on page 84

Susan Daleski Levy

Roasted Cauliflower and Pear Salad

1 large cauliflower
60 ml (¼ cup) olive oil
½ teaspoon sea salt
½ teaspoon granulated garlic
1 tablespoon ground cumin
2 firm beurre bosc (brown) pears
1 fennel bulb, trimmed
juice of ½ lemon
250 ml (1 cup) water
2 cups rocket (arugula) leaves
40 g (½ cup) shaved pecorino cheese

Dressing

60 ml (¼ cup) apple cider vinegar
60 ml (¼ cup) extra virgin olive oil
juice of 1 lemon
1 teaspoon sugar
¼ teaspoon cayenne pepper
½ teaspoon sea salt and ground
    black pepper

Preheat the oven to 220°C (425°F/Gas 7). Line a large baking tray.

Core the cauliflower, cut into small florets and toss with the olive oil, salt, garlic and cumin. Place on the prepared tray and roast for 20 minutes or until starting to brown and become crisp at the edges.

Quarter and core the pears. Finely shave the pear and the fennel and place in a bowl with the lemon juice and water.

Drain the pear and fennel well. On a shallow salad platter, layer the rocket, pear, fennel and cauliflower.

To make the dressing, in a bowl, whisk together the vinegar, olive oil, lemon juice, sugar, cayenne pepper, salt and pepper and taste for seasoning. Dress the salad and scatter the pecorino on the top. Serve immediately.

Serves 6–8 as a side dish

Michele's late mother loved to eat but not cook, so she made simple, fail-proof dishes. This is one of the few recipes Michele has from her mother and it is now understandably a favourite. It is a true heirloom recipe, which has become a part of Michele's Thanksgiving table and tradition. This salad is best made just before serving. ∼ *MMCC*

See Michele's story on page 84

Michele Wise

Wilted Spinach Salad

500 g (1 lb 2 oz) baby spinach leaves
225 g (8 oz) mushrooms, thinly sliced
1 red onion, quartered and very
   thinly sliced
75 g (½ cup) dried cranberries
90 g (¾ cup) candied pecans
   (see below)
60 ml (¼ cup) lemon juice
1 tablespoon dijon mustard
3 teaspoons honey
½ teaspoon sea salt or to taste
¼ teaspoon ground black pepper
125 ml (½ cup) olive oil
finely grated zest of 1 lemon

Candied Pecans

220 g (1 cup) sugar
1 teaspoon sea salt
1 egg white
1 tablespoon water
450 g (1 lb) pecans

Place the spinach, mushroom, onion and cranberries on a heatproof serving plate or salad bowl. Roughly chop the candied pecans and set aside.

In a small saucepan over medium heat, combine the lemon juice, mustard, honey, salt and pepper. Add the olive oil slowly and whisk to combine. Simmer for 5 minutes, then pour over the spinach, mushroom and onion. Toss very well to combine, then sprinkle over the pecans and lemon zest to serve.

Serves 10 as a side dish

Candied Pecans

This makes more than you will need for this recipe. Store the remainder in an airtight container for up to 3 months.

To make the candied pecans, preheat the oven to 120°C (250°F/Gas ½). Line a large baking tray. Combine the sugar and salt. Using a fork, whisk the egg white with the water and toss in the pecans and the sugar mixture. Mix well and spread the pecans in 1 layer on the prepared tray, then bake for 1 hour or until caramelised and golden, tossing from time to time. Allow to cool before using.

Makes 5 cups

This salad looks great using mixed colour and sized tomatoes. The simple feta dressing keeps well for up to two weeks in a jar in the refrigerator. Dress the salad just before serving. ~ *MMCC*

See Michele's story on page 84

Michele Wise

Heirloom Tomato Salad with Feta Dressing

2 kg (4½ lb) assorted heirloom tomatoes
2 teaspoons sea salt
¼ teaspoon ground black pepper
200 g (7 oz) feta cheese, crumbled
125 ml (½ cup) extra virgin olive oil
30 ml (1½ tablespoons) red wine vinegar
1 clove garlic, crushed
2 teaspoons dried oregano
1 avocado
½ red onion, halved and thinly sliced
sea salt and ground black pepper

Slice the larger tomatoes into thick slices and halve or quarter the smaller ones. Place them on a serving plate, alternating colour and sizes, and sprinkle with the salt and pepper.

To make the dressing, in a large bowl, whisk together half of the feta with the olive oil, vinegar, garlic and oregano until just combined. Season to taste with salt and pepper. Set aside.

Peel and slice the avocado, reserving some for garnish, and place it on top of the tomato.

Pour the dressing over the salad and top with the reserved avocado and onion. Sprinkle the remaining feta on top and serve.

Serves 10 as a side dish

SUSAN DALESKI LEVY

Things are certainly never dull when you are dealing with important moments in other people's lives. As caterers, we have seen it all over the years – the melting wedding cake in 44-degree heat, the guest who became a vegan just as dinner began and a groom who was 'missing in action'.

I have been in the cooking business for more than 30 years in Phoenix, Arizona. To this day, I still love going to work. Our catering business is primarily for large lifestyle celebrations, weddings, Bar Mitzvahs and corporate events within the Jewish community. We don't have set menus, as we like to take into account what the client likes, and design the menu accordingly.

I'm from a small family and was raised in Johannesburg, South Africa. When my mother died I was only 12 and had no choice but to take over running the house for some time. Thankfully my nanny was a wonderful cook who allowed me free rein to experiment with food and recipes. I am mostly a self-taught cook, and I have never been scared to adjust a recipe to suit my taste or even to have a few failures. I was just always hungry and needed to learn how to create food. I really love to cook for my family, and have the most wonderful memories of our long Sunday lunches.

SUSAN'S RECIPES

Roasted Cauliflower and Pear Salad: page 78
Citrus and Fennel Roasted Salmon: page 117

MICHELE WISE

Feed them and they will come! I send out a group message to my sons, 'Prime rib with horseradish sauce for dinner', and they materialise, with 12 friends, happy and full of news. When they were young, all I had to do was bake cookies, brownies and macaroni cheese to be their perfect mum.

Food has been the catalyst in bringing my family together for generations. My great-grandparents arrived at Ellis Island from Russia, with very little to their name. Family gatherings were always precious, and I remember travelling to the Bronx to visit. My grandma's five siblings were all married with large families, and every Sunday they would gather at my aunt's house for a huge brunch. Besides the 25 simultaneous conversations, a magnificent feast was served. Bagels and cream cheese, tons of smoked salmon and smoked white fish, Jewish stuffed pastries and New York black and white cookies.

I will never forget the joy of being part of this eclectic, tightknit family. I try to re-create that same feeling, especially when the high holidays are upon us, always including my boys' friends and girlfriends and anyone else who would like to join us. And when the conversation and food flows abundantly, I love it as I did when I was young.

Having lived all over the world with my husband, Simon, my life has been full of adventure, much of it revolving around food and family.

MICHELE'S RECIPES

Wilted Spinach Salad: page 81
Heirloom Tomato Salad with Feta Dressing: page 82
Standing Rib Roast with Horseradish Crust: page 166
Baked Potatoes with Horseradish Cream: page 203

GABRIELLE FRIEDMAN

It feels like I had three mothers growing up. My incredible grandmother 'Blondie', who lived with us, my aunt Etta, who was always at our place, and my mom. They entertained lavishly and frequently and I was always around them.

Oddly enough, when we were at Blondie's hospital bedside wondering if she would make it, it was her food that sustained us. Our freezer was stocked with her signature meat blintzes and we took comfort in her cooking. She handwrote a cookbook for me before she passed away, which I now treasure so much.

Due to political unrest my family left South Africa, where I grew up, in the late 1970s. My husband and I now live in Nashville, Tennessee, the music capital of America. Our daughters live near each other in California and I feel so proud that when one of them is sick or needs a little comfort the other nurtures her with a home-cooked meal. I keep all my recipes online so they can access them, but they still love coming home to my cooking!

My other consuming passion is jewellery making. On one day I will be in my studio, working with gold and silver and on the next I will be reading recipe books like most people read novels. I get totally lost in both and, together with family and a little travel, my life is an extraordinary and rich one.

GABRIELLE'S RECIPE

Kale Salad with Gouda: page 86

AMY KRITZER

Though I grew up in an all-American town in Connecticut, USA, my grandmother Bubbe gave me the taste of the Ashkenazi world with her authentic Jewish treats. I adored helping her braid *challah*, roll out *rugelach* or turn homemade crêpes into blintzes. There was nothing better than helping her in the kitchen and gossiping together while she prepared memorable food for the family.

I loved cooking these recipes so much, that eventually I quit my corporate job and went to culinary school at Le Cordon Bleu in Austin, Texas. This allowed me to fine-tune my cooking skills and further develop my passion for Jewish food. It is a cuisine that has evolved through the cooking traditions of Jews around the world, influenced by kosher living and traditional holidays.

Now I spend my days teaching cooking classes, developing recipes and food writing and I just wrote my first cookbook, *Sweet Noshings*. On my blog 'What Jew Wanna Eat' I combine Jewish flavours from around the world to put a modern spin on classic recipes. I love to use food as a way to honour the past, while tweaking it to fit our current needs and food choices. Why not add a little Texas heat to your Passover Seder brisket or a *shmear* of tahini on your bagel?

AMY'S RECIPE

Israeli Farro Salad: page 89

We were unsure about putting something as 'fashionable' as a kale salad into our book until we tasted this incredible Caesar-style salad originally created by the restaurant Five Leaves in Brooklyn, New York. We were blown away by how the dressing and gouda transformed the much-maligned kale into a salad we can't stop eating. ~ *MMCC*

See Gabrielle's story on page 85

Gabrielle Friedman

Kale Salad with Gouda

450 g (1 lb/about 1 bunch) kale

60 g (2 oz) aged gouda or parmesan
   cheese, shaved

80 g (½ heaped cup) hazelnuts roasted,
   roughly chopped

4 white anchovies, roughly chopped

Dressing

1 egg yolk

2 teaspoons Worcestershire sauce

2 teaspoons hot chilli sauce,
   such as Sriracha

finely grated zest and juice of 1 lime

2 tablespoons sherry vinegar

2 anchovy fillets, rinsed and chopped

2 garlic cloves, crushed

¼ teaspoon ground black pepper

60 g (2 oz) aged gouda or parmesan
   cheese, finely grated

250 ml (1 cup) extra virgin olive oil

sea salt

Remove the large stalks from the kale and discard. Chop the kale and set aside in a large bowl.

To make the dressing, whisk together the egg yolk, Worcestershire, Sriracha, lime zest and juice, vinegar, anchovy, garlic, pepper and grated gouda or parmesan. Continue to whisk and slowly drizzle in the olive oil until fully emulsified. Season to taste with salt and pepper.

Toss the chopped kale with sufficient dressing to coat lightly. Place on a serving plate and sprinkle with the shaved gouda, hazelnuts and white anchovy.

Serves 8 as a side dish

The addition of farro lifts the everyday Israeli salad to new heights. The za'atar in this recipe is also great on bread with olive oil and with chicken or fish. ~ *MMCC*

See Amy's story on page 85

Amy Kritzer

Israeli Farro Salad

200 g (1 cup) roasted farro
1 × 400 g (14 oz) tin chickpeas,
   rinsed and drained
60 ml (¼ cup) olive oil
1 tablespoon Amy's za'atar (see below)
100 g (4 cups) rocket (arugula) leaves
300 g (1½ cups) cherry tomatoes, halved
1 telegraph (long) cucumber
½ red onion, thinly sliced
100 g (3½ oz) feta cheese, crumbled

Dressing

80 ml (⅓ cup) lemon juice
160 ml (⅔ cup) olive oil
2 teaspoons sea salt
¼ teaspoon ground black pepper

Amy's za'atar

2 tablespoons sumac
3 tablespoons dried thyme
2 tablespoons dried oregano
3 tablespoons sesame seeds, toasted
1 teaspoon sea salt

Preheat the oven to 200°C (400°F/Gas 6).

In a large saucepan, bring plenty of salted water to the boil. Add the farro and bring back to the boil, reduce the heat to medium and simmer for 40 minutes or until tender. Drain and set aside.

Meanwhile, toss the chickpeas with the olive oil and spread on a baking tray. Roast for 15 minutes or until golden brown and crunchy, stirring occasionally; take care as they will splatter.

Remove the chickpeas from the oven and add the za'atar, tossing to coat well. Set aside.

Cut the cucumber into quarters, lengthways, remove the seeds and slice thickly. In a large bowl, place the farro, rocket, tomato, cucumber and onion. Dress with the lemon juice and olive oil and season to taste with salt and pepper. Add the roasted chickpeas, toss again and crumble the feta over the top.

Serves 6–8 as a side dish

Amy's za'atar

This makes more than you will need for this recipe. Store the remainder in an airtight container in a dark, cool place for up to 6 months.

Combine all the ingredients together in a small bowl and mix to combine.

Makes about ¾ cup

SOUP & SALAD 89

We love this salad – it is iconic deli food. Elizabeth says, 'You won't encounter a Jew from New York over the age of 50 who won't weep when eating it.' For true New York style, use only green cabbage, but you can mix in some red as an option if you prefer. This salad is best made the day before serving and refrigerated overnight. ~ *MMCC*

See Elizabeth's story on page 55

Elizabeth Schwartz

New York Deli Coleslaw

1 kg (2 lb 4 oz) green cabbage,
    finely shredded
½ large sweet or 1 white onion,
    finely grated
1 small carrot, peeled and
    coarsely grated

Dressing

125 ml (½ cup) white vinegar
150 g (½ cup) whole-egg mayonnaise
75 g (⅓ cup) white (granulated) sugar
80 ml (⅓ cup) cold water
1 teaspoon sea salt

Start this recipe a day before serving.

In a large container with an airtight lid, combine the cabbage, onion and carrot.

To make the dressing, whisk the vinegar, mayonnaise, sugar, water and salt together in a large jug. Pour the dressing over the cabbage mixture and toss to combine. Seal the container and refrigerate overnight, inverting the container from time to time.

Transfer into a serving dish with a slotted spoon, holding back some of the dressing.

Serves 10–12 as a side dish

Photo on page 125

Being a Sydneysider, I was very familiar with Dov's ground-breaking café of the 1990s and ate there all the time. He introduced the whole city to the very best and most delicious modern Israeli food. We are so thankful he has agreed to be part of our book, and has now shared some of his favourite salads with us all. ~ *Natanya, MMCC*

See Dov's story on page 93

Dov Sokoni

Beetroot and Walnut Salad

800 g (about 4 large) beetroot (beets)
125 ml (½ cup) water
1 small bunch dill, finely chopped

Roasted walnuts

100 g (1 cup) walnuts
1 teaspoon extra virgin olive oil
½ teaspoon sea salt

Tahina sauce

100 g (⅓ cup) tahini (raw sesame paste)
juice of ½ lemon, or to taste
100 ml (3½ fl oz) water
½ clove garlic, crushed
¼ teaspoon sea salt and ground
    black pepper

Balsamic dressing

2 tablespoons extra virgin olive oil
1 tablespoon balsamic vinegar
½ teaspoon sea salt and ground
    black pepper

Preheat the oven to 220°C (425°F/Gas 7).

Wash the beetroot, leaving the stems intact, and place in a roasting pan with the water. Seal very tightly with foil and roast for 2½ hours, checking the water level from time to time. If time permits, allow to cool completely in the foil-covered roasting pan.

To make the roasted walnuts, toss the walnuts in the olive oil and salt. Place on a small baking tray and roast for 8 minutes or until lightly browned and fragrant.

To make the tahina sauce, in a bowl, place the tahini and lemon juice and mix until thick. Add the water slowly, stirring until a runny sauce forms. Add the garlic, salt and pepper. Set aside.

To make the balsamic dressing, place the olive oil, vinegar, salt and pepper in a jar and shake well.

To assemble the salad, peel the beetroot, cut each into 6 wedges and place in a bowl. Pour over the balsamic dressing and toss to coat. Mix in the dill, reserving some for garnish.

On a serving platter, place half of the beetroot, drizzle with half of the tahina sauce, then roughly crumble half the walnuts on top. Repeat with the remaining beetroot, tahina sauce and walnuts, then garnish with the reserved dill.

Serves 4–6 as a side dish

Photo overleaf

DOV SOKONI

In Israel I grew up eating real food. My Eastern European parents had immigrated after the war to start a family and a new life. My mum, a good cook and an amazing baker, would stand in the kitchen every single week from Wednesday morning until Friday afternoon and the house would be filled with the aroma of freshly baked cakes and cookies, rising yeast and breads, buttery pastry and melting chocolate. There was always an abundance of fresh food, made from scratch.

After finishing school and doing my time in the army, I travelled the world for several years and ended up in Sydney. My life changed when I met Anders, who became my life and business partner, mentor, and the man who taught me everything I know. He was a chef and an artist, and so I learnt how to cook simple and delicious food in a visually appealing way, and how to transform those newfound skills into a professional career.

We opened Cafe Dov in Darlinghurst in 1990, which some say was ground-breaking at the time. To me, it was just food from my upbringing, the Middle East where I grew up and my European heritage. Food that was good, healthy, not complicated and real.

After Cafe Dov, we took over The Wharf in Walsh Bay with a spectacular design that was to see us through an incredible few years. I then opened Yulla in Bondi, which inspired the start of Yalla Foods. My restaurant customers always asked to buy my dips, relishes and salsas so I filled a fridge in the front of the restaurant with all the products they asked for, all made in my tiny restaurant kitchen. Everything sold out day after day; that was my testing ground. I was soon supplying delis and gourmet stores, taking orders and delivering. I wanted to prove that it was possible to make and sell real food that doesn't have a long shelf life, and doesn't contain artificial flavours or preservatives.

Yalla Foods has grown organically since its inception in 2003 and we now distribute across Australia. Our bestselling product has always been our authentic hummus, but in the last couple of years the chocolate mousse has become the jewel in our crown.

DOV'S RECIPES

Baba Ganoush: page 41
Beetroot and Walnut Salad: page 91
Roasted Pumpkin and Sweet Corn Salad: page 94

I lost a newspaper clipping of an earlier version of this salad from years ago, which I loved. I really must thank Dov for bringing it back to me – the matching of pumpkin with sweet corn and avocado is totally mouth-watering. ~ *Merelyn, MMCC*

See Dov's story on page 93

Dov Sokoni

Roasted Pumpkin and Sweet Corn Salad

2 teaspoons ground cumin

2 teaspoons ground cinnamon

1 teaspoon brown sugar

½ Japanese or Kent pumpkin (kobacha squash), skin on, seeded, cut into wedges

sea salt and ground black pepper

60 ml (¼ cup) olive oil

2 sweetcorn on the cob, husks and silk removed

100 g pepitas (pumpkin seed kernels)

1 avocado, thinly sliced

1 bunch coriander (cilantro), leaves only, roughly chopped

Tahina sauce

100 g (⅓ cup) tahini (raw sesame paste)

juice of ½ lemon, or to taste

100 ml (3½ fl oz) water

½ clove garlic, crushed

¼ teaspoon sea salt and ground black pepper

Preheat the oven to 200°C (400°F/Gas 6). Line a baking tray (or use a non-stick baking tray).

In a small bowl, mix the cumin, cinnamon and brown sugar together and sprinkle over both sides of the pumpkin wedges. Lay the pumpkin side by side on the prepared tray. Season with salt and pepper, drizzle with the olive oil and roast for 20 minutes or until soft and just starting to brown at the edges.

In the meantime, bring a saucepan of salted water to the boil and cook the sweetcorn for 5 minutes. Refresh in cold water. With a sharp knife, cut sections of the corn kernels off the cob, leaving some strips of kernels intact where possible.

In a small dry frying pan, toast the pepitas over medium heat for 5 minutes or until they start to pop and turn brown. Remove and set aside.

To make the tahina sauce, in a bowl, place the tahini and lemon juice and mix until thick. Add the water slowly, stirring until a runny sauce forms. Add the garlic, salt and pepper. Set aside.

On a serving platter, arrange the pumpkin slices and drizzle with half of the tahina sauce. Sprinkle with the sweetcorn, pepitas, avocado and coriander, leaving some for garnish. Drizzle with the remaining tahina sauce, then scatter with the garnish.

Serves 8 as a side dish

94   SOUP & SALAD

ain

2

Fish
Poultry
Lamb
Beef

I was the first one to try out this recipe in the MMCC kitchen. I had made the mash, poached the fish, squeezed the lemon, chopped the herbs and was just grinding in some fresh black pepper when the lid fell off the pepper grinder and 3000 black peppercorns fell into my fishcake mixture. Sigh. I spent the next hour picking them out before I could shape, crumb and fry the fishcakes. It was definitely worth it – they are irresistible. Lesley's recipe is adapted from Gordon Ramsay's fish cakes. ~ *Jacqui, MMCC*

See Lesley's story on page 100

Lesley Cohen

Fish Cakes

½ lemon, sliced

2 sprigs flat-leaf (Italian) parsley

2 teaspoons sea salt

300 g (10 oz) salmon fillet, skinned and pin-boned

300 g (10 oz) firm white fish fillets, skinned

300 g (10 oz/about 2) waxy potatoes

2 tablespoons olive oil

60 ml (¼ cup) lemon juice

finely grated zest of 1 lemon

½ bunch flat-leaf (Italian) parsley, chopped

½ bunch coriander (cilantro) leaves, chopped

1 tablespoon finely grated ginger

⅛ teaspoon ground black pepper

35 g (¼ cup/1 oz) plain (all-purpose) flour

2 eggs, lightly beaten

90 g (1 cup) panko breadcrumbs

80 ml (⅓ cup) olive oil, for frying

lemon halves and coriander (cilantro) sprigs, to serve

To poach the fish, you will need a saucepan wide enough to fit the fish fillets in 1 layer. Add the lemon slices, parsley, 1 teaspoon of the salt and enough water to cover the fish and bring to the boil. Slip in the fish fillets, cover with a lid and remove the pan from the heat. Allow to sit, covered, for 10 minutes. Remove the fish from the water, drain well, then set aside until cool enough to handle. Tear into large flakes.

Peel and chop the potatoes, place in a saucepan of salted water and bring to the boil. Cook until soft and then mash while still hot. Set aside to cool.

Combine the cooled potato and flaked fish, olive oil, lemon juice, lemon zest, parsley, coriander, ginger, remaining teaspoon of salt and pepper. Divide the mixture into 8 and shape into patties. Tip the flour onto a plate and season with salt and pepper. Coat the patties evenly in the seasoned flour, dip into the egg and coat with the breadcrumbs, reshaping if necessary. Place on a baking tray, cover with plastic wrap and chill in the fridge for at least 2 hours.

Preheat the oven to 180°C (350°F/Gas 4).

Heat the olive oil in a large frying pan over medium–high heat, then fry the fishcakes in batches for 2 minutes on each side or until golden brown. Remove and drain on paper towel.

Place on a baking tray and bake for 7–8 minutes.

Serve with lemon halves and coriander (cilantro) sprigs.

Makes 8

LESLEY COHEN

I am obsessed with cookbooks – my collection at its peak numbered over 450. I estimated it would take me 90 years to make each recipe just once – a sobering antidote to my unbridled acquisition of new cookbooks, which prompted me to do a vigorous culling. And now with access to unlimited recipes on the internet, cookbooks are mostly for entertainment.

I first became a confident cook back in the 1980s when I married. My husband was a fantastic audience – utterly appreciative and never critical of the occasional failures. We left Johannesburg and lived in Boston for a few years as I was studying postgraduate art history and my husband was doing an MBA at Harvard. It was the beginning of the era of contemporary delicatessens in the USA and the Silver Palate Deli on New York's Upper West Side was ground-breaking. Its food used the best quality, freshest ingredients, presented in a simple but so stylish way. I cooked my way through their inspiring and revolutionary *The Silver Palate Cookbook* and then its sequel, *The Silver Palate Good Times Cookbook*.

I was also mesmerised by Julia Child, whom I watched on TV every Saturday afternoon. In her somewhat exuberant (and possibly inebriated) state, she whipped out a seriously industrial blowtorch, with a slurred quip that every kitchen should have one, and proceeded to caramelise her *crème brûlée*.

I live in Johannesburg and absolutely love my work in strategy and development at the Wits Art Museum. My wonderful colleagues are often envious of my lunches, which are a selection of leftovers from the night before. In the early 2000s I was the founding editor of a gourmet produce magazine, inspired by the small-scale artisanal food producers and their commitment to quality. I had a team of food writers around South Africa researching the very best sources for meat, fish, baked goods, spices, olive oil, cheese and charcuterie makers.

When my sons were growing up I tried to encourage them to learn to cook with the promise that women find men who cook very sexy. Sadly, it didn't make them cook, but women find them gorgeous anyway!

LESLEY'S RECIPE

Fish Cakes: page 98

RACHEL DINGOOR

My grandmother Nani lived with us in Bombay (Mumbai), India, when I was growing up. She worked in our humble kitchen alongside my mother. Since there were no fridges or ovens in most Bombay homes, cooking was done every day. The most exciting times growing up were when I was lucky enough to go to the bazaar and help her with the shopping. Some staples, like eggs and bread, were brought to our front door every day by the various vendors.

Nani was from Basra, Iraq. She lost her young husband during the war and then bravely moved to Bombay with her two small sons to start her life over. She was a wonderful cook and I have vivid memories of sitting in our kitchen, transfixed, watching her. It was so inspiring to see Nani and my mother (her daughter-in-law) working side by side, creating food that I would remember for my entire life.

Every Rosh Hashanah it was customary to have delicious pastries and cookies. My mother and grandmother would prepare all the dough and shape the cookies the night before. Some would have dates inside, others almonds, and they were all different shapes. The next morning we would get up before sunrise to take the cookies to the local bakery to bake them. When we brought them home the aroma filled the house – I was in heaven.

I met my husband in Bombay and when we married we lived with my parents. After three years, which saw the arrival of our first daughter, we decided to move to Australia where the prospects were better. We were blessed with two more daughters once we settled in Sydney. In those early days, without anyone to teach me how to cook, I would draw on memories to help re-create the food of my childhood. I started with simple preparations and would add spices – a pinch of this and a sprinkle of that – to get the taste of the dish just right. It took many tries until I succeeded and I was thrilled when a dish was just like home.

It is now a great joy for me to cook for my own six grandchildren and four great-grandchildren and to share with them the Indian and Iraqi food of my heritage.

RACHEL'S RECIPES

South Indian Fish Curry: page 103
Kakas and Babas: page 274

One of my very favourite things about MMCC is documenting heirloom recipes like this one. Rachel came to our kitchen with the energy of a teenager and spent the morning teaching us some of her Sephardi secrets. As her granddaughter Orit told us, her nana's recipes are like gold. I wish we could see grandmothers and granddaughters all over the world cooking together. ∼ *Natanya, MMCC*

See Rachel's story on page 101

Rachel Dingoor

South Indian Fish Curry

Coconut base

250 ml (1 cup) coconut milk

2 teaspoons tamarind paste

2 tablespoons ground coriander

1 tablespoon ground cumin

1 teaspoon ground turmeric

1 tablespoon tomato paste
   (concentrated purée)

1 fresh long red chilli, seeded

1 teaspoon sea salt

Curry paste

1 onion, roughly chopped

2 tomatoes, roughly chopped

5 cloves garlic, peeled

1 tablespoon fenugreek seeds

1 teaspoon brown mustard seeds,
   dry roasted

½ teaspoon ground black pepper

1 fresh long red chilli, seeds removed,
   roughly chopped

60 ml (¼ cup) vegetable oil

8 fresh curry leaves

1 teaspoon sea salt

700 g (1½ lb) firm white fish fillets, halved

160 ml (⅔ cup) coconut milk

juice of ½ lemon

½ bunch coriander (cilantro), leaves only,
   finely chopped

steamed basmati rice, to serve

To make the coconut base, in a food processor or blender combine the coconut milk, tamarind paste, coriander, cumin, turmeric, tomato paste, chilli and salt and process until smooth.

In a deep, wide, heavy based frying pan, heat the vegetable oil over medium heat. Add the coconut base and bring to the boil. Reduce the heat to low and simmer for 15 minutes.

Meanwhile, to make the curry paste, in the food processor or blender, combine the onion, tomato, garlic, fenugreek, mustard seeds, pepper and chilli and process until smooth.

After the coconut base has cooked for 15 minutes, increase the heat to medium–high and add the curry paste. Simmer for 5 minutes, stirring. Add the curry leaves and salt, reduce the heat to low–medium and slip in the fish pieces. Cover the pan and cook for 5 minutes or until the fish is just about cooked through.

Remove the pan from the heat and add the coconut milk, shaking the pan gently to combine. Add the lemon juice and coriander leaves and season to taste with extra salt or lemon.

Serve with steamed basmati rice.

Serves 6

One of the many great cooks from our book *The Feast Goes On*, Ata, raved to me about Ronit's incredible food and wanted us to meet. He was right. Her food is wonderful and so quintessentially Byron Bay – healthy and vibrant – combined with bold Middle Eastern flavours. Her preference is for organic produce wherever possible. I've done a cooking workshop at Ronit's Open Table in the lush Byron hinterland and it was just brilliant. This dish works well with any firm white fish. ～ *Lisa, MMCC*

See Ronit's story on page 106

Ronit Robbaz

Sumac-Crusted Snapper with Roasted Chickpea Salad

2 eggs
½ teaspoon sea salt
¼ teaspoon ground black pepper
6 × 150 g (5½ oz) snapper fillets,
    each cut into 4
150 g (1¼ cups/5½ oz) potato flour
4 tablespoons za'atar
4 tablespoons ground sumac
1 teaspoon sea salt
125 ml (½ cup) vegetable oil
finely grated zest of 1 lemon, to garnish
coriander (cilantro) leaves, to garnish

Coriander and chickpea salad

1 × 400 g (14 oz) tin chickpeas,
    rinsed and drained
1 tablespoon extra virgin olive oil
2 bunches coriander (cilantro),
    roughly chopped
150 g (1 cup) pine nuts, lightly toasted

Dressing

60 ml (¼ cup) lemon juice
60 ml (¼ cup) extra virgin olive oil
3 cloves garlic, crushed
2 fresh bird's eye chillies (small hot
    red chillies), seeds removed,
    finely chopped
sea salt and ground pepper

Preheat the oven to 180°C (350°F/Gas 4).

To make the salad, toss the chickpeas with the olive oil on a baking tray and roast for 25 minutes or until golden. Allow to cool slightly. In a bowl, toss together the coriander, pine nuts and chickpeas.

To make the dressing, in a small bowl, combine lemon juice, olive oil, garlic, chilli, salt and pepper and whisk together well. Pour the dressing over the salad and toss to combine.

To prepare the fish, in a large bowl, lightly beat the eggs with the salt and pepper. Add the snapper fillets and allow them to sit for a few minutes. On a flat plate, mix the potato flour, za'atar, sumac and salt. Lift the snapper pieces, 1 at a time, out of the egg mixture and coat on both sides with the flour mixture. Set aside.

Heat the oil in a large heavy-based frying pan over medium–high heat until the oil is hot. Add the snapper pieces and fry for about 1 minute on each side or until golden.

Remove and drain on paper towel.

To serve, spread the salad on a wide serving platter and scatter the snapper pieces on top. Garnish with coriander and lemon zest.

Serves 6

104 ❖ MAIN FISH

RONIT ROBBAZ

Every Thursday after school my sisters and I helped with the prepping, chopping, frying and cooking for Shabbat dinner. The house was filled with the sound of chattering women in the kitchen, all laughing, shouting, giggling and at times screaming at each other while we were doing our kitchen chores. On Wednesdays we would shop at the farmers' market to source all the fresh veggies, fruits, nuts and seeds. I remember those days vividly, as I loved hanging around the stalls, eating dried apricots, figs and dates, soaking up the smell of the ocean mixed with the scent of citrus and stone fruits. Mum used to come home with baskets full of brightly coloured produce, and we kids would divide it into the rainbow colours.

Living in Israel with a young family, my mother's Moroccan heritage was evident as she prepared couscous from scratch. It was made from fine semolina flour, a beautiful ritual that could take up to three hours. I loved sitting with her on the kitchen floor, surrounded by bowls of water and oil to keep our hands moist while rubbing the semolina flour between our palms till couscous balls formed. It would then be placed in a *couscoussier*, to steam above the couscous broth until it was fluffy and airy and had absorbed the flavours from below. Mum would always keep some couscous aside for breakfast, as I loved mixing it with dried fruit, nuts, yoghurt or kefir and drizzling date syrup on top.

I now live in beautiful Byron Bay in New South Wales, Australia, and have a catering company, Open Table Catering. I am a chef and a cooking teacher and I love nothing more than to share my passion with others. My specialty is to fuse nutritional foods with a range of cuisines from around the world, perhaps inspired by my Spanish and Middle-Eastern heritage. For me, food is the bridge between cultures, worlds and people. It is about people coming together and sharing their love, their tribal ancestral memories, their passion and love for this earth and its abundant harvest.

RONIT'S RECIPES

Roasted Beetroot Dip: page 46
Sumac-Crusted Snapper with Roasted Chickpea Salad: page 104
Lamb Tagine with Dates: page 146
Coconut Rose Malabi: page 224

DEBBIE STRAUCH

LILA COHEN

Our household is one of eternally hungry men so it helps to be able to bake bread and bagels or whip up a great spaghetti bolognaise. I live in Melbourne, moving from Sydney when I met my husband, Leon. I have quite a mixed heritage with Polish, English and American roots but my mother was Melbourne-born and I feel quite content here.

My mother cooked simply and we survived on an uninspiring all-Australian diet of lamb chops and mash. I was determined to become a better cook, and wanted my children to understand how meals could be made from scratch. When my son Martin was small he would perch beside me on the kitchen bench and help me with simple jobs, like peeling garlic, while I cooked.

I started Little Cooks, a children's cooking class that developed into a cooking school for both kids and adults. My daughter Jacqueline was one of my first students and, decades later, she has a real interest in food and is now teaching me new tricks. I love my work at the National Council of Jewish Women, mainly with seniors. The time I spend with them is more than repaid by their happiness. Living in a Jewish part of Melbourne has made me realise that the traditions I grew up with – which at the time I thought were Australian – reflect both my Jewish and my diverse heritage.

One of the lovely parts of growing up in Poland was foraging for blueberries, raspberries and mushrooms in the summer months. I was born in Dagestan after my parents fled Krakow from the invading Germans, and returned to Poland after the war. We then immigrated to Australia in 1961.

My husband came from a Jewish Australian Anglo family so our food traditions were vastly different, but we both loved to explore new cuisines. We married young, and, equipped with four cookbooks covering French, Italian, Chinese and Jewish cooking, we started out on our culinary journey. He was always encouraging me, appreciative of what I served, and together we derived so much pleasure from the food we produced.

Meals with the family have always been an 'occasion' where we enjoy both the food and spirited conversation. I lost most of my family in the war, so preparing traditional dishes and sharing them is a vital part of my connection to the past. I'm living alone now, but love to invite my children, grandchildren and friends for meals. It brings me so much joy just thinking about which dishes to prepare, and of course I love to see the smiles my cooking brings to those around the table.

DEBBIE'S RECIPE

Steamed Ginger Snapper: page 108

LILA'S RECIPE

Fish with Ouzo (Lithri Plaki): page 110

This dish ticks all the boxes for my family. Light, healthy and so quick to make – the food that we love to eat midweek. I think this will be one of the go-to recipes of the book. The one that everyone will be making every week until our next book comes out. ~ *Natanya, MMCC*

See Debbie's story on page 107

Debbie Strauch

Steamed Ginger Snapper

6 snapper or other firm white fish fillets (about 900 g/2 lb in total), skinned

1 teaspoon sea salt

5 cm (2 inch) knob ginger, grated

125 ml (½ cup) light soy sauce

125 ml (½ cup) mirin or dry sherry

125 ml (½ cup) peanut or vegetable oil

4 spring onions (scallions), sliced on the diagonal

2 bird's eye chillies (small hot red chillies), seeds removed, thinly sliced

2 tablespoons toasted sesame seeds

½ bunch torn coriander (cilantro), to garnish

steamed jasmine rice, to serve

You will need a frying pan, with a lid, large enough to hold the fish fillets in 1 layer. Fill the pan with enough water so that it comes 5 mm (¼ inch) up the side and bring to the boil over high heat. Add the salt and ginger, reduce the heat to medium and slip in the fish fillets, cover with the lid and simmer for 4 minutes or until just cooked through.

Meanwhile, in a small saucepan over medium heat, combine the soy sauce, mirin (or dry sherry) and oil and bring to a simmer. Drain the fish fillets and place on a heatproof serving platter. Scatter the spring onion and chilli over the fish and pour the hot oil mixture over the top. Sprinkle with sesame seeds and coriander.

Serve with steamed jasmine rice.

Serves 6

This is a classic Greek Rosh Hashanah dish with interesting flavours that immediately transport us to the Mediterranean. The recipe is for a whole fish, but we've made it with great success using six fish fillets and cooking them for 20 minutes in total or until cooked through. ~ *MMCC*

See Lila's story on page 107

Lila Cohen

Fish with Ouzo (Lithri Plaki)

1 × 1.5–2 kg (3–4½ lb) whole snapper, cleaned, scaled and scored diagonally
2 onions, thinly sliced
60 ml (¼ cup) olive oil
4 large tomatoes, seeded and chopped
1 teaspoon honey
2 cloves garlic, crushed
1 bay leaf, crushed
few sprigs thyme
2 tablespoons orange juice
2 tablespoons lemon juice
60 ml (¼ cup) ouzo
150 g (1 cup) pitted kalamata olives
2 tablespoons salted baby capers, rinsed
1 bulb fennel, thinly sliced
sea salt and ground black pepper
steamed basmati rice, to serve

Preheat the oven to 180°C (350°F/Gas 4).

Place the fish in an oiled baking dish.

In a large frying pan over medium heat, fry the onion in the oil for 15 minutes or until translucent. Stir in the tomato, honey, garlic, bay leaf, thyme, orange and lemon juice and ouzo. Simmer over low heat for 10 minutes or until the sauce has thickened. Stir in the olives, capers and fennel and season to taste with salt and pepper. Pour the sauce over the fish and cover tightly with foil. Bake for 20 minutes, then remove the foil. Bake for a further 10 minutes or until the fish is just cooked through. Serve with the rice.

Serves 6

NADINE LEVY REDZEPI

I spent my early years in Portugal and London before moving to Århus, Denmark, very close to where my mother grew up. Those early years gave me such a strong respect for food and the land. My parents were street musicians and we lived on a farm where we grew a lot of our own produce. I would spend most days smelling flowers, tasting herbs and feeding the animals. It was natural to see what happened to crops and animals once they were picked or slaughtered.

I am married to one of the world's most exciting and innovative chefs and of course he influences my cooking. But it was my mother who really inspired me. Every time I eat roast chicken, potatoes and a crisp green salad it takes me right back. Luckily Mum now lives with us, and our three young daughters, in Copenhagen and helps keep our family running smoothly while we work crazy restaurant hours.

I met my husband, Rene, when I was working the floor at his restaurant, Noma. We had been dating for about three months when I made the brave decision to cook him dinner. I decided to make a Portuguese dish I had grown up with: spaghetti with chicken livers, garlic, chilli, tomatoes and parsley. I'd made this recipe so many times, I could make it with my eyes closed. It would be sure to impress him.

I wanted to use only natural ingredients, so instead of buying the usual canned tomatoes, I bought fresh. Sadly, the sauce was so bland that I added handfuls of sugar, salt, garlic and parsley to try and fix it. As I brought our plates of chicken livers to the table, I told Rene about my disaster in the kitchen all because I was concerned he would judge me using canned tomatoes. He laughed, thought I was sweet, and the rest is history.

I love to cook for family and friends, especially chef friends who like nothing more than a home-cooked meal. My book, *Downtime: Deliciousness at Home*, showcases simple, delicious home cooking that excites and inspires.

I also love the idea of heritage and tradition playing a part in my kitchen and my home. My own ancestry – part Danish, English and Jewish – together with Rene's diverse background – means we have our own melting pot and can create a new set of traditions for our own family.

NADINE'S RECIPES

Fish in a Salt Crust: opposite page
Risalamande: page 228

We were so happy to meet the lovely and charismatic Nadine. The story goes like this: MMCC's Paula and husband Gary had chef Rene Redzepi home for dinner and gave him a copy of our books. The following year, I went to his Noma pop-up in Sydney and introduced myself. He told me that his wife, Nadine, a great cook herself, loved the books, and asked if we knew she was Jewish. The obvious question popped out of my mouth, 'Would she like to give us some recipes for our next book?' And now, here we are! We love the addition of butter in her salt-crusted fish. Crack open the salt crust at the table and listen to the oohs and aahs. ~ *Lisa, MMCC*

Nadine Levy Redzepi

Fish in a Salt Crust

2 kg (4½ lb) whole white fish, such as snapper, scaled and gutted

2 kg (4½ lb) rock salt

75 g (½ cup/2¾ oz) plain (all-purpose) flour

2 egg whites, lightly beaten

250 g (9 oz) butter

500 g (1 lb 2 oz) green beans, trimmed

sea salt and ground black pepper

Preheat the oven to 200°C (400°F/Gas 6). Line a large roasting pan big enough to fit the fish.

In a large bowl, mix the salt and flour. Add the egg white and combine very well with your hand; you want to be able to squeeze the salt so that it almost sticks together – it is okay if it crumbles a little.

Place an even layer of salt on the bottom of the pan, over an area just wide enough for the fish; you do not have to cover the entire pan.

Wipe the fish dry with paper towel, inside and out. Cut half of the butter into slices and put inside the fish. Place the fish on the bed of salt in the roasting pan and cover with the rest of the salt mixture, pressing it softly to make sure the whole fish is covered all the way around except for the head and the tail.

Bake for 30 minutes, remove from the oven and allow to rest for 10 minutes. With a sharp knife, crack open the salt crust, then remove the crust and skin from the top of the fish and any remaining bits of salt. Remove the fish from the bones to a serving plate, then remove and discard the bones, head and tail. Gently remove the remaining fish, avoiding the skin and salt in the bottom of the pan, adding it to the serving plate.

To cook the green beans, bring 3 cups of water to the boil in a saucepan. Add the remaining butter and, once it has melted, add the green beans. Cook for 1–2 minutes or until the beans have turned a vibrant green colour and are just cooked. Using tongs, remove the beans from the water and season well.

Serve the fish with the green beans on the side.

Serves 6

Photo overleaf

We absolutely love recipes for a whole side of salmon that we can cook ahead of time. This is one of those, and it is a keeper. Roasted fennel can become a regular on everyone's table – it's also great with other dishes like roast chicken or as part of a warm salad. ~ *MMCC*

See Susan's story on page 84

Susan Daleski Levy

Citrus and Fennel Roasted Salmon

1 side salmon (about 1.5 kg/3 lb), skinned and pin-boned
juice of 1 orange and 1 lemon
2 tablespoons olive oil
finely grated zest of 1 orange and 1 lemon
½ teaspoon sea salt
½ teaspoon granulated garlic
¼ teaspoon ground fennel seed
¼ teaspoon dried chilli flakes
1 teaspoon brown sugar

Roasted fennel

2 fennel bulbs, sliced into thin wedges
60 ml (¼ cup) olive oil
juice of ½ lemon
1 teaspoon sea salt
¼ teaspoon granulated garlic
½ teaspoon dried chilli flakes

Preheat the oven to 230°C (450°F/Gas 8).

Line a baking tray and place the salmon on top.

Mix the orange and lemon juice with the olive oil and drizzle over the salmon. Mix together the orange and lemon zest, salt, garlic, fennel, chilli and sugar and sprinkle over the salmon. Roast for 12 minutes (for rare) or continue until cooked to your liking. Remove from the oven and reserve the pan juices.

To roast the fennel, line a baking tray. Toss the fennel with the olive oil and lemon juice and sprinkle with the salt, garlic and chilli. Roast for 25 minutes or until softened and browned at the edges.

To serve, scatter the roasted fennel over and around the salmon and drizzle with the pan juices.

Serves 8

Early in our MMCC journey, we were excited to be included in the Jewish episode of SBS television's *Food Safari* with Maeve O'Meara. At the launch of their *Food Safari* book, they served an unforgettable dish – Greg Malouf's tarator-style salmon – tender, soft, translucent salmon topped with a tahini–yoghurt sauce. The very next day I made it for my family, and over the years it has evolved into this, my version of Greg's recipe. This salad is great with ½ cup pickled red onion slices (page 120) in place of the red onion. ~ *Lisa, MMCC*

6 × 200 g (7 oz) salmon fillets, skinned and pin-boned
2 teaspoons sea salt
½ teaspoon ground black pepper
2 tablespoons olive oil

Quinoa herb salad

1 red onion, thinly sliced
juice of 1 lemon
1 tablespoon olive oil
250 g (1 heaped cup) quinoa
1 bunch flat-leaf (Italian) parsley, leaves only
1 bunch mint, leaves only
100 g (3 cups) baby rocket (arugula) leaves
100 g (1 cup) walnuts, toasted and roughly chopped
2 bird's eye chillies (small hot red chillies), seeds removed, thinly sliced
1 teaspoon ground sumac, to garnish

Tahini–yoghurt sauce

250 g (1 cup) plain Greek-style yoghurt
75 g (¼ cup) tahini (raw sesame paste)
2 tablespoons lemon juice
1 teaspoon sea salt

Dressing

80 ml (⅓ cup) extra virgin olive oil
2 tablespoons lemon juice
1 teaspoon ground sumac
sea salt and ground black pepper

Lisa Goldberg

Barbecued Salmon with Quinoa Herb Salad

Heat a barbecue grill-plate until hot. Sprinkle both sides of the salmon with the salt, pepper and olive oil. Cook the salmon on the first side for a few minutes, until a crust has formed. Flip and cook for another 3 minutes or so (for rare salmon) or continue until almost cooked to your liking, then remove from the heat; the salmon should be undercooked at this stage as it will continue to cook while it rests. Cover loosely with foil for at least 30 minutes.

To start making the quinoa salad, toss the sliced onion with the lemon juice and olive oil and set aside.

Meanwhile, bring a saucepan of salted water to the boil and cook the quinoa for about 10 minutes or until firm to the bite. Drain, rinse with cold water and drain well again. Reserve a few of the parsley and mint leaves for garnish, and roughly chop the remaining leaves, along with the rocket.

To make the tahini–yoghurt sauce, in a small bowl, mix the yoghurt with the tahini, lemon juice and salt. Stir until thickened and season to taste with extra lemon and salt. Cover with plastic wrap and refrigerate until needed.

To finish the salad, toss together the quinoa, parsley, mint, rocket, walnuts, chilli and drained red onion in a bowl. For the dressing, combine the olive oil, lemon juice and sumac and toss through the salad. Season to taste.

To serve, break up the salmon fillets into large chunks on a platter, and dollop the tahini–yoghurt sauce on top. Spoon the salad around and on top of the salmon and sprinkle with the sumac. Garnish with the extra parsley and mint leaves.

Serves 6

This spiced fish is served on a fresh corn tortilla with pickled red onion, Baja cream and slaw and a spoonful of your favourite (store-bought or homemade) tomato salsa. This dish has a few elements, and most can be made ahead. I personally fell in love with the pickled onion, and once I started adding them to all my daily salads, I began making them in bigger and bigger batches. Now all the MMCC girls are addicted too. *~ Lisa, MMCC*

See Sharon's story on page 246

Pickled red onion

1 large red onion, halved lengthways, thinly sliced
2 small green jalapeno chillies (peppers)
160 ml (⅔ cup) rice vinegar
1 tablespoon lime juice
1 heaped teaspoon sea salt

Baja cream

150 g (½ cup) whole-egg mayonnaise
120 g (½ cup) sour cream
2 teaspoons lime juice, plus extra to taste
1 teaspoon finely grated lime zest
pinch of sea salt

Baja cabbage slaw

2 tablespoons whole-egg mayonnaise
¾ teaspoon lime juice
2 drops jalapeno Tabasco sauce
200 g (½ small head) green cabbage, thinly sliced
sea salt and ground black pepper

Marinated fish

60 ml (¼ cup) olive oil
½ teaspoon chilli powder, or to taste
1½ teaspoons dried oregano
½ teaspoon ground cumin
¼ cup coriander (cilantro) leaves, chopped
1 green jalapeno chilli (pepper), chopped
450 g (1 lb) flaky white fish fillets
sea salt and ground black pepper

12 fresh corn tortillas
tomato salsa, to serve

Sharon Goldman

Baja Fish Tacos

To make the pickled red onion, place the onion and jalapeno in a heatproof medium bowl. In a small saucepan, combine the vinegar, lime juice and salt. Bring to the boil over high heat, stirring until the salt dissolves, then pour over the onion and jalapeno. Allow to stand at room temperature for at least 1 hour before using. (Leftovers will keep up to 1 week in the fridge.)

To make the Baja cream, whisk the mayonnaise, sour cream, lime juice, lime zest and salt in a small bowl, then taste for seasoning and lime juice.

To make the cabbage slaw, mix together the mayonnaise, lime juice and Tabasco in a bowl. Toss the cabbage with the mayonnaise mixture, season to taste and refrigerate.

To marinate the fish, mix the olive oil, chilli powder, oregano, cumin, coriander and jalapeno in a non-reactive dish. Add the fish and marinate for 20 minutes.

When ready to cook the fish, heat a non-stick frying pan over medium–high heat. Remove the fish from the marinade, place in the hot pan and season with salt. Cook the fish for 4 minutes, then turn over, season again with salt and cook for another 2 minutes or until just cooked through, depending on the thickness. Remove the pan from the heat and flake the fish with a fork, scraping up and mixing in any marinade that has stuck to the bottom.

Heat the tortillas according to the directions on the packet.

To assemble the tacos, place a heaped spoon of the fish onto the centre of a warm tortilla. Top with the pickled onion and japaleno, Baja cream, Baja cabbage slaw and tomato salsa.

Serves 4

Quite often, we get recipes that we just know will stay with us forever. We all find chicken breast fillets too easy to overcook, yet we like to chop them into a salad or shred them into a soup. Once you've poached, you'll never look back. We met Sheree when we did a charity cooking demonstration in Auckland, New Zealand, and she was brave enough to volunteer to braid a six-strand *challah* alongside us on the kitchen stage! ～*MMCC*

See Sheree's story on page 20

Sheree Stone

Poached Chicken with Lentils

2 litres (8 cups) water
1 onion, halved
1 dried bay leaf
5 sprigs thyme
1 tablespoon sea salt
1 tablespoon black peppercorns
4 chicken breast fillets, skin removed
extra virgin olive oil, for drizzling

Lentils

60 ml (¼ cup) olive oil
2 onions, finely chopped
2 leeks, white part only, thinly sliced
1 teaspoon thyme leaves
2 teaspoons sea salt
ground black pepper
2 cloves garlic, crushed
500 g (1 lb 2 oz) French green
   (Puy) lentils
2 carrots, peeled and finely chopped
4 celery stalks, thinly sliced
375 ml (1½ cups) chicken stock (broth)
2 tablespoons tomato paste
   (concentrated purée)
2 tablespoons red wine vinegar

To cook the chicken, place the water, onion, bay, thyme, salt and peppercorns in a stockpot. Bring to the boil over high heat, then add the chicken and cover with a lid. Remove the saucepan from the heat and allow to steep for 2 hours without lifting the lid. Remove 1 fillet and check it is cooked through at the thickest part. If not, allow the chicken to steep for a further 30 minutes.

To cook the lentils, place them in a heatproof bowl. Pour over boiling water until they are well covered and leave to sit for 15 minutes, then drain.

Meanwhile, heat the olive oil in a large wide saucepan over medium heat and add the onion, leek, thyme, salt and pepper. Sauté for about 15 minutes or until the onion and leek are translucent. Add the garlic and continue to cook for a further 2 minutes.

Add the lentils, carrot, celery, stock and tomato paste. Cover and simmer over low heat for about 25 minutes or until the lentils are tender. Season to taste with salt and pepper and stir through the vinegar.

To serve, cut the chicken into thick slices or tear into large pieces. Place on top of the warm (or room temperature) lentils. Drizzle with olive oil and sprinkle with salt and pepper.

Serves 8

Anita is the grandmother of a friend of ours, and one of the many highlights of our testing year was going to Anita's home in Sydney to cook with her. What a delight to meet her and what a privilege to hear her life story. We arrived in the morning to find everything prepped and ready to go, aprons for us all and the table set for lunch with linen and crystal, with a bottle of wine for us to enjoy. We watched, we helped, we listened and we learnt. And then we ate. The *backhendl* is best fried just before serving.

~ *Lisa, Merelyn and Natanya, MMCC*

See Anita's story on page 126

Anita Zweig

Fried Baby Chicken (Backhendl)

4 × size 5 (500 g/1 lb 2 oz) baby chickens (poussin)
75 g (½ cup/2¾ oz) plain (all-purpose) flour
2 teaspoons sea salt
¼ teaspoon ground black pepper
2 eggs
200 g (2 cups) dry breadcrumbs
500 ml (2 cups) light olive or vegetable oil

Quarter the chickens, remove the backbone and trim the pieces so you have 4 neat pieces from each chicken. Wash and dry the pieces well with paper towel.

Place the flour on a plate and add half of the salt and pepper. In a wide bowl, beat the eggs with a fork.

Place the breadcrumbs on a separate plate and toss with the remaining salt and pepper.

Taking 1 piece of chicken at a time, coat it with the flour, dip into the egg mixture and press straight into the breadcrumbs. Pat firmly and turn over so the breadcrumbs coat the whole piece. Set aside. Repeat with all the chicken pieces.

In a deep frying pan, heat the oil over medium heat until hot and fry the chicken in batches for about 5 minutes on each side or until crisp and golden. To check if each piece is cooked through, insert a skewer or sharp knife into the thickest part of the joint; if the juices run clear, it is ready.

Serve with German potato salad (page 202) and New York deli coleslaw (page 90).

Serves 8

ANITA ZWEIG

I was born and lived in the beautiful city of Vienna until I was 14, when my family fled for their lives following the *Anschluss* (annexation) of Austria by Nazi Germany in 1938. Our business and home were taken over by the SS and we were forced to leave Austria for Holland, where we had family. Unfortunately, when we arrived we were arrested and thrown in jail as we did not have visas. My family and I spent a week behind bars, a most frightening experience for a young girl.

After we were released, we spent six months with our family in Holland before we were able to make our way to Australia. We arrived in Sydney on the HMS *Jervis Bay* in January 1939, where I have lived ever since. I met my husband, Ernst, who was also a refugee from Vienna, when I was just 16 and had to wait until I turned 19 to marry him.

My mother-in-law was an exceptional cook, embracing the Central European traditions. I quickly worked out that if I was to have a happy and long marriage I would have to learn to cook. A remarkable teacher with a passion for food and family, she taught me how to do everything I know in the kitchen. Later on, as I grew more confident, I added new cuisines to the repertoire.

I still love entertaining my friends from the art world who I know from my 20 years working in the Barry Stern Art Gallery. I also adore feeding my family, and the Passover Seder is a very important annual meal for us. We each bring something to the dinner, and I bring the one dish I learnt from my own mother, a *matzo kugel*, which is hugely popular.

The generations continue and I now have seven gorgeous great-grandchildren living around the world. When my little Ofri comes to Sydney from Israel, she is just the right age to help me make cookies; it is her favourite thing to do and makes me so very happy.

I'll never forget the *nockerl* (egg noodle dumplings) I ate as a little girl, which I now always serve with chicken *paprikash*. My family and friends go mad for my *backhendl*, especially alongside my Viennese cucumber salad and potato salad.

ANITA'S RECIPE

Fried Baby Chicken (Backhendl): page 124

DEBRA GLASSMAN

A variety of influences help shape my culinary identity, but first and foremost, it was my mother who helped make me the cook I am today. She blossomed as a cook in the 1970s, when I was a teenager. She may not have been the most accomplished or well-trained chef, but she managed to make our family meals interesting and exciting. Being a teenager, I never helped or watched what she was doing in the kitchen, but I believe I learnt by osmosis that preparing a lovely meal for your family need not be an arduous task. Simple but beautiful meals. Simple but beautiful ingredients.

Once I was married and cooking on my own, I turned to Marcella Hazan's cookbooks (another thanks to my mother), whose rustic and down-to-earth recipes appealed to me and to my style of cooking and entertaining.

I'm a proud third-generation New Yorker from my mother's side, and my paternal grandparents came from Eastern Europe. Family and community are very important to me; both my parents and in-laws live near us, as do our siblings and their children. I have a father-in-law who is 103 years old and who often comes to our home for dinner! It is a treat to cook for him. We have a grandson, Asher, who lives in Boston with our daughter and her husband, and a son who lives in New York City with his wife.

My Jewish heritage has ensured that I have always been involved in community endeavours and has taught me many things, including the importance of sharing food with family and friends. One lesson I have learnt well: If someone in your family is sick, make chicken soup. If there is a holiday, make a brisket.

DEBRA'S RECIPES

Roast Chicken with Herbs, Garlic and Shallots: page 128
Baked Mustard–Herb Chicken Legs: page 131

Crisp-skinned yum – an awesome everyday recipe that you'll make over and over again. Why haven't we been cooking this combination and method forever? We particularly love it made with chicken marylands (leg/thigh pieces), as in the photo. ∼ *MMCC*

See Debra's story on page 127

Debra Glassman

Roast Chicken with Herbs, Garlic and Shallots

60 ml (¼ cup) olive oil

1 × 1.5 kg (3 lb) chicken, quartered

6 French shallots (eschallots), peeled and halved

8 cloves garlic, peeled

10 sprigs thyme, leaves only

10 sprigs rosemary, leaves only

1½ teaspoons sea salt

½ teaspoon ground black pepper

You will need a large roasting pan. Pour the oil into the roasting pan and place in the oven while it is preheating to 220°C (425°F/Gas 7).

Remove the hot pan and carefully place it on the benchtop. Add the shallot, garlic, thyme and rosemary and with a wooden spoon, swirl them around the pan to coat with the oil; take care as they will sizzle and spatter. Dredge the chicken pieces, skin-side down, in the oil and herb mixture, then arrange skin-side up in the pan. Season generously with salt and pepper.

Roast for 50 minutes or until the chicken is golden brown and crisp-skinned and cooked through.

Serve with the shallots and garlic from the pan.

Serves 4

Debra found this recipe of Mark Bittman's in the *New York Times* and we have reprinted it with permission below. When I first made it for my kids, they thought it tasted like a cross between chicken schnitzel and garlic bread. A nice combo indeed. We really wanted to include it in the book and so we agreed, as the *New York Times* requested, not to change the wording in any way, not even to reflect our Australian writing style. The recipe below is exactly as it appeared when it was originally published.

I also like it with skinless thigh fillets instead of chicken on the bone – simply reduce the cooking time to 25 minutes – and add a drizzle of olive oil before baking to add an extra crunch. ~ *Natanya, MMCC*

See Debra's story on page 127

Debra Glassman

Baked Mustard–Herb Chicken Legs

4 leg-thigh chicken pieces, cut in 2, or 8 thighs
1½ cups coarse fresh breadcrumbs
2 teaspoons minced garlic
2 tablespoons chopped parsley
1 teaspoon chopped fresh tarragon or other herb
salt and pepper to taste
6 tablespoons Dijon mustard

Heat oven to 200°C (400°F/Gas 6). Trim excess skin and fat from chicken. Combine breadcrumbs, garlic, parsley, tarragon and salt and pepper on a plate or waxed paper. Use a pastry brush to paint mustard lightly on chicken legs. Carefully coat chicken legs with breadcrumb mixture.

Gently place chicken in a roasting pan and bake for 30 to 40 minutes, or until completely cooked. Serve hot or cold.

Serves 4

Not sure what we're more excited about – a chook with a gluten-free stuffing or a dish that is a main and a side all in one. Either way, this dish is finger-licking good. ~ *MMCC*

See Nava's story on page 54

Nava Levy

Olive and Pistachio Chicken

2 kg (4½ lb) whole chicken
250 ml (1 cup) chicken stock (broth)

Stuffing

100 g (⅔ cup) shelled pistachio nuts
1 large onion, chopped
60 ml (¼ cup) vegetable oil
2 cloves garlic, crushed
½ teaspoon ground turmeric
½ teaspoon sweet paprika
130 g (1 cup) pitted green olives, chopped
2 tomatoes, chopped
½ cup, packed, flat-leaf (Italian) parsley, chopped
2 tablespoons sultanas (golden raisins)
2 cinnamon sticks
½ teaspoon sea salt
½ teaspoon black pepper

Chicken spice

1 teaspoon ground turmeric
1 teaspoon sweet paprika
1 teaspoon Moroccan seasoning or ras el hanout
½ teaspoon sea salt
½ teaspoon black pepper
2 tablespoons vegetable oil

Preheat the oven to 180°C (350°F/Gas 4). You will need a roasting pan large enough to fit the chicken.

To make the stuffing, place the pistachio nuts on a baking tray and roast for 20 minutes or until golden. Roughly chop.

Meanwhile, in a large frying pan over medium–high heat, sauté the onion in the oil for about 15 minutes or until golden. Add the garlic and stir for a minute, then add the turmeric and sweet paprika and stir for another minute until fragrant. One by one, add the pistachio nuts, olives, tomato, parsley, sultanas and cinnamon sticks, stirring after adding each addition. Stir in the salt and pepper. Set aside to cool.

To make the chicken spice, in a small bowl, mix together the turmeric, paprika, Moroccan seasoning (or ras el hanout), salt, pepper and olive oil. Place the chicken in the roasting pan and rub the spice mixture generously all over the chicken, including under the skin.

Fill the chicken with the stuffing and the cinnamon sticks. If there isn't enough room for all of the stuffing, put any remaining into the pan beside the chicken.

Pour the chicken stock into the pan, cover the dish with foil and roast for 30 minutes. Remove the foil and roast for a further 45 minutes or until the chicken is cooked through and the juices run clear when the chicken is pierced at the thigh joint. Remove from the oven, cover loosely with foil and allow to rest for 15 minutes before serving.

Serves 4–6

It's always fascinating to discover the origin of a recipe. This one was given to Amos's mother by a neighbour when she lived on the NATO air force base in Germany as a teenager. ~ *MMCC*

See Amos's story on page 234

Amos Cohen

Chicken Tarragon

1 × 1.5 kg (3 lb) chicken, cut into 8
handful of chopped flat-leaf (Italian)
 parsley, chopped, for garnish

Marinade

60 ml (¼ cup) olive oil
180 ml (¾ cup) white wine
2 tablespoons tarragon vinegar
 (see note)
2 cloves garlic, crushed
1 onion, finely chopped
1 celery stalk, finely chopped
½ teaspoon thyme leaves
a handful of chopped flat-leaf (Italian)
 parsley
1 teaspoon sea salt
¼ teaspoon ground black pepper

Start this recipe the day before serving.

Place the chicken pieces in a glass or ceramic baking dish so that they are in 1 layer.

To make the marinade, combine the olive oil, wine, vinegar, garlic, onion, celery, thyme, parsley, salt and pepper in a jug and pour over the chicken. Cover with plastic wrap and refrigerate overnight.

The next day, remove the dish from the refrigerator 30 minutes before cooking.

Preheat the oven to 180°C (350°F/Gas 4).

Remove the plastic wrap and bake the chicken for 1½ hours or until golden on top and cooked through.

Note – Tarragon vinegar can be found at gourmet food stores. To make it yourself, place a small handful of washed fresh tarragon leaves in a sterilised jar with 500 ml (2 cups) white wine vinegar. Seal and shake gently to combine and allow to steep for 1 week. Remove and discard the tarragon. Store the tarragon vinegar in a dark place for up to 6 months.

Serves 6

Linda created this dish from the flavours of her childhood. *Sambal goreng* – meaning 'fried chilli' – is a core element to Indonesian cooking. We've never come across *petai* (which actually means 'stinky bean') before but it can be found in Asian supermarkets; we're always so happy to have a new ingredient to play with, especially when it comes with an unbelievable list of health benefits. ～ *MMCC*

See Linda's story on page 139

Linda Enoch

Chicken Sambal Goreng

2 onions, finely chopped

2 tablespoons peanut oil

1 small red capsicum (pepper), seeds removed, chopped

3 cloves garlic, crushed

500 g (1 lb 2 oz) skinless chicken thigh fillets, quartered

6 Indonesian bay leaves (daun salam)

60 ml (¼ cup) kecap manis

2 fresh long red chillies, seeds removed, thinly sliced

1 × 170 g (6 oz) tin petai in brine (see above)

1 × 425 g (15 oz) tin young sweet corn spears, rinsed and drained

1 × 540 g (1 lb 4 oz) tin bamboo shoot strips, rinsed and drained

1 × 227 g (8 oz) tin sliced water chestnuts, rinsed and drained

1 × 270 ml (9 fl oz) tin coconut cream

chilli powder, to taste

300 g (10 oz) fried tofu (optional)

½ bunch coriander, leaves only, to garnish

steamed basmati rice, to serve

In a large, deep frying pan over medium heat, sauté the onion in the oil for about 15 minutes or until golden. Add the capsicum and sauté for a minute or two, then stir in the garlic. Add the chicken pieces and sauté for a few minutes or until just cooked through. Add the bay leaves, kecap manis and half the chilli, then the *petai*, including the brine. Reduce the heat to low and simmer for 10 minutes.

Add the corn, bamboo, water chestnuts and coconut cream. Check for chilli heat and add chilli powder, if needed.

Add the tofu pieces (if using) and place on top of the chicken, partially cover with the lid and simmer for 10 minutes. Turn over the pieces of tofu and cook for a further 10 minutes. Sprinkle with the remaining chilli and coriander and serve with steamed basmati rice.

Serves 6

ANDREA KREINER

Unlike many of my friends it was not my mother who taught me to cook, it was Julia Child and Graham Kerr via the television.

My family was always very good at making the traditional Eastern European and Jewish baked goods. Recipes, particularly those from my aunts and uncles who are no longer with us, make me feel connected to my past. I was born and raised in New York City, a second-generation American on my mother's side, with Romanian, Austrian and Russian roots.

Recently we were excited to discover relatives in Israel who we thought had perished in the Holocaust. One newfound cousin also loves cooking and we are getting to know each other through sharing recipes that we can trace back to our family heritage.

I love to cook with my son, Cameron. He first joined me in the kitchen when he was only three years old. I still laugh when I think about the time we had a blackout at home and he decided to make his own scrambled eggs on the gas stove wearing a headlamp so he could see what he was doing.

My husband's Persian family has enriched my food world. Our favourite food is Persian, and my sisters-in-law have taught me everything they know. Life is enriched with shared food and tradition, and using fresh produce from my garden.

ANDREA'S RECIPE

Persian Lamb and Eggplant: page 144

LINDA ENOCH

My siblings and I were each born on a different island in the Dutch East Indies. This was a testament to our adventurous life, thanks to my father's job at the Shell oil refinery, travelling from island to island for work. In each place, my mother would add the local cuisine to her already extensive repertoire.

I loved sitting with my mother in our kitchen '*soojarning*', or skewering satays – she was from Singapore – in preparation for special banquets for our family and friends.

I was born in Sumatra, Indonesia, and we can trace my father's heritage back to the Iraqi Jewish community, which came to Burma in the 19th century during the era of the British Empire.

Moving to Sydney when I was two years old and integrating into a larger and diverse Jewish community was wondrous. As a busy Sephardi family, food was a central part of our culture. We entertained often, and Mum's cooking was delicious even when Asian ingredients were scarce in Australia. I was never taught to cook, as the kitchen was her domain, so I learnt by tastes, smells and watching carefully.

I have developed my own style of cooking over the years. My family giggles at the rows of jars of baked treats that regularly line up on my kitchen counter ready to be given to friends, family, or people in need.

LINDA'S RECIPE

Chicken Sambal Goreng: page 137

This is old-world continental cooking from a time and place when sour cherries were a staple ingredient. The great thing about this dish is that the ducks can be roasted and the cherry sauce made the day before serving, then reheated in the oven. Sometimes, when we don't want to deal with whole ducks, we roast eight duck marylands for about one hour at the same temperature. Excellent with mashed or roast potatoes. ~ *MMCC*

See Naomi's story on page 143

Naomi Penny

Duck in Cherry Sauce

2 × size 22 (2.2 kg/5 lb)
   best-quality ducks
4 cloves garlic, crushed
sea salt and ground black pepper
1 onion, sliced

Cherry sauce

2 × 600 g (1 lb 5 oz) jars pitted sour
   cherries
80 ml (⅓ cup) orange juice
2 cloves garlic, bruised
3 dried bay leaves
½ teaspoon sea salt
¼ teaspoon ground black pepper
110 g (½ cup) sugar
125 ml (½ cup) white vinegar
1 heaped tablespoon cornflour
   (corn starch)
juice of 1 lemon

Preheat the oven to 220°C (425°F/Gas 7).

Wash and trim the ducks, removing excess fat and the wing tip. Pat dry with paper towel, prick all over with the point of a sharp knife, rub with the garlic and season generously with salt and pepper, inside and out. Place the onion inside the ducks, then place, breast-side down, in a shallow roasting pan.

Roast for 1½ hours, basting from time to time. Tip the fat into a large bowl and, when it cools and separates, tip off the fat and save any brown duck roasting juices left behind to add to the cherry sauce.

When the ducks are cool, quarter and trim each piece into a nice shape. Place skin-side up in a shallow baking dish.

To make the sauce, you will need 2 saucepans, one medium and one large. Drain the cherries, reserving the juice, then place the cherries in the medium pan. Tip half of the cherry juice in with the cherries and set the remainder aside. Add the orange juice, garlic, bay leaves, salt and pepper to the cherries. Simmer over medium heat for about 15 minutes.

In the large saucepan, combine the sugar and vinegar and cook over medium heat for about 10 minutes or until golden and caramelised, then add the reserved cherry juice. Bring to a gentle simmer. In a small bowl, mix the cornflour with ¼ cup of the hot liquid from the large saucepan until smooth, then pour back into the large saucepan and continue to simmer for about 10 minutes, stirring from time to time, or until the sauce has thickened. Add in half of the cherries and juice from the medium saucepan. Set aside the remaining half until you reheat the duck. Add any duck juices reserved from roasting. Stir well and add enough lemon juice, starting with 1 teaspoon and tasting, to balance the sweetness. Season to taste with salt and pepper.

Around 45 minutes before serving, preheat the oven to 180°C (350°F/Gas 4).

Remove the garlic and bay leaves from the medium saucepan and pour the liquid and cherries over the duck. Cover the duck with foil and heat for 20 minutes or until hot. Remove the foil and place the duck under the hot oven grill (broiler) to crisp the skin before serving.

Place the duck with the cherries from the roasting pan on a serving platter. Pour the thickened sauce (from the large saucepan) over the duck pieces or offer it on the side.

Serves 6–8

Photo overleaf

NAOMI PENNY

I was born on the first night of Pesach. Perhaps that explains my passion for cooking around Jewish festivals and Shabbat, using recipes handed down from my grandmother, mother and mother-in-law.

Granny-Girl, as she was affectionately known, was my father's mother. She was born in Russia and eventually settled in Sydney. As a child, I would often sit in her kitchen, watching her cook beautiful Jewish dishes. I will never forget the aroma of freshly baked *challah* and rich golden chicken soup being prepared for Shabbat.

Many of my favourite dishes did not survive to be part of the modern Jewish repertoire. The dish I loved the most, *helzel*, is the skin of the chicken neck, stuffed with bread crumbs, fried onion, chicken fat and lots of pepper, then sewn up and simmered in chicken soup. When ready, Granny-Girl would whisper to me, 'Don't tell the others, but come and taste.' I also recall with relish chicken *schmaltz* and *gribenes* – a combination of chicken fat and onions rendered down until the fat has melted, leaving some small, very crispy pieces. She would spread it on bread, sprinkle with a little salt, and I was in heaven.

My mother, Bessie, was born in Lithuania, spent her childhood in England and then, aged eleven, moved to Sydney, tragically losing her dear mother not long after they arrived. When she married my father, she was lucky to find a wonderful mother-in-law in Granny-Girl, who then taught her many treasured recipes.

My culinary world changed in the 1960s when I married Ron. His mother, Cynthia, exposed me to the Polish–Jewish style of cooking. We lived overseas for two years with our children, where new ingredients, different national dishes and tips from friends and cookbooks continuously expanded my repertoire. We became more health conscious due to Ron's research – gone were the days of cooking with chicken fat, we had our cholesterol levels and our hearts to think of! By the time we returned to Australia, a vast and wonderful variety of ingredients had become available, and new styles of cooking meant we could be adventurous and healthy.

To this present day, one of my greatest joys is to sit around our table on Shabbat and *yom tov* with our children and grandchildren, and to share both our traditional dishes and an array of modern foods.

NAOMI'S RECIPE

Duck in Cherry Sauce: page 140

Once we get to know a recipe really well, we'll often look for short cuts and put a bit of our own personality into the dish when making it for our families. In this case, we've found that we can skip peeling the eggplant and save one step of prep. ~ *MMCC*

See Andrea's story on page 138

Andrea Kreiner

Persian Lamb and Eggplant

1 large eggplant (aubergine)
sea salt
olive oil, for frying the eggplant
500 g (1 lb 2 oz) stewing lamb, cut into
    bite-sized pieces
1 onion, roughly chopped
½ teaspoon ground turmeric
1 × 400 g (14 oz) tin Italian diced
    tomatoes
125 ml (½ cup) hot water
steamed basmati rice and Persian pickled
    vegetables, to serve

You will need a large, heavy-based, deep frying pan or flameproof casserole dish with a lid.

Peel and slice the eggplant lengthways into 5 mm (¼ inch) slices. Place in a colander and sprinkle with salt. Allow to sit in the sink for at least 20 minutes, then rinse and pat dry with paper towel.

Place about 5 mm (¼ inch) of oil in the pan or casserole dish and heat over medium–high heat. Once the oil is hot, working in batches, fry the eggplant for about 3 minutes on each side or until well cooked and golden brown. Remove the eggplant and drain on paper towel. Repeat with the remaining eggplant.

Tip out any excess oil, increase the heat to high and add the lamb and onion. Brown the lamb quickly for a couple of minutes on all sides, then add the turmeric and salt to taste. Stir to combine. Top the lamb with the tomatoes, then add the water. Lay the eggplant on top, overlapping the pieces to cover the tomatoes and lamb.

Cover with the lid and cook over low heat for 2 hours or until the lamb is fork-tender. Check after 1½ hours and add more water if the pan or dish is too dry.

Serve with steamed basmati rice and Persian pickled vegetables.

Serves 4

A dish of celebration – Ronit often prepares this tagine for weddings and parties. The cinnamon is a sign of abundance and warmth, while the ginger balances the sweetness and adds more depth. It is a layered and complex dish, and reheats brilliantly. ～ *MMCC*

See Ronit's story on page 106

Ronit Robbaz

Lamb Tagine with Dates

2 onions, roughly chopped
80 ml (⅓ cup) olive oil, plus 1 teaspoon extra
1 teaspoon ground ginger
1 teaspoon ground cinnamon
1 tablespoon ground cumin
½ teaspoon ground black pepper
1.2 kg (2 lb 10 oz) boneless lamb shoulder, cubed
410 ml (1⅔ cups) water or beef stock (broth)
1 tablespoon coconut or raw sugar
pinch of saffron threads
sea salt and ground black pepper
2 tablespoons lemon juice
150 g (5½ oz) medjool (fresh) dates, pitted and halved
½ preserved lemon
40 g (½ cup) flaked or slivered almonds
coriander (cilantro) leaves, to garnish
couscous, to serve

In a large heavy-based deep frying pan or heavy-based flameproof casserole dish over medium heat, sauté the onion in the oil for about 10 minutes or until softened. Add the ginger, cinnamon, cumin and pepper and stir for about 1 minute or until fragrant. Increase the heat to high, add the lamb and, tossing from time to time, brown on all sides.

Add the water (or stock), sugar, saffron and 1 teaspoon salt. Reduce the heat to low, cover and simmer for 2 hours, stirring occasionally to prevent the sauce from sticking.

Add the lemon juice and season to taste with salt and pepper. Place the dates on top, cover and simmer for a further 10 minutes or until the dates are plump.

Meanwhile, rinse the preserved lemon under cold water, remove and discard the membrane and pulp, then cut into thin strips and add to the lamb. Mix gently and cook for a further 15 minutes or until the lamb is fork-tender.

Heat the extra olive oil in a small frying pan over medium heat and add the almonds. Cook for 2 minutes, stirring often, until golden, then immediately tip onto a plate to prevent burning.

Serve the lamb tagine on a bed of couscous, sprinkled with the almonds and coriander.

Serves 6

Myrna Rosen is a legend, having taught two generations of South Africans how to cook. We, with our mothers and grandmothers, learnt our way around the kitchen, following her every recipe. I think this is one of her most iconic – slow cooked, a little sweet and SO SO succulent – a lamb of all lambs. The same sauce is good with browned lamb chops or ribs.

~ *Lynn, MMCC*

See Myrna's story on page 220

Myrna Rosen

Roman Lamb

1 × 2 kg (4½ lb) lamb shoulder, bone-in
3 cloves garlic, crushed
1 teaspoon sea salt
1 teaspoon dried oregano
1 teaspoon rosemary leaves, finely
   chopped
2 tablespoons olive oil

Sauce

3 onions, roughly chopped
2 tablespoon olive oil
1 teaspoon sweet paprika
½ teaspoon cayenne pepper
400 ml (13 fl oz) tomato purée or passata
250 ml (1 cup) water
2 tablespoons white vinegar
2 tablespoons Worcestershire sauce
2 tablespoons brown sugar
1 teaspoon sea salt

Preheat the oven to 200°C (400°F/Gas 6). You will need a roasting pan or casserole dish large enough to hold the shoulder.

Cut small slits all over the lamb. Mix together the garlic, salt, oregano and rosemary and rub all over the lamb and in the slits. Pour the oil over the top. Roast, uncovered, for 1 hour. Remove from the oven and carefully tip out the fat that has accumulated in the pan.

While the lamb is roasting, make the sauce. In a deep frying pan over medium heat, sauté the onion in the oil for about 20 minutes or until golden, then add the paprika and cayenne pepper. Stir for a minute, then add the purée or passata, water, vinegar, Worcestershire, brown sugar and salt. Stir to combine and cook for 5 minutes. Set aside.

After the lamb has been in the oven for 1 hour, reduce the temperature to 120°C (250°F/Gas ½). Pour the sauce over the lamb, cover with a lid or a double layer of foil and cook for a further 5 hours, basting occasionally.

Serves 4–6

I was the first to try out this recipe and was amazed that a dish so easy to make, with so few ingredients (apart from the spices), could be so complex in flavour. I now think of it as my go-to lamb dish; it takes only 20 minutes to prep and then I can forget about it once it goes into the oven.

∼Natanya, MMCC

See Lauren's story on page 63

Lauren Carmichael

Yemenite Rosh Hashanah Lamb

60 ml (¼ cup) olive oil

1 onion, finely chopped

1 teaspoon sea salt

1 teaspoon ground black pepper

2 teaspoons ground cumin

1 teaspoon ground cardamom

1 teaspoon ground cinnamon

1 teaspoon sweet or smoked paprika

1 teaspoon ground turmeric

½ teaspoon mixed spice

¼ teaspoon ground cloves

1.5 kg (3 lb 5 oz) boneless lamb shoulder, cubed

steamed basmati rice or Israeli rice pilaf (page 212), to serve

Preheat the oven to 160°C (325°F/Gas 3).

In a flameproof casserole dish, heat the oil over low–medium heat. Sauté the onion for 15 minutes or until soft and lightly golden. Remove the dish from the heat.

In a large bowl mix together the salt, pepper, cumin, cardamom, cinnamon, paprika, turmeric, mixed spice and cloves, add the lamb and toss until coated. Place the lamb in the casserole dish and mix with the onion. Cover, place in the oven and cook for 1½ hours or until the meat is fork-tender. The juices from the meat should keep the dish moist, but check after 1 hour of cooking and add a little water if necessary.

Serve with steamed basmati rice or Israeli rice pilaf (page 212).

Serves 8

Over the last ten years we've been on an ongoing quest to uncover great brisket recipes – we believe we can never have enough. This one takes the elements of a number of more traditional recipes and puts them together with great success. Mikki originally made this dish with veal brisket, which can be hard to find. If you do make this recipe with veal, it's smaller in size so needs less spice rub and glaze and a shorter cooking time. ~ *MMCC*

See Mikki's story on page 154

Mikki Fink

Glazed Beef Brisket

7 onions, sliced
500 ml (2 cups) veal or beef stock (broth)
2 kg (4½ lb) beef brisket, some fat left on

Spice rub

1 tablespoon mustard powder
1 heaped tablespoon garlic granules
1 heaped tablespoon dried parsley flakes
2 teaspoons sea salt

Glaze

55 g (¼ cup) brown sugar
60 ml (¼ cup) tomato sauce (ketchup)
60 ml (¼ cup) dijon mustard

Preheat the oven to 160°C (325°F/Gas 3). You will need a large roasting pan.

Put the onion into the pan and pour over the stock.

To make the spice rub, in a bowl mix the mustard powder, garlic, parsley and salt together and rub over both sides of the brisket. Place the brisket on top of the onion.

Cover the dish with foil, place in the oven, and roast for 2 hours. Uncover and continue to roast for a further hour or until fork-tender, basting from time to time.

Meanwhile for the glaze, in a bowl, mix together the sugar, tomato sauce and mustard. Spread on top of the cooked brisket and roast for an additional 30 minutes.

To serve, place the brisket on a platter, pile the onion on top and slice thickly.

Serves 10

MIKKI FINK

I couldn't cook and was still in college when I was married in 1953. After I graduated, my husband sent me to a Viennese cooking school in New York for a whole year. We cooked so many different dishes, then enjoyed them for lunch with matched wines – what an indulgence! I have loved cooking and baking ever since, and I adore sitting around the table sharing food with my family and friends.

I'm a second-generation American with a diverse heritage, now living in California with my husband. My grandparents cover a few continents – Ireland, Portugal, Austria-Germany and Finland. My parents loved to travel so we had the chance to experience many different cultures and cuisines. As a child, I thought we were on a never-ending adventure, especially as my parents loved dining at the very best 'in restaurants' all over the world.

I actually think cooking was always in my blood, as my grandmother was a fabulous cook and hostess. She never wrote anything down, but as a child I remember watching her and keeping certain things in my head, which I carefully recorded after I finished cooking school. I always have *schmaltz* in my fridge, which reminds me of my grandmother, and the *gribenes* and rye bread of my childhood. I remember watching her bake, and licking the bowl after the batter was poured into the tin. When my own grandchildren were old enough to understand baking, I did exactly the same thing. They spent a lot of time in my kitchen, at first just licking the bowl and then cooking with me.

My grandson David particularly loved cooking when he was young. As he grew older, it was such a joy to cook together. At college he took a cooking course and then came home and cooked for us and it was just amazing – the warmth and enjoyment we shared as we ate his wonderful meal is a memory I will treasure forever. I still bake for my grandchildren and send Passover packages so they don't forget my macaroons, or me!

MIKKI'S RECIPES

Glazed Beef Brisket: page 152
Pecan-Glazed Noodle Kugel: page 240

My philosophy on food is there should be no waste, as I have lived through times where food was very scarce. As a child living in Siberia, my family received United Nations Relief Organisation packages. One parcel contained dehydrated chicken breasts. My mother didn't know what to do with this gem at first, but she decided to soak the chicken in water, pound out the reconstituted breasts, add what spices and ingredients we had, and turn it into her own *gefilte* fish. It was mouth-watering and I remember the meal to this day.

It is my Jewish heritage that has led me to appreciate food and its importance in fostering friendship and love. I am both Ashkenazi and Sephardi. My mother's heritage is Eastern European and I was born in Warsaw, Poland. On my father's side, we can trace our Sephardi heritage right back to the Spanish religious conversions of the 15th century.

I was just six months old when my father insisted our family leave Poland, as he could see the threat of war descending on Europe and feared for our lives. Many of our extended family remained behind and, as a result, perished. While my father was in Russian-occupied Poland, my mother planned our escape, which involved carrying me across a river. The man who helped us warned that I must not cry or we would be caught, so my mother gave me a piece of chocolate to keep me quiet.

We lived in Siberia and my father worked as a slave labourer in an armaments factory for the Russian government, in freezing cold conditions, often reaching minus 40 degrees. After the war, we returned to Poland before making our way to Australia. We left without a single member of our extended family – they did not survive the Warsaw Ghetto.

When I was 21, we arrived in Sydney without any family or money. We worked exceptionally hard and managed to buy a house within one year of arriving. When we moved into our new home in Greenwich our neighbour arrived with a batch of moreish Anzac biscuits and a pot of tea, the quintessential Australian welcome. My parents remained friends with them for life. I am now a guide at the Sydney Jewish Museum and am constantly inspired as I tell my story to adults and children so they can learn the harsh lessons of history.

GEORGE'S RECIPE

Rack of Veal with Herbs: page 156

I first met George, the most special man, at the Sydney Jewish Museum, where he is a Holocaust Survivor Volunteer Guide and I am a Community Stories Volunteer. We love chatting about all things food, and his 'Gourmet Group' has always fascinated me. Five couples meet every month to try out a different cuisine. The host couple provides drinks, decoration and music, while the guests cook and bring the food. George cooks this veal on the barbecue but we do ours in the oven. ~ *Jacqui, MMCC*

See George's story on page 155

George Sternfeld

Rack of Veal with Herbs

8-bone rack of veal
2 teaspoons sea salt
1 teaspoon ground black pepper
60 ml (¼ cup) olive oil
2 cloves garlic, crushed
1 bunch rosemary
1 bunch sage
4 large onions, quartered
250 ml (1 cup) water
beetroot confit, to serve

Beetroot Confit

50 g (1¾ oz) butter or margarine
1 tablespoon olive oil
½ onion, thinly sliced
2 cloves garlic, crushed
450 g (1 lb/about 3 medium) beetroot
   (beets), peeled and grated
90 g (½ cup, loosely packed)
   brown sugar
60 ml (¼ cup) balsamic vinegar
60 ml (¼ cup) dry sherry
80 ml (⅓ cup) orange juice
1 tablespoon finely grated orange zest
½ teaspoon ground cinnamon
½ teaspoon ground nutmeg
100 g (⅔ cup) currants or sultanas
   (golden raisins)

Preheat the oven to 250°C (500°F/Gas 10). You will need a flameproof roasting pan and a wire rack to fit.

Rub the veal with the salt, pepper, olive oil and garlic. Cover with the rosemary and sage (on their stalks) and truss with butcher's twine to secure. Alternatively, ask your butcher to tie the veal, leaving enough room so you can tuck the herbs under the twine.

Put the onion into the roasting pan, then add the water.

Place a wire rack over the onion, arrange the veal on top and roast for 15 minutes.

Reduce the temperature to 180°C (350°F/Gas 4) and roast for a further 25 minutes (for rare). Remove the roasting pan from the oven. Transfer the veal and onion to a large plate, cover with foil and allow to rest for 20 minutes.

Meanwhile, on the stove top, place the roasting pan over medium heat and simmer for a few minutes or until the cooking juices are reduced by half.

Serve with the cooking juices and onion from the roasting pan, and beetroot confit (see below) on the side.

Serves 6–8

Beetroot Confit

In a heavy-based saucepan over medium heat, melt the butter or margarine and add the olive oil. Add the onion and garlic and sauté for 15 minutes or until soft. Add the beetroot and the remaining ingredients. Stir to combine. Cover and simmer gently over low heat for 1 hour, stirring occasionally, until the beetroot is fork-tender. Uncover, increase the heat to medium–high and simmer to reduce any excess liquid. Allow to cool before serving.

Store in the refrigerator for up to 2 weeks.

Makes 2½ cups

156 MAIN BEEF

This recipe was created by Lainie to honour her grandmother's Persian cooking, and I was lucky enough to spend an afternoon watching Lainie make them. These little torpedoes of spiced beef, onion and pine nut are delicious at any time of the year but are especially popular during the Jewish festival of fried food, *Chanukah.* ∼ *Lisa, MMCC*

See Lainie's story on page 179

Lainie Cadry

Kibbeh

vegetable oil, for shallow-frying
lemon wedges, to serve

Filling

3 onions, finely chopped
125 ml (½ cup) olive oil
1 teaspoon ground cumin
1 teaspoon ground turmeric
1 teaspoon garlic powder
1 teaspoon onion powder
½ teaspoon sea salt
½ teaspoon ground cinnamon
½ teaspoon ground black pepper
250 g (9 oz) minced (ground) beef
80 g (½ cup) toasted pine nuts

Dough

320 g (2 cups) fine burghul (bulgur)
500 g (1 lb 2 oz) finely minced
    (ground) beef
2 eggs
1 onion, processed in a food processor
1 teaspoon ground cumin
1 teaspoon garlic powder
1 teaspoon onion powder
½ teaspoon ground turmeric
¼ teaspoon ground cinnamon
1 teaspoon sea salt
1 teaspoon ground black pepper

Soak the burghul in cold water for 1 hour, then drain very well.

To make the filling, in a frying pan over low heat, fry the onion in ¼ cup of the olive oil for about 30 minutes or until well caramelised. When almost done, add the cumin, turmeric, garlic powder, onion powder, salt, cinnamon and pepper and toss for 2 minutes. Remove from the pan and set aside. In the same pan, over high heat, add the remaining oil and sauté the minced beef for a few minutes until browned and cooked through. Return the onion to the pan, add the pine nuts and stir to combine. Season to taste and set aside.

To make the dough, in a large bowl, mix the burghul, beef, egg, onion, cumin, garlic powder, onion powder, turmeric, cinnamon, salt and pepper together in a large bowl. Season to taste with extra salt and pepper. With wet hands, make a walnut-sized ball and, with your index finger, make a deep hole for the filling, rotating your finger to make the hole quite large.

Place a generous teaspoonful of the filling in the hole and close to seal. With wet hands again, gently mould the ball into an almond shape with pointy ends, patching with more dough where necessary. Be quite firm and fast with your moulding and make sure there are no cracks. Repeat with all the dough and filling. Place the kibbeh on a tray, cover with plastic wrap and refrigerate for at least 1 hour. When you remove them from the fridge, seal any cracks then shape the ends so they are quite pointy.

To fry the kibbeh, pour 2.5 cm (1 inch) of vegetable oil into a saucepan. Heat the oil over medium heat and fry the kibbeh in batches for 2 minutes on each side or until golden brown all over.

Drain on paper towel and serve immediately with lemon wedges.

Makes about 40

We met Solomon's daughter Naomi, also a wonderful cook, through her work with Breville when we presented a Mother's Day cooking demonstration. She has become a firm friend, with a generous soul and a wealth of cooking and appliance knowledge. She brought several of her dad's dishes to our kitchen for tasting, and we just couldn't resist the satay sticks. Supermarket peanut butter is quite salty, so use both a low-salt soy sauce and chicken stock to balance it. ～ *MMCC*

See Solomon's story on page 162

Solomon Sassoon

Beef and Chicken Satay

32 wooden skewers
800 g (1 lb 12 oz) rump steak, cubed
800 g (1 lb 12 oz) chicken thigh fillets, cubed
1 × 2.5 cm (1 inch) piece ginger, grated
2 cloves garlic, crushed
80 ml (⅓ cup) low-salt soy sauce
3 teaspoons sesame oil

Satay sauce

375 g (13 oz) crunchy peanut butter
250 ml (1 cup) low-salt chicken stock (broth)
2 tablespoons low-salt soy sauce
1 tablespoon lemon juice
2 teaspoons sambal oelek or hot chilli sauce
1 clove garlic, crushed
2 teaspoons sugar
2–3 tablespoons boiling water

lime wedges, to serve

Start this recipe at least 6 hours before serving.

Soak the wooden skewers in cold water for 30 minutes.

Place the rump steak in a bowl. Place the chicken in another bowl. To make the marinade, in a small mixing bowl, combine the ginger, garlic, soy sauce and sesame oil. Divide the marinade between the chicken and beef and mix well. Cover with plastic wrap and refrigerate for at least 6 hours or overnight.

To make the satay sauce, in a saucepan over medium heat, place the peanut butter, stock, soy sauce, lemon juice, sambal oelek (or hot chilli sauce), garlic and sugar and stir until combined; do not bring to the boil. Remove from the heat and set aside. The satay sauce will thicken as it cools.

Just before serving, add the boiling water to the satay sauce and stir until smooth.

Thread about 4 pieces of the beef onto each skewer until all the beef has been used. Repeat with the chicken.

Heat a barbecue grill-plate to high. Barbecue the skewers for a few minutes on each side, until cooked to your liking, ensuring the chicken is cooked through.

Lay the skewers on a platter and drizzle with the satay sauce. Serve with lime wedges for squeezing and the remaining satay sauce in a bowl alongside.

Serves 8

SOLOMON SASSOON

I was born in a Japanese internment camp in Singapore in 1943, during the tumultuous time of the Japanese occupation of World War II. It must have been a very difficult time for my mother, with five small children and an infant son to care for in such harrowing conditions. In search of a better life, I moved to Sydney when I was 17.

My love of Eastern food is inspired by my childhood in Singapore and Iraqi heritage. I remember as a child watching my mother, elder brother and our local Chinese helper create the tastiest meals. I was so curious and eager to help that I was soon part of the action. One of my most delicious memories is eating mouth-watering satay in the steaming heat at the Singapore Satay Club.

My wife was born in Sydney and luckily she has been more than happy to eat my style of food. My daughters are also passionate cooks, perhaps inspired by all the entertaining we did. As youngsters they would help me prepare for dinner parties by threading the meat onto the satay skewers. We all laughed so hard when they answered the phone with 'Sol's House of Satay!'

I'm retired now and while I do love gardening and karaoke, my great passion is still most definitely cooking; I still love a great curry and a bowl of dahl.

SOLOMON'S RECIPE

Beef and Chicken Satay: page 160

YOSSI BENDAYAN

I grew up in a Moroccan family where food was the centre of the home and the family. We were all involved in cooking dinner, from deciding what to cook, to preparing ingredients and finally critiquing the food as each course was served.

My mother always had great attention to detail. It was equally important to her which spices to use in each dish and its presentation at the table. Even now I associate saffron with special occasion foods, which take me back to the celebration meals of my youth. When I made *aliyah* (immigrated to Israel), I was lucky to cook with my paternal grandmother, who years earlier had also taught my mother, her daughter-in-law, all her secrets.

I studied to be a chef and worked my way to the top of the hospitality ladder when I realised how much I love teaching others how to cook. Now I am a roving ambassador for Israeli food and have my own restaurant, Shulchan Orech, in Jerusalem.

Israeli food is continually evolving from many diverse cultures and for me it is about the fusion of modern Israeli cooking with forgotten ethnic cuisines. It is a beautiful time for the culinary arts in Israel. With our abundance of fresh produce and a great passion for eating, you can enjoy everything from falafel and hummus on the street corner to kosher fine dining.

YOSSI'S RECIPE

Meatball Tagine with Chickpeas: page 164

I had the pleasure of working with Yossi when he visited Sydney as a guest chef. This dish is pure unadulterated deliciousness (if that's even a word). When we first made it we stood around the pot, spoons in hand, digging in and going back for more. If you prefer no bread, Yossi suggests using one grated, raw desiree potato instead. ~ *Lynn, MMCC*

See Yossi's story on page 162

Yossi Bendayan

Meatball Tagine with Chickpeas

200 g (1 cup) dried chickpeas
2 red capsicums (peppers), quartered, seeds removed
sea salt and ground black pepper
60 ml (¼ cup) olive oil
6 cloves garlic, crushed
1½ tablespoons ground cumin
1½ tablespoons sweet paprika
1 teaspoon dried chilli flakes
2 bunches coriander (cilantro), leaves only

Meatballs

2 slices white bread, crusts removed
1 onion, finely chopped
3 cloves garlic, peeled
1 bunch flat-leaf (Italian) parsley, leaves only
500 g (1 lb 2 oz) minced (ground) beef
60 ml (¼ cup) olive oil
1 tablespoon ground cumin
1 tablespoon sweet paprika
sea salt and ground black pepper

Start this recipe a day before serving.

Soak the chickpeas in a bowl of cold water overnight. The next day, drain the chickpeas, rinse under cold water and drain again.

In a large saucepan, place the chickpeas and cover generously with water. Bring to the boil over high heat, then reduce the heat to medium and simmer for 1 hour or until the chickpeas are soft. Drain and reserve the cooking water.

Meanwhile, preheat the oven to 200°C (400°F/Gas 6). Line a baking tray.

Place the capsicum on the lined tray, season and drizzle with olive oil, then roast for 30 minutes. Cool, then slice into strips and set aside.

To make the meatballs, soak the bread in water for a few minutes. Drain and squeeze the bread and place in a food processor with the onion, garlic and parsley and pulse until a paste forms. In a large bowl, mix the paste with the minced beef, olive oil, cumin and paprika. Season generously. With wet hands, shape into walnut-sized balls. Set aside. (Makes about 35 meatballs.)

You will need a deep, heavy based frying pan with a lid. Heat the olive oil in the frying pan over low–medium heat, and sauté the garlic, cumin, paprika and chilli flakes for a minute, until the spices are fragrant. Add the chickpeas with 2 cups of the reserved cooking liquid, stirring well. Bring to the boil, then reduce the heat to low and place the meatballs on top. The liquid should half-cover the meatballs; if not, add more. Cover and simmer for 15 minutes.

Reserving a handful for garnish, chop the coriander leaves. Add to the frying pan with the roasted capsicum and simmer vigorously over medium–high heat for 20 minutes, stirring gently from time to time, until the sauce reduces and thickens. Season to taste.

Sprinkle with the reserved coriander, then serve.

Serves 6

We were really keen to put this recipe into the book, as we were missing a big roast that can feed the whole family. Michele has adapted and made her own version of Tyler Florence's prime rib of beef with horseradish crust. The salty crust works perfectly with the juicy meat, and the vegetables are spectacular. ~ *MMCC*

See Michele's story on page 84

Michele Wise

Standing Rib Roast with Horseradish Crust

2 kg (4½ lb) standing beef rib roast (prime rib of beef)
4 carrots, peeled and cut into chunks
16 French shallots (eschallots), peeled
4 potatoes or parsnips, cut into chunks
2 tablespoons olive oil
sea salt and ground black pepper

Horseradish crust

60 ml (¼ cup) olive oil
4 cloves garlic, crushed
45 g (½ cup) horseradish, grated fresh or prepared
8 sprigs thyme, leaves only
2 tablespoons sea salt
1 tablespoon ground black pepper

Preheat the oven to 200°C (400°F/Gas 6). Place a large roasting pan in the oven to heat up.

To make the horseradish crust, in a bowl, combine the olive oil, garlic, horseradish, thyme, salt and pepper and spread over the beef.

In a separate bowl, toss the carrots, shallots and potatoes or parsnips with the olive oil. Season with salt and pepper.

Remove the hot roasting pan from the oven and carefully place the beef in the pan, bone-side down. Scatter the vegetables around the beef. Roast for 15 minutes, then reduce the oven temperature to 180°C (350°F/Gas 4) and continue to roast for about 1 hour (total cooking time) for rare, 1¼ hours for medium–rare and 1½ hours for medium. The cooking time depends on the size of the roast but a good guide is 16 minutes per 500 g (1 lb 2 oz) for rare, 20 minutes for medium and 24 minutes for well done.

Remove the roasting pan from the oven, cover loosely with foil and allow the beef to rest for 20 minutes before carving. Serve the beef with the roasted vegetables.

Serves 6

Frederique is one of my dear sisters-in-law. Her cooking is delectable. I had heard of her family's couscous many times over the years, and just knew I had to lay my hands on the recipe for this book. I love that all the women in her family make this recipe, but add their own personal touch. It is a feast that will feed a whole crowd and then some. The couscous is traditionally served in a large bowl at the centre of the table, with the meat and vegetables on a separate platter. Serve with grilled capsicum salad (*salade cuite*), and Moroccan carrot and chard salad (both page 170) and harissa on the side.

~ *Merelyn, MMCC*

See Frederique's story on page 171

Frederique Halimi-Frank

Algerian Beef Couscous

300 g (10 oz) dried chickpeas

Base stock

2 beef shin bones, whole or in pieces
3 onions, quartered
1 roma (plum) tomato, quartered
1 celery stalk
2 bay leaves
water, to cover
½ tablespoon peppercorns
sea salt and ground black pepper

Start this recipe a day before serving.

Place the chickpeas in a large bowl and cover generously with water. Allow to soak overnight.

To make the base stock, place the bones, onion, tomato, celery, bay leaves and peppercorns in a stockpot. Pour in enough cold water to cover the ingredients, around 3 litres (3 quarts). Bring to the boil and skim off the scum that rises to the surface. Partially cover with a lid, reduce the heat to low–medium and continue to simmer for 4 hours or until there is a flavoursome stock, topping up with extra water as required.

Add salt and pepper to taste. Allow to cool slightly, then remove the bones and strain the liquid. It should yield about 2.5 litres (2.5 quarts) stock. Discard the bones and vegetables. Cool, then cover with plastic wrap and refrigerate overnight.

Beef and vegetable broth

1 quantity base stock (see opposite)

1.5 kg (3 lb 5 oz) chuck steak (braising beef), in large pieces

3 tomatoes, roughly chopped

3 onions, halved

6 small carrots, peeled

2 turnips, peeled and quartered

¼ white cabbage

300 g (10 oz) pumpkin (squash)

2 bunches coriander (cilantro), leaves only, roughly chopped

1 head garlic

1 tablespoon ground cumin

500 g (1 lb 2 oz) zucchini (courgettes), ends trimmed

sea salt and ground black pepper

Couscous

500 ml (2 cups) chicken or vegetable stock (broth)

1 tablespoon olive oil

1 teaspoon harissa, or to taste

400 g (2 cups) regular or wholegrain couscous

To make the beef and vegetable broth, skim off the fat from the top of the stock and place in a stockpot. Add the beef, tomato and onion and bring to the boil. Skim off the scum that rises to the surface, partially cover with a lid and simmer over low heat for about 1½ hours or until the meat is fork-tender. Remove the beef from the liquid and set aside.

Drain the soaked chickpeas, rinse with cold water and drain again. Add the chickpeas to the broth and simmer over low heat for 30–45 minutes or until just cooked. Add the carrots, turnip, cabbage, pumpkin, coriander, garlic and cumin and simmer for about 30 minutes or until the carrots are just cooked through. Add more water if the broth becomes too thick – there should be enough liquid to almost cover the vegetables. Add the zucchini and simmer for a further 15 minutes or until just cooked and still bright green.

Just before serving, remove and discard the garlic. Return the beef to the broth to reheat.

To cook the couscous, in a large saucepan, place the stock, olive oil and harissa and bring to the boil. Add the couscous and cook over high heat, stirring continuously, for a couple of minutes or until the stock is almost completely absorbed. Remove from the stove, cover with a lid and set aside for 20 minutes or until the grains have completely swelled. Using a fork, break up and separate the couscous.

The couscous can be served immediately, or reheated in the top section of a *couscoussier*, in a covered drum sieve set over the stockpot or in a microwave.

Serve with grilled capsicum salad (*salade cuite*, page 170) and Moroccan carrot and chard salad (page 170), and harissa on the side.

Serves at least 10

Photo on pages 172–173

Grilled Capsicum Salad (Salade Cuite)

5 large red capsicums (peppers)
2 large green capsicums (peppers)
2 tablespoons extra virgin olive oil
3 cloves garlic, crushed
1 × 400 g (14 oz) tin Italian diced
   tomatoes
1 teaspoon sea salt

Preheat the oven to 230°C (450°F/Gas 8). Line a baking tray.

Place the capsicums on the baking tray and roast for 30 minutes or until the skins blister and blacken, turning regularly. Remove from the oven and put them into a plastic bag. Twist the top of the plastic bag to enclose the steam and leave for 20 minutes or until just cool enough to handle.

Peel and remove the seeds from each capsicum, leaving the others in the bag to stay warm. Do not run them under running water to wash off the seeds or skin, as it also washes off the roasted flavour. Cut the capsicums into 2 × 1 cm (¾ × ½ inch) pieces.

In a large saucepan over medium heat, heat the olive oil and add the garlic, stirring until it is sizzling and pale. Add the tomatoes and salt and simmer for 20 minutes or until thick, stirring regularly. Add the capsicum and cook for 15 minutes or until the sauce is thick.

Allow to cool and refrigerate until ready to serve. Serve cold or at room temperature.

Serve alongside the Algerian beef couscous (previous page)

Moroccan Carrot and Chard Salad

1 bunch chard or silverbeet (about
   1 kg/2 lb 4 oz)
6 carrots (800 g/1 lb 12 oz)
3 cloves garlic, crushed
60 ml (¼ cup) extra virgin olive oil
1 tablespoon ground cumin
2 tablespoons white wine vinegar
½ teaspoon sea salt
ground black pepper

Rinse the chard (or silverbeet) well, remove and discard the stems, and roughly chop. Peel and thickly slice the carrots.

Bring a large saucepan of salted water to the boil. Add the carrot and cook over high heat for about 3 minutes or until just starting to soften. Place the chard (or silverbeet) on top of the carrot, cover and steam over high heat for 2 minutes or until wilted. Drain well.

In a saucepan over low–medium heat sauté the garlic in the oil for 1 minute or until sizzling. Add the cumin and sauté for 1 minute, then add the vinegar and salt, taking care as the mixture may spit. Add the carrot and chard (or silverbeet) and cook, stirring, for 5 minutes or until the vegetables are soft and there is very little liquid left in the pan. Season with extra salt and pepper. Allow to cool and refrigerate until ready to serve. Serve cold or at room temperature.

Serve alongside the Algerian beef couscous (previous page)

Photo on pages 172–173

FREDERIQUE HALIMI-FRANK

I love the process of cooking, which for me is almost a form of meditation. I am the product of a lineage of excellent cooks who each put their heart and soul into the food they prepare and eat. It's certainly a mixed heritage, full of eclectic cooking styles that are a fusion of my ancestors' histories. My father is from Algeria, and my mother from Morocco. I was born in Morocco, grew up in Marseille, France, and have lived in Israel since the mid-1980s. I discovered a wonderful life when I came to Israel on a holiday to reconnect with my roots, and never left.

It was partly because I lived in Israel that I learnt to cook. I realised there was nothing ready-made here, so if I wanted to eat, I needed to make it from scratch. At first I re-created dishes I had enjoyed as I travelled around the world, mainly from Asia and India. Then I started to cook the holiday feasts from my childhood – traditional dishes I had grown up with.

My mother and her sisters are all very independent cooks and their kitchens have always been their own domains, off-limits to the children. Growing up, it was almost impossible to cook with them as they never measured and cooked according to the variable number of guests and to taste. We could watch and chat but could not ask too many questions. Over the years, by trial and error, I have mastered their dishes. Even checking this Algerian couscous recipe took a trip to Marseille – and three generations in the kitchen – to ensure Maman told us the correct measurements and tips.

The long line of excellent cooks continues into the next generation, as my three children and my husband all love to cook. For our 25th wedding anniversary, the kids sent us away and took control of the kitchen. They spent the whole day together, preparing a feast. It was a joyous celebration, full of charades and games, stories and laughs, but what I loved the most was that the three of them had spent the day together, creating lifelong memories.

FREDERIQUE'S RECIPES

Algerian Beef Couscous: page 168
Grilled Capsicum Salad (Salad Cuite): opposite page
Moroccan Carrot and Chard Salad: opposite page

We learnt something very interesting about Silvia's Italian connection to Libyan food. There is a large, thriving Libyan–Jewish community in Rome, who mostly came from Tripoli in 1967, escaping persecution by Gaddafi. Incredibly, in just one month, the Italian Navy helped evacuate more than 6000 Jews to Rome. Like many Jewish communities in the diaspora, the Libyan people took their own cooking traditions and ingredients with them, and this dish has become a popular Italian dish for Shabbat. ∼ *MMCC*

See Silvia's story on page 198

Silvia Nacamulli

Libyan Beef with Beans

250 g (1⅓ cups) dried cannellini beans

300 g (10 oz) beef marrow or shin bones

1.25 litres (5 cups) cold water

1 tablespoon salt

2 onions, finely chopped

80 ml (⅓ cup) olive oil

2 teaspoons ground cumin

2 teaspoons sweet paprika

2 teaspoons ground cardamom

1–2 teaspoons harissa or chilli paste

1 teaspoon sea salt

1 teaspoon ground black pepper

3 cloves garlic, crushed

1.2 kg (2 lb 10 oz) chuck or stewing beef, cubed

140 g (½ cup) tomato paste (concentrated purée)

couscous or rice, to serve

Start this recipe a day before serving.

You will need a large flameproof casserole dish with a lid.

Cover the beans generously with water and soak overnight or for at least 12 hours.

In a large saucepan, place the marrow bones with the cold water and tablespoon of salt. Bring to the boil, skim off the scum that rises to the surface, then cover and simmer over low heat for 40 minutes. Set aside.

In a large flameproof casserole dish, fry the onion in the oil over low–medium heat for 5 minutes. Add the cumin, paprika, cardamom, harissa or chilli paste, salt and pepper. Cook over low heat for 10 minutes, stirring from time to time. Add the garlic and continue to cook for another 2 minutes, stirring. Add the beef and sear for 8–10 minutes over medium–high heat.

Drain and rinse the cannellini beans and add them to the casserole dish with the tomato paste. Stir well, cover with a lid and continue to simmer for 10 minutes. Remove the marrow bones, reserving the cooking liquid and add them to the casserole dish, along with as much of the liquid as is needed to come three-quarters of the way up the side of the beef. Reserve the remaining liquid.

Simmer over low heat, covered, for 3 hours or until the beef is fork-tender, stirring occasionally. Halfway through cooking, add more of the reserved liquid if needed to keep the dish moist and to allow the beans to cook properly.

Serve with couscous or rice.

Serves 6–8

We are so excited by this fusion of an iconic Jewish dish with the flavours of the Berbers of North Africa. ~ *MMCC*

See Michael's story on page 178

Michael W. Twitty

Berbere Brisket

2 kg (4½ lb) beef brisket, some fat left on

2 tablespoons berbere spice mix (see below)

5 cm (2 inch) knob ginger, peeled, finely grated

2 cloves garlic, crushed

60 ml (¼ cup) olive oil

3 onions, roughly chopped

2 × 400 g (14 oz) tins Italian diced tomatoes

2 red onions, sliced into thick rings

500 ml (2 cups) chicken or beef stock (broth)

1 tablespoon brown sugar

1 sprig rosemary

sea salt and ground black pepper

Berbere Spice Mix

1 tablespoon sweet or hot paprika

1 tablespoon garlic powder

1 tablespoon onion powder

1 tablespoon chilli powder

1 tablespoon sea salt

½ teaspoon ground ginger

½ teaspoon ground cinnamon

½ teaspoon ground cardamom

½ teaspoon dried basil

½ teaspoon ground cumin

½ teaspoon chilli flakes

½ teaspoon ground fenugreek

Preheat the oven to 160°C (325°F/Gas 3). You will need a flameproof roasting pan large enough to fit the brisket.

In a small bowl, combine the spice mix, ginger, garlic and 1 tablespoon of the olive oil. Rub into both sides of the brisket.

Heat the remaining olive oil over high heat in the roasting pan. Sear the brisket for a few minutes on each side, until well browned. Remove from the pan and set aside.

Add the chopped onion to the roasting pan, adding a splash more oil if needed, and sauté for about 15 minutes or until soft. Add the tomatoes and toss through. Turn off the heat, remove the tomato mixture from the roasting pan and set aside.

Place the red onion in the roasting pan and lay the browned brisket on top. Pour the tomato mixture on top of the brisket.

Stir the sugar into the stock and pour around the brisket. Add the rosemary and season well with salt and pepper.

Cover tightly with foil (aluminium foil) and bake for 3½ hours or until the brisket is fork-tender.

If you are not serving the brisket immediately, remove from the oven, allow to cool and refrigerate. When chilled, remove the excess fat from the sauce, slice the meat and place in an ovenproof serving dish, piling the red onion on top. To serve, reheat gently at 160°C (325°F/Gas 3) for 30 minutes or until heated through.

Serves 10

Berbere Spice Mix

This makes more than you will need for this recipe. Store the remainder in an airtight container for up to 6 months.

Combine the paprika, garlic powder, onion powder, chilli powder, salt, ginger, cinnamon, cardamom, basil, cumin, chilli flakes and fenugreek in a jar, seal, shake well.

Makes about ½ cup

MICHAEL W. TWITTY

People say to me, 'I don't understand you – you're Black and you're Jewish.' And then, when I feed them, they get me immediately. But how could I possibly understand what it's like to be really Jewish? Being Black is great preparation. I talk with my hands, I eat chicken, I complain, I survived my oppression. What else do you need to know?

My lifelong interest in Judaism, and Jewish food, began as a child. Growing up outside Washington, DC, the treat in my house every weekend was *challah*, a taste my mother developed during her childhood in Cincinnati, where the only baker open on Sundays was Jewish. When I was seven, after seeing Chaim Potok's *The Chosen*, I informed my mother that I was Jewish. Over the next few years, when I visited my Jewish friends' homes, I would be mesmerised by their Jewish grandmothers as they prepared food for us. For many of my friends, I became the culinary memory of the family as I would ask the questions, watch the cooking – especially their hands – and collect knowledge about the food and the recipes. If their grandmother put cinnamon and meat in her *kneidlach*, I knew she came from Lithuania.

This, among other things, led to my conversion to Judaism in my 20s in a Sephardic Synagogue, which was very welcoming to African-Americans.

I'm a food writer and culinary historian, a Judaic studies teacher and historical interpreter. Jewish and African diasporas are all around the world, so I have amazing access to almost every cuisine. Over time I began to fuse Southern and African-American food with Jewish and called it 'Kosher/Soul'. I believe we express our identities through food and this new fusion said so much. It is about melding the histories, tastes, flavours and diasporic wisdom of being Black and Jewish. Both express many of their cultural and spiritual values through the plate and this is what my food journey is all about.

There are a lot of parallels between Jewish and African-American people. There's not a thing that the Southern White folk did that Black men and women did not touch, influence or revolutionise to the point that they did not know where we ended and they began. And it's the same thing with *Yehudim*. You can't throw a stone in Europe without finding the Jewish influence, or Jewish genes, there.

It's funny how oppressed people end up being everywhere and everything. You can't get rid of us – and you can't put us down. We use our food to empower ourselves. What I do with kosher/soul is combine the survival gene in the Jews with the survival gene in Black folk, and I make it work.

MICHAEL'S RECIPES

Black-Eyed Bean Hummus: page 48
Berbere Brisket: page 176

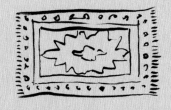

LAINIE CADRY

My grandparents' journeys have shaped the way I cook. The food I love is not bound by one tradition or cuisine but being Jewish is at its core. On our Shabbat table, the traditions of Eastern Europe are seen in the *challah* – with caramelised onions on top, my own touch – and in the chopped liver and the egg dip, in the *matzo* balls and the *lokshen kugel*. My rich Persian heritage is evident in the *gondi* and spiced chicken soup, in the *khoresht* (stews) loaded with exotic ingredients and in the crunchy *tahdig* (crispy rice).

My *bobba* (my maternal grandmother), Betty, was born in Lithuania and my *zaida* (my maternal grand-father), Gershon, escaped from Nazi Germany and made it to British Mandate Palestine when he was only a 13-year-old boy. My father's parents, Jacqueline and Jack, were born in Persia (Iran) and came to Australia in search of a safer life.

Omi (Jacqueline) taught my mother, Judy Wilkenfeld, the secrets of her Persian kitchen. Mum soon mastered these treasured recipes and, when I was old enough, shared them with me, together with her own Eastern European traditions. I also cooked with my grandmother's Russian helper Tania, adding yet another dimension to my repertoire.

The one Persian dish that Mum never learnt from Omi was how to make *gondi*. It is one of the most unique dishes to the Jews of Iran, probably originating in the Jewish ghetto in Tehran. We went to our Persian friend Angie, who shared her cooking method with us. It has taken me many years, attempts, subtractions and additions to get to where it is today. I remember when I finally got the recipe correct, Mum couldn't believe it – she said they were even better than my grandmother's.

Baking has never been a priority in my family. I started by making packet mixes and decorating Marie biscuits with coloured icing and sprinkles with my cousin Debbie. I then taught myself by watching cooking shows and YouTube videos until I had the techniques covered.

Mum was fundamental in establishing my love of cooking. She taught me to cook with intuition and to use whatever is already in the house. She taught me to cook instinctively, with complexity in flavour and simplicity in style and, most importantly, to do so with generosity, abundance and love. We adore being in the kitchen together and when we are cooking we move in complete unison – we call it 'our dance' – and you can taste the love in everything we make.

To me, family is everything. I am studying to become a mothercraft nurse and midwife and can't wait to assist women in welcoming their families into the world.

LAINIE'S RECIPES

This dish of green beans in tomato with mince and *tahdig* (crispy rice) is like a Persian version of a cottage pie. Lainie spent the morning in the MMCC kitchen taking us through her recipes, step by step. We madly scribbled notes and tasted everything, as we followed her instructions. Lainie developed this recipe out of necessity when she was travelling with her dad to a Persian rug fair, and found herself having to make a traditional Persian *khoresht* (stew) in less than two hours. Using minced (ground) meat instead of stewing beef saved her hours, and the crusty rice is genius. ∼ *MMCC*

See Lainie's story on page 179

Lainie Cadry

Lubia Polow

60 ml (¼ cup) vegetable oil

Meat mixture

500 g (1 lb 2 oz) green beans, trimmed
2 tablespoons olive oil
2 onions, halved and sliced
500 g (1 lb 2 oz) minced (ground) beef
1 onion, puréed with 60 ml (¼ cup) water
1 teaspoon sea salt
½ teaspoon ground white pepper
½ teaspoon ground turmeric
½ teaspoon ground cinnamon
½ teaspoon ground cumin
210 g (7 oz) tomato paste
   (concentrated purée)
210 g (7 oz) tomato purée
125 ml (½ cup) water

To make the meat mixture, slice the beans into 4 cm (1½ inch) pieces. In a wide, heavy-based, non-stick saucepan over medium heat, cook the beans in 2 teaspoons of the olive oil for about 10 minutes, covered, stirring occasionally. Remove the beans and set aside.

In the same pan over medium heat, sauté the onion in the remaining oil for about 20 minutes or until soft and golden. Remove the onion from the pan and set aside.

Increase the heat to medium–high and add the beef, onion purée, salt, pepper and turmeric to the pan. Toss well and cook until the beef is well browned and the liquid has evaporated. Add the cinnamon and cumin and cook for 2 minutes or until fragrant. Stir through the tomato paste. Add the beans, onion, tomato purée and water. Stir to combine and bring to the boil. Reduce the heat to low and simmer for 20 minutes or until most of the liquid has evaporated. Season to taste. Remove the meat mixture from the pan and set aside.

Rice

330 g (1½ cups) basmati rice
½ teaspoon sea salt

Saffron water

pinch of saffron threads (8 threads)
½ teaspoon sugar
60 ml (¼ cup) hot water

While the meat is cooking, make the rice. Thoroughly rinse the rice in a fine-mesh strainer under cold running water for 2 minutes or until the water runs clear. Fill a large saucepan with water and bring to the boil. Add the rice and salt and cook at a rolling boil for 7 minutes or until the rice is just firm to the bite (al dente). Drain and rinse under cold water. Set aside.

To make the saffron water, grind the saffron and sugar together with a mortar and pestle, then stir in the hot water.

To assemble the dish, cover the bottom of the wide, heavy-based, non-stick saucepan with the vegetable oil. Spread one-third of the rice over the oil covering the base of the pan and sprinkle with one-third of the saffron liquid. Layer with half the meat mixture, leaving a 2 cm (¾ inch) border of rice around the meat. Add another one-third of the rice, taking it to the side of the pan, and sprinkle with the second third of saffron water. Add the remaining meat mixture once again leaving a 2 cm border. Finish with the remaining rice, taking it to the side of the pan, and sprinkle the remaining saffron liquid. Using the handle of a wooden spoon, poke 6 holes in the mixture that reach almost to the bottom of the pan.

Cover the saucepan with a lid wrapped in a tea towel (dish cloth) and cook over low–medium heat for 45 minutes or until the rice starts to come away from the edge of the pan.

To serve, gently invert onto a large platter. The base of the rice, now the top, should be golden brown and crunchy.

Serves 6

Photo on page 181

Potato

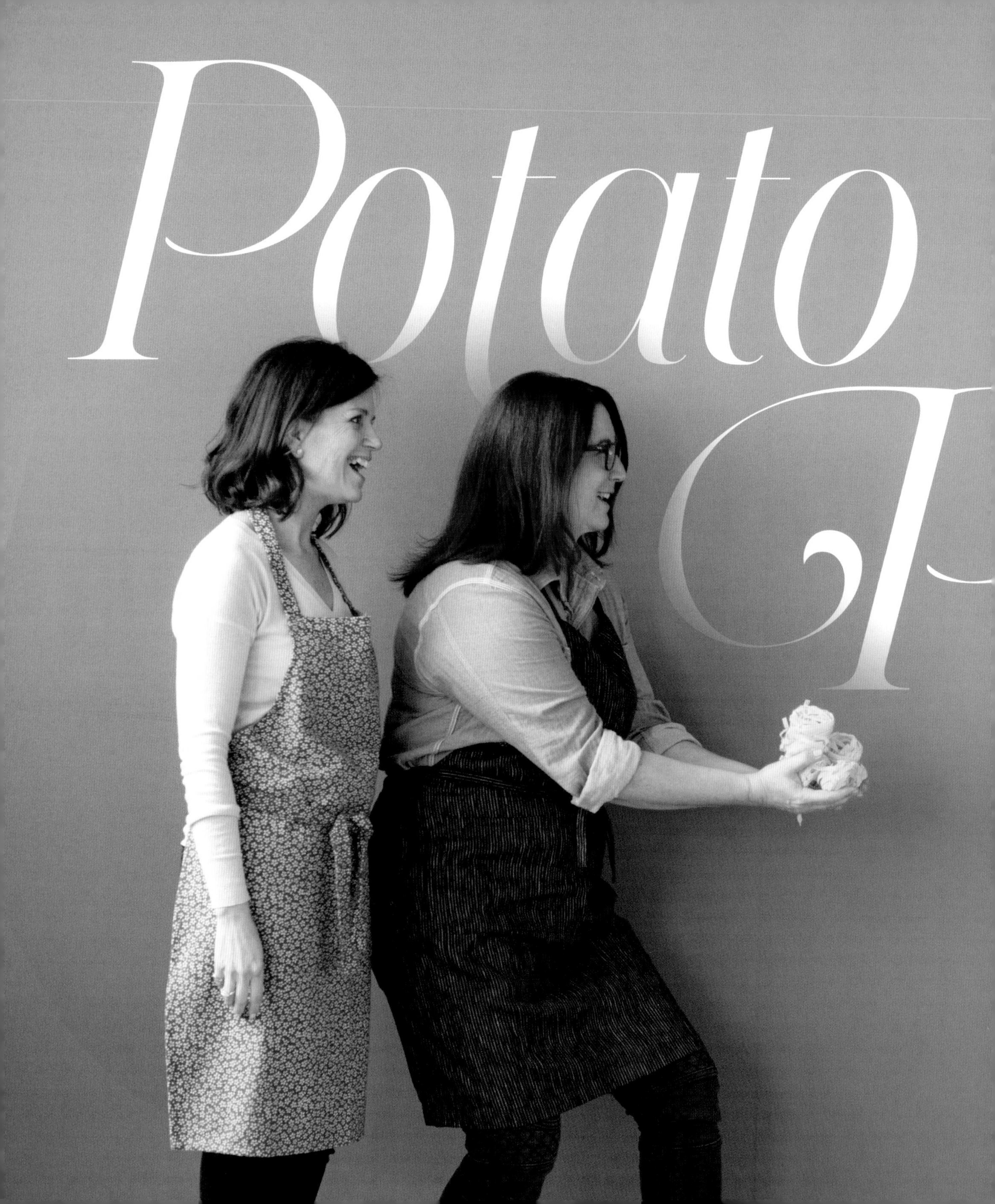

Pasta
Veg

LAURELLE RITZ

It is no secret that Jewish people love to feed others as much as they love to eat. Having Jewish grandparents almost guarantees you spend most of your life overeating whenever in their company – and most of us wouldn't have it any other way.

My family has always been the type to sit and eat together. My father's mum, Luba, was a huge influence in my ongoing love of food. Everything she made was perfectly cooked and she gave me a deep appreciation of practice and patience in the kitchen. I wish I had paid more attention when Luba was alive; she still plays such a big role every time I cook or explore recipes, even though she's no longer here.

I still dream of those days when I was a little girl and slept over at her house. We would make pikelets the next morning, spooning the batter into the frying pan in the shape of letters to spell my name, drenching them in maple syrup and then devouring them together.

I'm a second-generation Australian and I'm thankful for my Russian and Eastern European heritage. Living in multicultural Melbourne gives me a unique take on food and flavour and I love combining my Jewish heritage with modern food to create new dishes for my family and friends.

LAURELLE'S RECIPE

Spinach and Ricotta Gnudi: page 188

This recipe intrigued me, as, like so many people, I love the combination of spinach and ricotta. When I saw the photo after Lisa first made it and heard how her family raved, I couldn't wait to retest it myself. It is a light meal, so simple to make, and beautiful with MMCC's essential tomato sauce, which we always have in the freezer, ready to use. ~*Lynn, MMCC*

See Laurelle's story on page 186

Laurelle Ritz

Spinach and Ricotta Gnudi

500 g (1 lb 2 oz) ricotta cheese
2 French shallots (eschallots), finely
   chopped
1 clove garlic, crushed
20 g (1 tablespoon) butter
100 g (3½ oz) English spinach leaves
1 egg, lightly beaten
65 g (½ cup) grated parmesan cheese,
   plus 25 g (⅓ cup) extra
75 g (½ cup) plain (all-purpose) flour
sea salt and ground black pepper
1 litre (4 cups) MMCC's essential tomato
   sauce (see opposite)

Preheat the oven to 180°C (350°F/Gas 4). You will need a large baking dish, at least 30 × 22 cm (12 × 9 inches).

Place the ricotta in a paper towel-lined colander and leave to drain until needed.

In a heavy-based frying pan over medium heat, sauté the shallot and garlic in the butter for a couple of minutes or until golden. Add the spinach leaves, reduce the heat to low and cook, stirring from time to time, for a couple more minutes, until softened. Tip into a separate colander and push out any liquid with the back of a spoon. Remove from the colander and roughly chop.

In a bowl, mix together the ricotta, egg, parmesan, flour, a pinch each of salt and pepper and the spinach until well combined. Season again to taste.

Bring a large saucepan of salted water to the boil. With two dessertspoons, mould the mixture into quenelles (oval shapes) and slip into the boiling water. Do this in batches of about 5 or 6 at a time. Simmer for a few minutes or until they float to the surface. Remove with a slotted spoon and place on paper towel to drain. Repeat until all the *gnudi* are cooked. (Makes 20–24.)

Pour the tomato sauce into the baking dish. Place the *gnudi* on top of the sauce and sprinkle with the extra parmesan. Bake for 20 minutes or until the *gnudi* are hot and the sauce is bubbling.

Serves 4

Photo on previous page

MMCC's Essential Tomato Sauce

60 ml (¼ cup) extra virgin olive oil

2 onions, finely chopped

4 × 400 g (14 oz) tins Italian diced
  tomatoes or 20 roma (plum) tomatoes

60 ml (¼ cup) tomato paste
  (concentrated purée)

2 cloves garlic, bruised

1 teaspoon sea salt, or to taste

½ teaspoon ground black pepper

In a deep frying pan over low–medium heat, heat the olive oil. Sauté the onion for about 20 minutes or until very soft but not brown. If using fresh tomatoes, cut a cross into the end of each tomato and put them into a large bowl. Cover with boiling water and allow to stand for 10 minutes. Tip off the water and peel the tomatoes. Chop the tomatoes, keeping the seeds and juice and set aside.

Increase the heat to medium–high, add the tomato paste and cook for a minute or so, stirring. Add the garlic, tomatoes, salt and pepper. Stir and bring to the boil, reduce the heat to low and simmer for 2 hours, stirring from time to time. Remove the garlic cloves and discard. Taste for seasoning.

Makes about 6 cups

I tried out this recipe on a Sunday night before running out the door to a radio interview. Needless to say, the family was so impressed that I could make an irresistible vegetarian dinner while frantically prepping for the radio. Dana says you can substitute other cheeses, flour or vegetables – make sure you shred them finely so they cook through. ~ *Merelyn, MMCC*

See Dana's story on page 192

Dana Slatkin

Zucchini Fritters with Green Goddess Dressing

4 (about 675 g/1½ lb) zucchini (courgettes)

1 teaspoon salt

4 spring onions (scallions), thinly sliced

1 clove garlic, crushed

½ cup combined chopped chives, dill and mint

65 g (½ cup) grated parmesan cheese

100 g (3½ oz) feta or goat's cheese, crumbled

75 g (½ cup/2¾ oz) chickpea flour (besan)

½ teaspoon baking powder

1 egg, lightly beaten

250 ml (1 cup) olive oil

lemon wedges, to serve

Green goddess dressing

1 ripe avocado

125 ml (½ cup) buttermilk

75 g (¼ cup) whole-egg mayonnaise

juice of 1 lemon

1 clove garlic, crushed

¼ cup chopped combined chives, dill and flat-leaf (Italian) parsley

sea salt and ground black pepper

Coarsely grate the zucchini. Place in a colander over the sink, sprinkle with the salt and leave for at least 1 hour to drain.

To make the green goddess dressing, in a food processor, combine the avocado, buttermilk, mayonnaise, lemon juice, garlic, chives, dill and parsley. Process until you have a smooth dressing. Season to taste with salt and pepper and refrigerate until ready to serve.

After the zucchini has drained, wrap it tightly in a clean tea towel (dish cloth) and wring out any residual liquid. Transfer to a medium bowl. Add the spring onion, garlic, chives, dill, mint, parmesan, feta or goat's cheese, chickpea flour and baking powder and mix well. Add the egg, mix again and season generously.

In a large heavy-based frying pan over medium heat, add enough of the oil to reach a depth of at least 5 mm (¼ inch). When the oil is hot, working in batches, carefully add tablespoons of the mixture to make the fritters. Fry over medium heat for a few minutes on each side, until golden brown. Drain on paper towel. Continue frying the fritters in batches, adding more oil to the pan if necessary.

Serve warm, with the green goddess dressing, Persian cucumber salad (see opposite) and lemon wedges on the side.

Makes about 20

Photo on page 193

This is an American-style 'salad', like egg or tuna salad, something delicious to serve alongside the zucchini fritters (see opposite) or as a shmear. To us Australians, it's a dip. We like to drain it very well in the fridge, so it becomes like labne in texture. ~ *MMCC*

See Dana's story on page 192

Dana Slatkin

Persian Cucumber Salad

3 Lebanese (short) cucumbers, finely grated
450 g (1 lb) plain Greek-style yoghurt
1 spring onion (scallion), finely chopped
3 sprigs mint, leaves only
sea salt and ground black pepper
25 g (¼ cup) walnuts, toasted, finely chopped
35 g (¼ cup) currants

Place the grated cucumber in a sieve and press down with the palm of your hand to release as much liquid as possible. Transfer the drained cucumber to a medium bowl and stir in the yoghurt, spring onion and mint. Season to taste with salt and pepper. Stir in the walnuts and currants, reserving a few to garnish.

Transfer the salad to a sieve lined with paper towel and placed over a bowl. Cover with plastic wrap and allow to drain in the refrigerator for at least 1 hour and up to 6 hours.

Spoon into a serving bowl and scatter with the reserved walnuts and currants.

Makes 2½ cups

Photo on page 193

EYDIE DESSER

DANA SLATKIN

I am the only one in my family who makes my grandmother's *mandelbrot*. Maw Maw, my Russian-born grandmother, took great pride in teaching me. She never measured any ingredient, she just knew instinctively the right texture and taste. Years after she died, I made them as a surprise for my dad. I felt Maw Maw was right beside me as I measured flour using her sifter, sprinkled in the right amount of cinnamon and smoothed the dough with wet hands, just like she used to. They were *almost* as good as hers; I do wish for just one more lesson.

We live in California. After a long career with CBS Radio, teaching cooking has become my life. I trained at the French Culinary Institute in New York City, which I think inspired my husband to propose! My new focus is promoting a wholefood, plant-based, nutrient-rich diet. I'm on the board of an international organisation called The Plantrician Project, which educates doctors on how prescribing a wholefood diet can prevent and even reverse disease. I also teach these inspiring cooking classes to individuals and charitable organisations out of my home.

My mum, Jane, was a wonderful cook and entertainer. She was always replicating gourmet meals from fancy restaurants, setting the table just so, exploring other food cultures, and urging my brothers and me to taste everything. I'm sure she had a grand plan to keep us close through a love of food. Now she is no longer here and the three of us are always on the phone talking about what we are cooking; it's an unbreakable bond that keeps Mom's memory alive every single day.

When I was nine we took a family vacation to Colorado Springs. I don't remember much of it, except the snow and the best thing I had ever dipped bread into: a buttery garlicky *escargot* sauce at my first fancy French restaurant.

As a child, I always adored helping my mother in the kitchen and relished the smells from the many bubbling pots, enjoying the closeness we shared. After graduating UC Berkeley, I almost became a lawyer, as I wanted to help people fight for their rights and justice. But after working in a trattoria in Venice, Italy, during my junior year, I fell in love with the way cooking could bring people together, day after day. That's when I knew I was destined for a career in food.

When I was studying at the Culinary Institute of America, I was given a cookbook by Georges Blanc, and I became obsessed with his enchanting, locally sourced style of cooking. I wrote to Chef Blanc to ask if he would accept me as an intern, and he generously accepted. I moved to France for a year to work for him, then Michel Guèrard, the bakery Poilane, and the famous gastronomic emporium Fauchon. What a heady time. That year taught me discipline and precision, to utilise the best seasonal ingredients and to constantly improvise on classic techniques. It also inspired me to launch the Beverly Hills Farmers Market and subsequently my Beverly Hills Farmgirl cooking school.

DANA'S RECIPES

Zucchini Fritters with Green Goddess Dressing:
page 190
Persian Cucumber Salad: page 191
Strawberry Rhubarb Cobbler: page 239

EYDIE'S RECIPES

Egg Strata Pudding: page 192
Buttermilk Scone: page 277

When we were interviewed on Martha Stewart radio about heirloom recipes, Eydie phoned in to tell us about her mother's legacy, a cookbook called *Just Add Butter*. They compiled and collated the recipes together but her mum passed away, leaving Eydie to finish it. We were so thrilled to then meet Eydie at our book launch in LA, where she gave us a copy. I cried when I read it back in Sydney. Eydie has become such an important example to us of preserving recipes and memories of the older generation, and a dear friend of our project. And, surprisingly, we had never come across a cheesy, savoury bread and butter pudding before this landed in our kitchen.

~ Merelyn, MMCC

See Eydie's story on page 192

Eydie Desser

Egg Strata Pudding

1 loaf (600 g) challah bread or brioche, crusts removed
115 g (4 oz/1 stick) butter, softened
450 g (1 lb) extra sharp (strong) cheddar cheese, grated
9 eggs
750 ml (3 cups) milk
3 teaspoons mustard powder
¼ teaspoon Tabasco sauce, or to taste
1½ teaspoons sea salt
½ teaspoon ground black pepper

Start this recipe a day before serving.

Butter a 2.5 litre (10 cup) baking dish.

Slice the challah or brioche into 1 cm (½ inch) thick slices and spread the butter on both sides. Layer the sliced bread with the grated cheese until all the bread and cheese are used.

In a large bowl, beat the eggs. Add the milk, mustard powder, Tabasco, salt and pepper and beat until well combined. Pour over the bread and cheese, cover with plastic wrap and refrigerate overnight or for at least 6 hours.

The next day, preheat the oven to 180°C (350°F/Gas 4).

Remove the plastic wrap and bake the pudding for 1½ hours. If the top gets too brown, cover with foil. The pudding is ready when it is golden brown on top and there is only a slight jiggle when you shake the dish.

Remove from the oven and allow to rest for 15 minutes before serving.

Serves 8–10

It's so amazing for us to come across recipes we have never seen, from places we've never been, from Jewish communities we never knew existed. This traditional Welsh recipe uses ingredients that, in the olden days, would have been available from the cook's 'smallholding' (a small farm with a home). It is a substantial gratin-style dish that makes a perfect meal with a fresh green salad on the side. ∼ *MMCC*

See Diana's story on page 198

Diana Soffa

Anglesey Eggs

550 g (1 lb 4 oz) floury (starchy) potatoes
6 leeks, trimmed, quartered and sliced
20 g (1 tablespoon) butter
2 teaspoons sea salt
¾ teaspoon ground black pepper
8 eggs, hard-boiled and peeled

Sauce

20 g (1 tablespoon) butter
1 tablespoon plain (all-purpose) flour
250 ml (1 cup) milk, warmed
100 g (¾ cup/3½ oz), grated sharp
   cheddar cheese
sea salt and ground black pepper

Preheat the oven to 180°C (350°F/Gas 4). Grease a 2 litre (8 cup) baking dish.

Peel the potatoes and cut into large chunks. Place the potato in a saucepan of well-salted water over high heat and bring to the boil. Reduce the heat to medium and simmer for 20 minutes or until the potato is fork-tender. Drain well and mash in a large bowl. Set aside.

At the same time, bring another saucepan of salted water to the boil, add the leek and simmer for 5 minutes or until soft. Drain well and add to the hot mashed potato. Add the butter, salt and pepper and beat well with a wooden spoon until well combined and fluffy. Tip the mixture into the prepared dish. Bury the eggs (halved if you prefer) in the potato mixture.

To make the sauce, heat the butter in a small heavy-based saucepan and whisk in the flour until there are no lumps. Add the milk, a little at a time, whisking well to combine. Reduce the heat to low and stir with a wooden spoon for 10 minutes or until the mixture thickens and coats the back of the spoon. Add two-thirds of the cheese, stir to melt and pour over the potato mixture. Sprinkle with the remaining cheese and bake for 40 minutes or until the top is golden and crisp.

Serves 4–6

What a privilege to be a part of the wonderful Jewish community in Cardiff, Wales. There are only 2000 Jewish people in all of Wales, and as the coal mines closed and small communities from the valleys moved away the only viable community became my home town. My great-grandfather came here from Russia in 1880 and enjoyed a cosmopolitan city full of continental and European accents, different cultures and myriad food and cooking styles that still exist to this day.

I developed my love of cooking from my mother, grandmothers, assorted aunts and women who I knew through the synagogue community. These women not only taught me to cook, but they gave me an understanding of how important the Jewish traditions are, and the links they build between generations. My family has always been involved in Jewish life, especially the synagogue, and, more recently, interfaith work in the wider community. We shared a very special meal with the congregants of a local mosque and all felt how powerful this simple act was in bringing people together.

Wales is a stunning country and we are fortunate to live close to the coast. However, times change and our adult children have moved away to seek work and opportunity elsewhere. But when they do come home, we love to share a family meal, based on the traditions that have been forged over the generations.

When I left Rome over 24 years ago to study abroad I thought it would be temporary. But after studying political science in Israel for six years, I moved to London to do a master's degree and it became home. You can take the girl out of Italy, but you can't take Italy out of the girl – no matter where I am, the Italian way of living and cooking is part of me.

I learnt to cook from my mother and grandmothers, absorbing the smells, tastes and flavours, and understanding the importance of seasonal, fresh produce. A highlight was baking with Mum for Pesach until late at night, while she told enchanting stories about our family. Many years ago, when my grandmother Nonna Bianca turned 80, she decided it was time for my sister and me to learn to make her wonderful gnocchi. We had an incredible day and I treasure the piece of paper with her handwritten recipe on it.

My twin daughters, named Bianca and Thea after their great-grandmothers, are keeping these traditions alive. They make great little assistants, rolling meatballs, mixing cake dough, baking biscuits and happily tasting all the food we prepare together.

I'm a cook, not a chef, even though I work 24/7 in my business, Cooking for the Soul. I teach, cater, write and lecture about Italian–Jewish cuisine and I've now written my first cookbook, *Jewish Flavours of Italy*. The book celebrates my heritage – my mother's family have lived in Rome for at least 14 generations – which truly brings food to life.

DIANA'S RECIPE

Anglesey Eggs: page 197

SILVIA'S RECIPES

EDVERNA 'EDDY' GILBERT

Julia Child, the famous chef, author and television presenter, was one of the greatest influences on my mother Edverna's culinary life, along with her mother and mother-in-law. She was fascinated by Julia's television show, which she would watch religiously, and my brother and I would often hear her laughing hysterically at the antics.

Eddy, as she was known, was born in Detroit, Michigan, and spent her life in the Detroit area where both her parents had grown up. Friends in the large Jewish community introduced her to my father, Al, and they married. My brother and I were also born in Detroit, and even though my parents had both gone to Jewish public schools, they chose not to bring us up as part of the community. My mother, however, remained very active in the local JCC (Jewish Community Center). My father, Al, changed his name from Ginzberg to Gilbert on his 21st birthday in August 1945, to match his older brother, a novelist and screenwriter, who had done it years earlier for assimilation.

My brother and I were always well fed; Mom initially learnt to cook from her own mother and, soon after she got married, Dad's German-born mother took great care in showing and teaching her the wonders of delicious European cooking. Eddy loved to entertain and even though she didn't make Friday night dinners, she made sure that all the festivals were celebrated together with her sister and their families. Her traditional Jewish dishes such as brisket and *matzo* ball soup were my introduction to Jewish tradition, but everything always had her special touch.

Eddy was an avid traveller and for 40 years explored the world. She spent at least three weeks each year travelling the breadth of France, a country very close to her heart. Her family had migrated from Canada, Poland, Russia and Romania – all had found a home in the US – but they each brought and maintained their rich cultural heritage, which inspired her to seek out new places to visit.

My mother's American and European heritage gave her the basics of what and how to cook, but she modernised her repertoire with the help of Julia Child and her own creativity. Mom passed away in 2002 and will always be remembered as a strong and confident woman of her generation.

– *Martin Gilbert, Edverna's son*

EDVERNA'S RECIPE

German Potato Salad: page 202

When my family goes on holiday, we eat with gusto. In Sicily, we ate this rich, beautifully oily eggplant pasta, finished with grated salted ricotta, every single night for dinner. Imagine my excitement when we were introduced to Silvia – an Italian–Jewish cook living in London – who gave us pasta alla Norma. No need to go back to Sicily. ~ *Lisa, MMCC*

See Silvia's story on page 198

Silvia Nacamulli

Pasta alla Norma

60 ml (¼ cup) extra virgin olive oil
2 cloves garlic, thinly sliced
1 × 400 g (14 oz) tin Italian diced tomatoes
1 teaspoon sea salt
½ teaspoon ground black pepper
2 (about 500 g/1 lb 2 oz total) eggplant (aubergines)
375 ml (1½ cups) olive or sunflower oil
6 basil leaves
400 g (14 oz) penne or other short pasta
sea salt and ground black pepper
75 g (¾ cup/2¾ oz) grated salted ricotta (ricotta salata) cheese

In a large deep frying pan or saucepan, heat the olive oil together with the garlic over low–medium heat. Add the tomatoes, salt and pepper. Increase the heat to medium and simmer for 25 minutes, partially covered and stirring occasionally to ensure the sauce doesn't catch on the bottom of the pan.

Meanwhile, trim the ends off the eggplant and cut into 2 cm (¾ inch) cubes. In a separate large heavy-based frying pan, heat half of the olive or sunflower oil over high heat and, when hot, fry half of the eggplant, turning occasionally, for about 5–10 minutes or until golden. Repeat with the remaining oil and eggplant. Drain on paper towel.

Add the fried eggplant to the tomato sauce and cook for a final 10 minutes over medium heat. Turn off the heat and tear in the basil leaves.

Meanwhile, bring a large saucepan of salted water to the boil. Cook the pasta, stirring from time to time, until it is firm to the bite (al dente).

Drain the pasta, add it to the eggplant and tomato sauce and toss well over medium heat for a couple of minutes. Season to taste. Transfer to a large serving bowl or platter and sprinkle with the salted ricotta. Serve immediately.

Serves 4–6

My friend Marty's late mum used to make this potato salad, a recipe she got from her German mother-in-law. No recipe was ever written down. Marty described it and I followed his instructions – potatoes just-cooked, sliced thinly and dressed while still warm with olive oil, vinegar, fresh herbs and sliced green onions. He tried it at my place the very next night and looked at his husband, Matt – with a tear in his eye – and said THIS IS IT!!!

~ Lisa, MMCC

See Edverna's story on page 199

Edverna Gilbert

German Potato Salad

6 small (750 g/1 lb 10 oz total)
    waxy potatoes
125 ml (½ cup) extra virgin olive oil
60 ml (¼ cup) white wine vinegar
2 teaspoons sea salt
½ teaspoon ground black pepper
1 bunch chives, thinly sliced
½ bunch flat-leaf (Italian) parsley, leaves
    only, chopped
6 spring onions (scallions), thinly sliced
sea salt and ground black pepper

This recipe is best made at least 2 hours ahead of time. You will need a wide, shallow serving bowl.

Peel the potatoes and place in a large saucepan with plenty of cold water and a large pinch of salt. Bring to the boil over medium heat, then reduce the heat to low and simmer gently for about 30 minutes or until the potatoes are firm but cooked. Insert a skewer into a potato to check if it is done; there should be a little firmness as the potatoes will continue to soften as they cool.

Meanwhile, make the dressing by whisking together the olive oil, vinegar, salt and pepper in a small bowl.

Drain the potatoes and, as soon as you are able to touch them, slice thinly (3–5 mm/⅛–¼ inch) with a sharp knife or mandoline straight into the serving bowl. Immediately pour the dressing over the warm potatoes and toss gently. Add the chives, parsley and spring onion and toss gently once again.

Season to taste.

Serves 6–8

Photo on page 125

Through trial and error, I now understand why the best baked potatoes are made using the floury, starchy variety. These give a fluffy white filling inside the baked shell, just waiting to be topped with the horseradish cream. This horseradish cream is also a great match with roasted or grilled fish.

~ Merelyn, MMCC

See Michele's story on page 84

Michele Wise

Baked Potatoes with Horseradish Cream

6 medium floury (starchy) potatoes
2 tablespoons olive oil
55 g (¼ cup) table salt

Horseradish cream

250 ml (1 cup) crème fraîche or
  sour cream
75 g (¼ cup) whole-egg mayonnaise
3 teaspoons dijon mustard
140 g (½ cup) fresh grated or prepared
  white horseradish
⅓ cup chopped chives
3 teaspoons lemon juice
sea salt and ground black pepper

Preheat the oven to 200°C (400°F/Gas 6).

Wash the potatoes and dry well. Poke them all over with a fork. Just before baking, toss the potatoes in the olive oil and sprinkle the salt all over each potato. Place in a small roasting pan and roast for 1½ hours or until the skins are golden and crisp.

To make the horseradish cream, combine the crème fraîche (or sour cream), mayonnaise, mustard, horseradish, chives and lemon juice in a bowl and mix well. Season to taste. Cover with plastic wrap and refrigerate until needed.

Serve the potatoes with the horseradish cream.

Serves 6

This recipe gives the simple carrot and parsnip a spicy, crisp makeover. The recipe makes more chermoula than you need but it can be refrigerated in an airtight container for up to one month. ~ *MMCC*

See Ronnie's story on page 62

Ronnie Fein

Chermoula-Spiced Carrots and Parsnips

3 large carrots (about 500 g/1 lb 2 oz)
3 large parsnips (about 500 g/1 lb 2 oz)
¼ cup chermoula (see below)
sea salt

Chermoula

½ bunch flat-leaf (Italian) parsley
½ bunch coriander (cilantro)
3 cloves garlic, roughly chopped
2 teaspoons sweet or smoked paprika
1 teaspoon ground cumin
¼ teaspoon cayenne pepper
80 ml (⅓ cup) olive oil
60 ml (¼ cup) lemon juice

Preheat the oven to 230°C (450°F/Gas 8). Line a baking tray or roasting pan.

To make the chermoula, roughly chop the leaves and stems of the parsley and coriander. Place in a food processor with the garlic and pulse a few times to mix and chop the ingredients. Add the paprika, cumin, cayenne pepper, olive oil and lemon juice and process for about 30 seconds or until thoroughly blended.

Peel the carrots and parsnips and cut them into 10 × 1 cm (4 × ½ inch) strips. Place the vegetables in a bowl and toss with ¼ cup of the chermoula paste to coat them evenly. Sprinkle with salt.

Transfer to the prepared tray or pan and roast for 20 minutes, turning occasionally, or until the vegetables are golden and a little crisp around the edges.

Serves 6–8 as a side dish

I took my kids to Hunter's Lodge, and then 21 Espresso, for many years to get our fix of continental cooking. Their creamed spinach was legendary, and this recipe takes me right back. I think it is best made ahead of time, refrigerated and then reheated for the flavours to meld. ~ *Merelyn, MMCC*

See George's story on page 208

George Fischer

Hunter's Lodge Creamed Spinach

1 kg (2 lb 4 oz) frozen finely chopped spinach

7 cloves garlic, crushed

30 g (1 oz) butter

375 ml (1½ cups) pure (35% fat) cream

3 teaspoons plain (all-purpose) flour

2 teaspoons sea salt

½ teaspoon ground black pepper

In a large heavy-based saucepan, place the spinach over low heat and cook for about 30 minutes, uncovered, or until thawed and almost dry.

In a small frying pan over low heat, sauté the garlic in half of the butter for about 15 minutes or until the garlic is well cooked but not brown. Add to the spinach along with 1 cup of the cream. Stir well and set aside.

In the same frying pan, melt the remaining butter over medium heat. Add the flour and stir until smooth. Continue to cook for a minute or two or until pale golden, then add to the spinach mixture. Cook the spinach mixture over medium heat for 5 minutes, whisking from time to time, taking care that it does not catch on the base of the saucepan. Add the remaining cream, salt and pepper and stir well. Simmer for a further few minutes, whisking from time to time until the mixture is thick and well combined. Season to taste before serving.

Serves 6–8 as a side dish

GEORGE FISCHER

Over 50 years ago, the Hunter's Lodge Restaurant opened its doors in a little cottage at 18 Cross Street, Double Bay. The owners, Mama and Papa Fischer and their son George, were recent immigrants from Hungary, having escaped during the Hungarian Revolution of 1956. George was my father.

Back in Hungary, my grandparents Mama and Papa Fischer were renowned for their restaurants and they brought their culinary talents and delicacies to Double Bay in the eastern suburbs of Sydney, Australia. It was December 1963 and the perfect place for their first restaurant; Double Bay was fast becoming the coffee and cake destination for many post-war immigrants who were homesick for conversations with friends from the old country, and continental cooking was eagerly embraced by the locals.

Papa was the flamboyant chef for the first few years and Mama ran the kitchen with an iron fist until 1990. For over 30 years, Dad was the charming and charismatic front of house who entertained more than one million people – from local diners to prime ministers, from famous movie and rock stars to petty criminals. Every night was a party, and there are literally thousands of Sydneysiders who can proudly recall their birthday dinners, weddings, wedding anniversaries and first dates at the Hunter's Lodge.

The food was simple continental fare, executed to perfection. Whether it was veal schnitzel or filet mignon, crêpes suzette prepared at the table or the magnificent bombe alaska that was brought alight from the kitchen, it was prepared with love by the chefs and cooks who were trained under the watchful eye of the Fischer family.

The Hunter's Lodge closed in 1998. It was one of the longest surviving restaurants in Sydney's history, being under one ownership and in the same location for more than 36 years. In 2004 the opportunity arose to take over the iconic 21 Espresso in Knox Street, Double Bay. Dad and Tom, my brother, jumped at the opportunity to return to their roots doing what they do best, serving delicious continental food to their loyal customers. They continued this tradition, serving thousands of schnitzels with mashed potato and creamed spinach, until Dad's retirement in 2011.

Dad passed away in 2014, leaving behind an incredible legacy that generations of Sydneysiders will always remember.

– *Vivienne Mohay (née Fischer), daughter*

GEORGE'S RECIPES

Paprika Chicken Livers: page 44
Hunter's Lodge Creamed Spinach: page 206

TAMI WEISER

Cooking meaningful food is my way of searching for *mazel*, aligning my stars and finding my place in the world.

I come from a long line of sacramental kosher winemakers in New York City who proudly made wine for the Lubavitcher Rebbe. Now a deeply secular Jew living in Connecticut, I grew up in a more religious world, attending Yeshiva until I went to college then doing graduate work at a Jewish theological seminary.

My mom's family hailed from Franco–German stock but she is a New Orleans native, the only 'Yankee' in her family. Perhaps that's why I have a deeply Southern take on so many things – and I love spices. As a trained attorney with an undergraduate degree in anthropology, I love bringing out my inner geek by researching Jewish food history. Understanding religious history helps us find context in the modern global world and integrate with the past.

I have done so many varied things in my life, including ethnomusicology, working on archaeological digs and teaching adults how to read Hebrew. A goal has always been to teach people how to be intuitive, fearless cooks. I am now a trained chef, writer, recipe developer, culinary educator and caterer. My website, TheWeiserKitchen.com, is an inspiring and popular resource for creative cooks, celebrating, among other things, culinary tradition, the cornerstone of global Jewish food.

TAMI'S RECIPE

Bengali Rice with Cauliflower: page 210

We were interviewed by Karen Berman, of *The Weiser Kitchen*, a *blogzine* published by food writer Tami Weiser. Karen wrote a beautiful review of *The Feast Goes On* (such nachas!) and later gave us her recommendations for Jewish cooks – it was a huge help in our quest. Of course, Tami was on the list and she, in turn, gave us her list. This rice dish of Tami's is the flavour bomb, packed with texture, spice and zing. ~ *MMCC*

See Tami's story on page 209

Tami Weiser

Bengali Rice with Cauliflower

440 g (2 cups) basmati rice
1 litre (4 cups) coconut water
1 litre (4 cups) water
1 cinnamon stick
4 bay leaves
3 teaspoons sea salt
1 small head cauliflower, trimmed and
    cut into florets (about 6 cups)
2 tablespoons olive or coconut oil
1 teaspoon ground cumin
2 teaspoons garam masala
1 teaspoon ground turmeric or
    5 cm (2 inch) piece turmeric,
    peeled and grated
5 cm (2 inch) knob ginger, peeled
    and grated
4 cloves garlic, crushed
1 tablespoon tomato paste
    (concentrated purée)
1 tablespoon light brown sugar
finely grated zest and juice of 1 lemon
1 red onion, halved and thinly sliced
220 g (1½ cups) roasted, salted cashews
½ bunch coriander (cilantro), leaves only

Place the rice in a fine-mesh strainer and rinse under cold running water until the water runs clear.

Pour the coconut water and the water into a large saucepan, add the cinnamon stick, bay leaves and salt and bring to a boil over high heat. Add the rice and stir well. Reduce the heat to medium and simmer, uncovered, for 7 minutes or until the rice is firm to the bite (al dente). Drain the rice and set aside, removing and discarding the cinnamon and bay.

Place the cauliflower in a saucepan with a small amount of water, bring to the boil and steam, covered, for 5 minutes or until just tender. Drain and set aside.

In large frying pan over medium–high heat, heat the oil. Add the cumin and garam masala, stir, then cook for about 20 seconds, until fragrant. Add the turmeric, ginger and garlic and stir well. Add the tomato paste and sugar, stir well, and cook for about 20 seconds. Add the lemon zest and juice and stir. Add the onion, stir to coat, and reduce the heat to low. Cover and cook, stirring from time to time, for 5 minutes or until the onion is soft and translucent.

Add the rice and cauliflower and stir to coat. Cook, stirring regularly, for a few minutes, until heated through completely. Season to taste. Add the cashews and coriander to serve.

Serves 8–10

I received an email from 'Gloria from Nova Scotia' who had read about MMCC in *Tablet Magazine* and asked for some dining recommendations for her upcoming Sydney trip. Gloria returned from her fabulous trip, having bought both our books and, over much email 'chatter', told me all about her love of cooking and entertaining. This recipe of hers caught our attention immediately. Yum. ~ *Lisa, MMCC*

See Gloria's story on page 247

Gloria Jacobson Pink

Israeli Rice Pilaf

75 g (2½ oz) dried vermicelli noodles
60 ml (¼ cup) olive oil
440 g (2 cups) basmati or long grain rice
1 litre (4 cups) chicken stock (broth)
1 teaspoon sea salt
1 onion, roughly chopped
40 g (¼ cup) pine nuts
40 g (¼ cup) currants or sultanas
 (golden raisins)

Break up the vermicelli noodles into short pieces, about 4 cm (1½ inches) long.

In a large, preferably non-stick, saucepan, heat half of the oil over medium heat and cook the vermicelli, watching carefully, for a minute or two or until they turn brown; take care, as they burn easily. Add the rice and sauté for a few minutes until it becomes opaque.

Add the stock and salt, bring to the boil, cover and reduce the heat to low. Simmer, undisturbed, for 20 minutes.

While the rice is cooking, heat the remaining oil in a small frying pan and sauté the onion for about 15 minutes or until golden. Add the pine nuts and currants (or sultanas), tossing to toast them lightly. Remove from the heat. Turn the cooked rice onto a serving platter and fluff with a fork. Top with the onion, pine nuts and currants (or sultanas).

Serves 8 as a side dish

eet

Dessert
Cake & Tart
Biscuit & Slice

Imagine a cross between cheesecake, custard and cream with the exotic fragrance of Indian sweets. Seekhund is a unique dessert from Karyn's Indian friend Nimoo, which we had never seen before. It is wonderful not only with poached white peaches, but as an accompaniment to roasted winter fruits. ~ MMCC

See Karyn's story on page 300

Karyn Moskow

Poached Peaches with Seekhund

6 white peaches
330 g (1½ cups) sugar
3 strips lemon rind
2 sprigs mint
1.5 litres (6 cups) water
½ teaspoon rosewater

Seekhund

250 g (9 oz) cream cheese
110 g (½ cup) white (granulated) sugar
250 g (1 cup) plain Greek-style yoghurt
250 ml (1 cup) buttermilk
½ teaspoon ground cardamom
35 g (¼ cup) roasted slivered almonds, plus extra

You will need a saucepan that can fit the 6 peaches in 1 layer. Put the sugar, lemon rind, mint and water into the saucepan and bring to the boil. Slip in the peaches, reduce the heat to medium and place a piece of baking paper on top of the peaches, then weigh it down with a plate. (This stops the peaches from bobbing up to the surface and allows them to poach evenly.) Simmer for 8 minutes or until the peaches are just soft. Remove the peaches from the liquid and peel off the skin under gentle running water, reserving the skins.

Place the skins back in the saucepan with the poaching liquid and bring to the boil and reduce the liquid to ¾ cup. Add the rosewater to the reduced syrup, strain and pour over the peaches.

To make the *seekhund*, using an electric mixer, beat the cream cheese and sugar until smooth and creamy. Add the yoghurt, buttermilk and cardamom and mix for a few minutes. Fold in the almonds.

Cover with plastic wrap and refrigerate for at least 2 hours. Pour a little of the *seekhund* in each bowl and top with a peach. Serve any extra *seekhund* in a bowl alongside. Scatter with the extra slivered almonds.

Serves 6

I suggested to the MMCC gals they might like my baked apples and brought my written recipe along one Monday. The feedback was, 'delicious but too sweet'. I realised that over the years I had altered the recipe without ever noting my changes. When I told the girls to double the lemon juice, they loved it. I like making these baked apples the old-fashioned British way, with sultanas, but you can up the ante by using dates and currants, and replacing the golden syrup with honey, maple syrup or silan (date syrup).

~Merelyn, MMCC

Merelyn Chalmers

Baked Apples

8 granny smith apples
125 ml (½ cup) water
230 g (1 cup) caster (superfine) sugar
2 tablespoons golden syrup
   (light treacle)
grated zest and juice of 1½ lemons

Stuffing

30 g (1 oz) unsalted butter
40 g (¼ cup) brown sugar
1 teaspoon ground cinnamon
160 g (1 cup) sultanas (golden raisins)

Preheat the oven to 180°C (350°F/Gas 4). You will need a baking dish that fits the apples snugly in 1 layer.

Remove the core from the apples with an apple corer, score around the middle with a paring knife and set aside.

To make the stuffing, in a bowl, stir together the butter, brown sugar and cinnamon, then mix through the sultanas. Stuff each apple tightly with the mixture, mounding some on top and place in the baking dish. Any leftover stuffing can be scattered around the apples in the baking dish.

Combine the water, caster sugar, golden syrup, lemon zest and juice in a small saucepan and stir over medium heat until the sugar dissolves. Taste and add more lemon juice, if desired. Pour over the apples, taking care to not break up the mounds of stuffing.

Bake uncovered for 45 minutes or until the apples are soft but still holding their shape. Allow to cool slightly and serve warm with some of the syrup.

Serves 8

LIBBY SKURNIK

Food, for me, means gathering family, friends and even their families, into our home, around the table and ultimately into our lives.

Growing up in Winnipeg, Canada, meant endless cold days, but they offered the perfect excuse for my mother to get together with her friends to cook special warming dishes. She would regale us with stories of the food and happy times together. She was always having dinner parties, with fancy dishes and beautifully presented food. She wanted to feast with the eyes as well as the taste buds.

We moved to Melbourne when I was nine. At an early age, I became aware of my mom's interest in cooking and baking. She kindled my enthusiasm for the kitchen.

It is a privilege to share the Jewish festivals with others and to celebrate the Lithuanian and Polish heritage of my parents, in-laws and grandparents. We had our own little cooking club in my family – grandmothers, granddaughters and I would come together to cook the traditional foods for the *chagim*. My daughters waited with glee to make *hamantashen* and *kreplach*, though I must say they preferred to eat (rather than cook) my mother-in-law's palm-sized *gefilte* fish.

Now both my girls teach me delicious ways of cooking, baking and food presentation. I am happily learning from the younger generation.

LIBBY'S RECIPES

Pea and Lamb Soup: page 76
Passionfruit Ice Cream: page 222

MYRNA ROSEN

Who would have thought my first love was dressmaking? Luckily my father discouraged me from making it my career – he thought it was not commercial enough. Instead, I took inspiration from my late mother and grandmother, who were both superb cooks. Grandmother Leah was a trailblazer. She emigrated from Lithuania to South Africa, had nine children and ran a successful restaurant at the gold diggings. I can't imagine how difficult the working conditions would have been for a young woman with a large family in the mines so many years ago.

My mother used to help bake and cook for the restaurant and home. She was a huge support and became an exceptional cook, even better than my grandmother.

My knowledge and love of cooking is entirely due to the interest sparked by my mother. Her experience and knowledge have been an endless source of inspiration. Growing up, I lived in the small towns of Potchefstroom and Germiston, and when I married Ron we moved to Johannesburg. I always cooked and baked with my friends and neighbours, until one enthusiastic neighbour suggested I teach cooking to keep me busy while my children were at school. Ron supported me in this endeavour, and the rest is history.

I have written five cookbooks. My first book, *Cooking with Myrna Rosen*, was published in 1978 and has recently been reprinted. It continues to sell all over the world.

MYRNA'S RECIPES

Roman Lamb: page 149
Lime Ice Cream: page 223

This recipe, originally from South Africa, has been passed around the Melbourne Jewish community over the years, and arrived in our kitchen from Libby. We were absolutely astounded that a dairy-free ice cream could be so lush. It has become Libby's tradition to serve it for dessert at the end of Seder, but we'll take it anytime. ～ *MMCC*

See Libby's story on page 220

Libby Skurnik

Passionfruit Ice Cream

6 eggs, separated
230 g (1 cup) caster (superfine) sugar
125 ml (½ cup) vegetable oil
250 ml (1 cup) passionfruit pulp (about 10 passionfruit)

Start this recipe a day before serving.

In an electric mixer, whisk the egg whites until soft peaks form, then add half of the sugar and continue to whisk until stiff. Set aside.

In a separate bowl, whisk the egg yolks and remaining sugar for 5 minutes or until very pale and thick, then gradually add the oil until fully amalgamated. Fold the egg white into the egg yolk mixture.

Add the passionfruit pulp and gently fold through with a spatula. Pour into a freezer-proof container and freeze overnight or for at least 6 hours.

Serves 10

Photo on previous page

When we first tested this recipe, there was no doubt from any of us it had to be shared with the world. We then took the recipe home and made it for our own family dinners. It was a runaway success. What a treat to have a smooth ice cream that doesn't need to be churned. Myrna's original handwritten recipe calls for key limes, which are pretty much impossible to get in Australia. If you can get your hands on some, please substitute. This ice cream will become a necessary and permanent part of your table, as it has ours. ~ *MMCC*

See Myrna's story on page 220

Myrna Rosen

Lime Ice Cream

5 eggs, separated
2 × 395 g (14 oz) tins sweetened
  condensed milk
180 ml (¾ cup) lime juice
finely grated zest of 3 limes
300 ml (1¼ cups) thickened (whipping)
  cream
roasted macadamias and shaved
  coconut, to garnish

Start this recipe a day before serving.

In the bowl of an electric mixer, beat together the egg yolks and the condensed milk until well combined, then stir in the lime juice and zest. In a separate bowl, whisk the egg whites until soft peaks form. Fold gently into the egg yolk mixture. Using the same bowl, whisk the cream until stiff peaks form and fold into the lime/yolk mixture. Pour into a freezer-safe container or the prepared tins (see note). Wrap in plastic wrap, then foil and freeze overnight.

Scoop out or slice the ice cream and serve with roasted macadamias and coconut shavings.

Note – This ice cream can be frozen in a freezer-safe plastic container, then scooped out to serve. It is also suitable to pour into 2 small loaf tins, each lined with baking paper with an overhang of at least 10 cm (4 inches) on each side. If using tins, unmould before serving, then remove the baking paper and slice to serve.

Serves 12

Photo on page 221

I went nuts for this do-ahead, dairy-free dessert. It takes me back to family holidays in Israel, where we used to devour it for breakfast. Add the rosewater slowly, tasting as you go, as some brands have a stronger flavour than others. ~ *Merelyn, MMCC*

See Ronit's story on page 106

Ronit Robbaz

Coconut Rose Malabi

1 litre (4 cups) coconut cream (or milk)
½–1 tablespoon rosewater, or to taste
150 g (1 cup) coconut sugar
65 g (½ cup) cornflour (corn starch)

Syrup and topping

250 ml (1 cup) water
150 g (1 cup) coconut sugar
½ pomegranate, seeds only
1 tablespoon coconut oil
40 g (¾ cup) shaved coconut

Start this recipe at least four hours before serving.

To make the malabi, in a large heavy-based saucepan over medium heat, add the coconut cream or milk, rosewater and sugar and stir until the mixture just starts to boil. Remove from the heat. Place the cornflour in a heatproof bowl. Ladle 1 cup of the coconut cream mixture into the cornflour and whisk until smooth. Return this mixture to the pan, whisking continuously to avoid lumps, then stir over low heat for about 5 minutes or until thickened; the mixture should coat the back of a spoon. Pour into 6 glasses or ramekins or a larger serving bowl. Cover with plastic wrap and refrigerate for at least 4 hours before serving.

To make the syrup, in a small saucepan over medium–high heat, add the water and sugar and simmer for about 10 minutes or until it becomes syrupy. Set aside to cool. Stir in half of the pomegranate seeds.

In a hot frying pan over medium heat, place the shaved coconut and add the coconut oil. Quickly sauté or until the coconut is golden brown. Set aside.

Just before serving, spoon the pomegranate syrup on top of the malabi and top with the toasted coconut. Sprinkle with the remaining pomegranate seeds.

Serves 6

This is a traditional Danish dessert typically served at Christmas. It is made from cooled rice pudding, which is then folded through whipped cream and almonds, served cold with cherry sauce. Nadine, as a child, along with her maternal grandfather, never liked cherry sauce and together they created a sublime caramel sauce. When we first made this sauce in the MMCC kitchen, we literally could not stop eating it. Our caramel was so dark – one step before burnt – and the resulting sauce was so intense in flavour and super-smooth in texture. ∼*MMCC*

See Nadine's story on page 112

Nadine Levy Redzepi

Risalamande

300 ml (1¼ cups) water
180 g (6½ oz) Arborio rice
1.25 litres (5 cups) milk
1 vanilla bean, split and seeds
    scraped out
75 g (⅓ cup) caster (superfine) sugar
pinch of sea salt
200 g (7 oz) whole blanched almonds,
    coarsely chopped
1 litre (4 cups) thickened
    (whipping) cream
caramel sauce (see opposite), to serve
cherry sauce (see opposite), to serve

Start this recipe a day before serving.

In a large heavy-based saucepan with a lid, bring the water to a boil over medium–high heat. Add the rice and cook, stirring, for 3 minutes. Add the milk and the vanilla bean and seeds and bring to the boil. Reduce the heat to low and partially cover the pan. Simmer, stirring occasionally to avoid catching on the bottom, for 40 minutes or until most of the liquid is absorbed and the rice is tender. Remove from the heat and stir in the sugar and salt. Allow to cool, cover with plastic wrap and refrigerate overnight.

The next day, stir the almonds into the pudding. In an electric mixer, whip the cream until stiff peaks form. Fold the cream into pudding. Serve with the caramel sauce and cherry sauce (see opposite) for drizzling on top.

Serves 8–10

Photo on previous page

Cherry Sauce

Nadine's original recipe calls for 2 cups sweet cherry juice and 225 g (8 oz) frozen pitted sweet cherries. Both are quite hard to find in Australia, so in the recipe we have replaced them with tinned cherries. ~ *MMCC*

2 × 425 g (15 oz) tins pitted
  black cherries
1 heaped teaspoon cornflour
  (corn starch)
110 g (½ cup) sugar
1 vanilla bean, split and seeds
  scraped out

Drain the cherries, reserving the syrup. Place the cherry syrup in a large measuring jug and top up with water until the liquid measures 500 ml (2 cups).

In a small bowl, whisk together ¼ cup of the cherry syrup and the cornflour until a smooth slurry forms.

In a saucepan over high heat, bring the remaining cherry syrup, sugar and vanilla bean and seeds to the boil. Add the cherry syrup/cornflour slurry and cook, whisking from time to time, for 5 minutes or until the sauce turns clear and the bubbles appear slightly thicker. Remove the vanilla bean and stir in the cherries. Cook for a further 5 minutes or until the sauce has thickened a little.

Allow to cool, transfer to a bowl, cover with plastic wrap and refrigerate until needed.

Caramel Sauce

220 g (1 cup) sugar
125 ml (½ cup) boiling water
300 ml (1¼ cups) thickened
  (whipping) cream

To make the caramel sauce, in a heavy-based stainless steel saucepan over medium heat, cook the sugar, stirring with a wooden spoon, for 10 minutes or until the sugar has melted. Continue to cook over low–medium heat, stirring and swirling the pan, for 10 minutes or until the mixture is a rich, dark brown caramel (and reaches 175°C/345°F) on a candy thermometer). Remove from the heat and slowly and very carefully pour the boiling water into the pan, little by little, whisking thoroughly until combined. Carefully pour the hot caramel liquid into a large heatproof bowl and allow to cool.

In an electric mixer on medium speed, whip the cream until soft peaks form. Fold the cream into the caramel until incorporated. Cover with plastic wrap and refrigerate until needed.

Over the last ten years we've come to realise the importance of honouring a recipe's provenance and the journey it made to get to our kitchen here in Sydney. Amos delivered this recipe to us. He learnt it from Gabriela Llamas's cooking school in Madrid and, coincidentally, Amos's mother cut out the same recipe from a New Zealand magazine and gave it to him. We've since been in touch with Gabriela and have discovered that her original version is from Anita Bensadón, and is a traditional Sephardi Jewish dairy-free dessert. The texture of this mousse is like no other – thick, silky and nougat-like. ~ *MMCC*

See Amos's story on page 234

Amos Cohen

Olive Oil Chocolate Mousse

150 g (5½ oz) best-quality dark chocolate (70%)
125 ml (½ cup) fruity extra virgin olive oil
4 eggs, separated
115 g (½ cup/4 oz) caster (superfine) sugar
1 tablespoon Grand Marnier
pinch of sea salt

Start this recipe at least 4 hours before serving.

Melt the chocolate in a heatproof bowl over a saucepan of simmering water, then slowly stir in the olive oil. Remove from the heat and set aside.

In an electric mixer, beat the egg yolks with half of the sugar until pale and creamy. With a spatula, gently stir the chocolate mixture into the egg yolk mixture, a little at a time while stirring gently, then add the Grand Marnier. Set aside.

In a separate bowl, whisk the egg whites with the salt until soft peaks form and gradually add the remaining sugar, whisking until stiff peaks form. Gently fold one-third of the egg white mixture into the chocolate mixture, then fold in the remainder. Pour into a serving bowl or individual serving glasses or bowls. Cover with plastic wrap and chill overnight, or for at least 4 hours.

Serves 4–6

Amanda worked for a London family when she finished university and this was the one recipe she brought home. As soon as I saw her recipe – some 25 years later – the original title and the food processor method sounded familiar. I had been to the Gretta Anna Teplitzky Cooking School for a few inspiring classes back in 1988 and Gretta Anna taught us the identical recipe. I think I made it for every dinner party between 1988 and 1998! We haven't been able to find a connection between the London family and the late Gretta Anna but it is possibly the best sticky date pudding I've come across. ~ *Lisa, MMCC*

See Amanda's story on page 235

Amanda Berman

Warm Date Cake with Pecan Caramel Sauce

230 g (1 cup/8 oz) caster
   (superfine) sugar
185 g (6½ oz) unsalted butter,
   at room temperature
3 eggs
190 g (1¼ cups/6¾ oz) self-raising
   (self-rising) flour
1½ teaspoons vanilla extract
1 heaped teaspoon baking powder
150 ml (scant ⅔ cup) water
75 ml (scant ⅓ cup) milk
250 g (9 oz) pitted medjool (fresh) dates
ice cream, to serve

Pecan caramel sauce

300 g (1⅓ cups, firmly packed) dark
   brown sugar
50 g (2 oz) butter
300 ml (1¼ cups) thickened
   (whipping) cream
1 tablespoon pecans, chopped (optional)
1 teaspoon vanilla extract

Preheat the oven to 180°C (350°F/Gas 4). Line a 23 cm (9 inch) round cake tin.

In a food processor, place the sugar, butter, eggs, flour, vanilla, baking powder, water and milk and process for 15 seconds or until well combined. Roughly chop the dates, add to the mixture and process for a further 30 seconds, scraping down the side about halfway through, or until the dates are finely chopped and well distributed through the batter. Pour the batter into the prepared tin and bake for 1 hour or until golden and a skewer inserted into the cake comes out clean.

While the cake is in the oven, make the caramel sauce. In a heavy-based saucepan, place the sugar, butter, cream and pecans (if using) and vanilla and bring to the boil. Simmer over medium heat for 5 minutes, stirring, until it is a well combined sauce.

To serve, remove the cake from the tin and pour the sauce over. Serve warm with ice cream.

Serves 10

232 🕎 SWEET DESSERT

AMOS COHEN

I inherited an appreciation of food that embraces diverse traditions, freshness, seasonality and doing things from scratch. The kitchens of Eastern European Jews, the British Raj, Mediterranean Israel and Spain, Canada and California all influenced our family dinners in Palmerston North in New Zealand. In a town where you could barely muster a *minyan* at *shul*, my Jewish heritage was celebrated with homemade *challah* and *sufganiyot*, *charoset* and *mandelbrot*, *gefilte* fish and *kneidlach*.

Food has always been a large part of the glue that binds our family together, to the point that outsiders are often bemused by the extent to which it dominates our conversations. There was no restaurant food culture where we lived in the 1970s and 1980s, no farmers' markets or ethnic street food festivals. Our food culture was a homegrown bubble – a garden full of seasonal fruit and vegetables, a mother who cooked for five of us, seven days a week, with occasional assistance from my father, who was also responsible for elaborate brunches, exotic breads, jams and preserves, yoghurts and ice creams. My first tentative culinary steps were taken at my mother's side, learning how to cook Bolognese, curry and chilli con carne for my family.

Reading about, preparing and consuming food was, in part, escapism – the next best thing to actually being elsewhere. As a teenager I was fuelled by encounters with Elizabeth David and Julia Child. Many years before *Julie & Julia* I was poring over *From Julia Child's Kitchen*, where sketchy black and white photos helped me master the technique behind a perfect omelette. I still remember Elizabeth David's vivid description of a picnic outside Marseilles 'not long before the war'. Recipes needed to be well written, and come with a story, to capture my imagination.

Now that I am a journalist and filmmaker living in modern, multicultural Melbourne, Australia, it's no longer necessary and not always possible to do most things from scratch, but it's one of the main things that stands out from my childhood. My mother used to make her own *challah* every Friday. I recall with joy being allowed to braid my own 'mini-*challah*', glazing the loaves with beaten egg and sprinkling them with poppy seeds. Oh, and being allowed to punch the risen dough! I've now developed my own traditions as far as maintaining quality is concerned and generally travel with my own pepper grinder, salt and knives – which is always a challenge going through security.

AMOS'S RECIPES

AMANDA BERMAN

Freshly baked bagels meant it was Sunday morning at our house. My grandmother Gaga not only made exceptional bagels from scratch but also the most perfect *bulkas*, *kreplach* and *tsimmes* one could imagine. She never used a recipe or scales; it was just how the weight of an ingredient felt in her hands. She tried to teach me how to bake her famed *bulkas* and it was quite the challenge to weigh every extra handful of everything she kept adding.

Growing up in Cape Town, I had South African parents and, like many of my peers, grandparents who came from Lithuania. The loss of my mother when I was 16 had a profound effect on my life and left a huge gap in my family, leaving my older sister and me to look after Dad. We were in charge of the household and cooking, thankfully with Gaga's help.

I left for Australia in my 20s and now have my own family in Sydney. I'm grateful that my sister and her family also live nearby. We are so lucky to live in a place with incredible produce so meals at home can be equally delicious and healthy, alongside a good glass of wine! Traditional Jewish foods are not really part of my repertoire, but nothing beats the expression on my kids' faces when they come home and smell the *challah* baking.

CANDY GOLD

Our family thrives on being together and creating feasts. Every Father's Day, all three generations get together to bake *streuselkuchen*, a cherished cake recipe from Omi – my father's grandmother. I treasure these special moments. My passion for cooking started as a child in Cape Town when I learnt to cook from my grandmother Bobba, Mom and our special maid, Agnes, who was a part of the family. We grew up surrounded by food; my parents were always entertaining and we were constantly encouraged to try new cuisines and engage in different cultures.

As a third-generation South African, I never imagined my passion for food would open so many doors. After my daughters were born, friends begged me to teach them how to cook the food I served at our dinner parties. What started out as one cooking lesson for eight friends grew into a cooking school and consulting business in Sydney, my home for more than three decades.

I'm always experimenting and tweaking until I have something perfect that I can teach my students. Some years ago I came across a wonderful recipe with ginger. That was the beginning of my obsession with anything ginger, which ultimately evolved into my ginger pudding. When I taught the recipe at one of my classes, the ladies decided it was my best dessert ever.

AMANDA'S RECIPE

Warm Date Cake with Pecan Caramel Sauce:
page 232

CANDY'S RECIPES

Cauliflower Soup with Pangrattato: page 66
Crystallised Ginger Pudding: page 236

See Candy's story on page 235

135 g (¾ cup/4¾ oz) crystallised (candied) ginger

225 g (1½ cups/8 oz) plain (all-purpose) flour

1½ tablespoons baking powder

1 teaspoon bicarbonate of soda (baking soda)

150 g (5½ oz) butter, at room temperature

250 g (9 oz) brown sugar

3 eggs

1 teaspoon vanilla extract

1 tablespoon ground ginger

250 ml (1 cup) buttermilk

Topping

125 g (4 oz) raw almonds

110 g (½ cup) sugar

100 g (3½ oz) butter

60 ml (¼ cup) thickened (whipping) cream

Yoghurt cream

250 ml (1 cup) thickened (whipping) cream

500 g (2 cups) plain Greek-style yoghurt

125 g (¾ cup) icing (confectioners') sugar, sifted

1 teaspoon vanilla extract

Candy Gold

Crystallised Ginger Pudding

Preheat the oven to 170°C (340°F/Gas 3–4). Grease a 2.5 litre (10 cup) baking dish.

In a food processor or blender, process the crystallised ginger until finely chopped and set aside; if the ginger is hard, add 1 tablespoon hot water to make it easier to process. In a small bowl, combine the flour, baking powder and bicarbonate of soda.

In an electric mixer, beat the butter and sugar together until thick and pale. Add the eggs and vanilla, beating briefly. Add the crystallised ginger, ground ginger, flour mixture and buttermilk and beat just until the batter is combined and smooth. Pour the batter into the prepared dish and bake for 30 minutes or until the pudding has risen.

While the pudding is in the oven, prepare the topping. In the food processor, process the almonds until very finely chopped. Place the sugar, almonds, butter and cream in a heavy-based saucepan. Without stirring, bring to the boil over medium heat and, shaking the saucepan from time to time, simmer for 5 minutes or until the bubbles are thick and glossy. Set aside.

Remove the pudding from the oven and spread the topping evenly over the surface. Return it to the oven and bake for a further 20 minutes or until the topping is bubbling. Serve immediately or reheat to serve.

To make the yoghurt cream, whisk the cream until soft peaks form. Stir in the yoghurt, icing sugar and vanilla. Serve alongside the warm ginger pudding.

Serves 10–12

We still pinch ourselves at how generous Dana was to us, inviting us to run a class at her cooking school. She has the most gorgeous set up in LA and we were so warmly welcomed. I've stayed in touch with Dana over the years, and she has become a true friend. This mouth-watering cobbler comes from her cookbook *The Summertime Anytime Cookbook*, a recipe from Shutters on the Beach, one of her family's hotels. ∼ *Merelyn, MMCC*

See Dana's story on page 192

Dana Slatkin

Strawberry Rhubarb Cobbler

2 bunches rhubarb, trimmed
    (about 600 g/1 lb 5 oz)
170 g (¾ cup) caster (superfine) sugar
1 heaped tablespoon plain
    (all-purpose) flour
450 g (2 heaped cups/1 lb)
    strawberries, hulled and halved
vanilla ice cream or crème fraîche,
    to serve

Cobbler topping

150 g (1 cup/5½ oz) plain
    (all-purpose) flour
2½ tablespoons caster (superfine) sugar
1½ teaspoons baking powder
pinch of sea salt
60 g (2 oz) cold unsalted butter, cubed
60 ml (¼ cup) milk
2 tablespoons thickened
    (whipping) cream

Preheat the oven to 200°C (400°F/Gas 6). Grease a 28 × 18 cm (11 × 7 inch) baking dish.

Cut the rhubarb into 1 cm (½ inch) slices and toss with the sugar and flour, then place in the prepared dish. Bake for 15 minutes or until the rhubarb is starting to break down and juices bubble around the edges. Remove from the oven; do not pour off the juice.

While the rhubarb is cooking, make the topping. Combine the flour, sugar, baking powder and salt in a large bowl. Using your fingers or a pastry cutter, mix in the butter until coarse crumbs are formed. Add the milk and the cream, mixing until just combined and sticky; the topping will be quite thick.

Place the strawberries on top of the rhubarb, then drop clumps of the topping over the fruit. The fruit need not be covered entirely, as the batter will spread while baking. Bake for 25 minutes or until the topping is golden and the filling is bubbling.

Serve with vanilla ice cream or crème fraîche.

Serve 8–10

Picture a group of five women standing around a kitchen benchtop picking the glazed pecans off a hot kugel, straight from the oven, burning their tongues, but heading straight back for more. That's us! Noodle kugel is a truly Jewish dessert, and this version comes topped with shiny golden pecans and a sweet caramel. ~ *MMCC*

See Mikki's story on page 154

Mikki Fink

Pecan-Glazed Noodle Kugel

400 g (14 oz) flat egg noodles

115 g (4 oz/1 stick) butter, melted

115 g (½ cup) caster (superfine) sugar

1 teaspoon vanilla extract

1 heaped teaspoon ground cinnamon

pinch of sea salt

4 eggs, separated

2 large granny smith apples,
  peeled and grated

Pecan caramel

50 g (2 oz) butter

370 g (2 cups, lightly packed)
  brown sugar

60 ml (¼ cup) water

240 g (8 oz) pecans

Preheat the oven to 170°C (340°F/Gas 3–4). Grease a 1.2 litre (12 cup) ring tin.

To prepare the pecan topping, combine the butter, brown sugar and water in a saucepan and melt over low heat. Increase the heat to medium and simmer for about 6 minutes or until the mixture thickens. Add in the pecans, stir and bring back to a simmer. Pour the pecan mixture into the prepared tin.

Cook the noodles in a large saucepan of salted boiling water until they are just firm to the bite (al dente). While they are cooking, combine the melted butter, caster sugar, vanilla, cinnamon and salt in a jug. In a small bowl, beat the egg yolks with a fork to combine. In a separate bowl, whisk the egg whites until stiff peaks form.

Drain the noodles and tip into a large bowl. Pour the melted butter mixture over the warm noodles and mix in the egg yolks and apple. Fold the egg whites into the noodle mixture and pour into the tin on top of the pecans.

Bake for 1½ hours or until dark golden and crisp on the top. Allow to cool for a couple of minutes, then invert onto a heatproof serving plate. Allow to cool and slice to serve.

Serves 12

When Lisa told me that this was now her favourite cake in the world and suggested that I try it again at home, I didn't see the need for what I thought was a basic butter cake. How wrong I was – there is nothing basic about this cake. (And yes, we had another typical MMCC debate on whether a recipe should be 'in' or 'out'.) How can anyone resist this gorgeous, moist, deep-yellow cake with its fluffy white topping reminiscent of the colours of a summer frangipani flower? *~ Natanya, MMCC*

See Helen's story on page 290

Helen Carp

Frangipani Cake

115 g (4 oz/1 stick) unsalted butter, at room temperature

3 egg yolks

170 g (¾ cup/6 oz) caster (superfine) sugar

150 g (1 cup/5½ oz) self-raising (self-rising) flour

125 ml (½ cup) milk

Topping

3 egg whites

115 g (½ cup/4 oz) caster (superfine) sugar

90 g (1 cup) desiccated coconut

Preheat the oven to 160°C (325°F/ Gas 3). Line a 20 cm (8 inch) spring-form cake tin.

In an electric mixer, beat the butter, egg yolks and sugar until thick and creamy. Gently fold in the flour and milk. Pour the batter into the prepared tin.

To make the topping, in a separate bowl whisk the egg whites until soft peaks form, then, with the motor running, add the sugar slowly, continuing to beat until the sugar is dissolved and stiff peaks form. With a metal spoon or spatula, gently fold in the coconut.

Spread the topping over the batter.

Bake for 1 hour or until a skewer inserted in the middle comes out clean.

Serves 8–10

We're happy to learn traditions from others and let them also become our own. Sweet potato pie is a typical dish from the southern USA. It is an all-American pie, something quite foreign to Australians, where we mostly use sweet potato (and pumpkin for that matter) as a vegetable. The pie crust is traditionally made from a blend of butter and solid vegetable shortening (such as Crisco) to give a light, flaky crust. In places where solid vegetable shortening is unavailable, substitute with an equal quantity of butter. ~MMCC

See Sharon's story on page 246

Sharon Goldman

Sweet Potato Pie

Pastry

90 g (3¼ oz) very cold unsalted butter

225 g (1½ cups/8 oz) plain (all-purpose) flour, plus extra

1½ teaspoons caster (superfine) sugar

¼ teaspoon sea salt

2 tablespoons cold vegetable shortening or 40 g (1½ oz) butter

60 ml (¼ cup) iced water

Filling

1 large sweet potato (450 g/1 lb)

115 g (4 oz/1 stick) butter, softened

165 g (¾ cup) sugar

125 ml (½ cup) milk

2 eggs

½ teaspoon ground nutmeg

½ teaspoon ground cinnamon

1 teaspoon vanilla extract

double cream, to serve

Preheat the oven to 180°C (350°F/Gas 4). You will need a 23 cm (9 inch) pie dish.

Start with the filling. Place the sweet potato in a saucepan and cover with water. Bring to the boil and simmer for 45 minutes or until soft. Drain and rinse under cold water, remove and discard the skin and break the flesh in into pieces.

While the sweet potato is cooking, make the pastry. Cut the butter into 1 cm (½ inch) pieces and return it to the refrigerator while you prepare the flour mixture. In a food processor, place the flour, sugar and salt and pulse a few times to mix. Add the butter and shortening (or butter, if using). Pulse until the butter is in pea-sized pieces. With the motor running, pour the iced water down the feed tube, then pulse until it comes together. Tip out onto a floured benchtop and shape it into a ball. Cover in plastic wrap and refrigerate for 30 minutes.

With a rolling pin, roll out the pastry on a well-floured benchtop into a circle slightly larger than the pie dish. Place into the pie dish and press into the base and side of the dish, then trim and crimp the edge. Set aside.

To make the filling, in an electric mixer, beat the sweet potato and butter until smooth. Add the sugar, milk, eggs, nutmeg, cinnamon and vanilla. Beat on medium speed until the mixture is smooth. Pour the filling into the pastry-lined pie dish.

Bake for 1 hour or until the filling only has a slight wobble when the pie is gently shaken; it will puff up as it cooks and sink as it cools. Serve at room temperature with a dollop of cream.

Serves 8–10

SHARON GOLDMAN

❧

I grew up in 'farm and ranch country' in Omaha, Nebraska, and moved to Chicago years ago to explore the exciting metropolitan city with its diverse population. I loved going to its countless ethnic restaurants and over time started to duplicate the dishes at home.

I've been part of a cooking club for over 35 years, 'The Gourmet Group'. We were all from the same neighbourhood but from different backgrounds. Four times a year a host decides on a theme. Over the decades we have enjoyed a huge range of flavours such as Texas barbecue and Southern fare, and international cuisines like French, Spanish, Russian, Japanese and Italian. We have also done low calorie, vegan and holidays – both Jewish and secular. The most memorable was the 'Diet Dinner'. It was awful and ended up being truly low calorie as no one could eat a thing!

We all love to travel and explore foods from different countries. We talk to chefs, take cooking courses wherever we go and bring back interesting ideas. Happily, the latest trip often becomes the theme for the next dinner. Food and cooking has created great friendships for more than three happy decades.

ELANA JACOBS

❧

As a little girl I learnt that good food tastes even better when shared with others, especially those you love the most. For many years, our Sundays were spent at a cousin's farm. Mornings were devoted to tending cucumbers and tomatoes in the greenhouses, and afternoons to large groups of guests over languid lunches. The experience of communal cooking and eating made for beautiful memories.

For me, food is one of the primary ways that culture is transmitted from one generation to the next. From the *shtetls* of Lithuania to South Africa in the early twentieth century, my grandparents brought many rich traditions, which provided the context in which my parents grew up, which then coloured the way my siblings and I were raised. I learnt to cook from my grandparents and parents, who were skilled in creating beautiful meals with limited ingredients and without reference to recipe books, and from our wonderful nanny who was unsurpassed in producing traditional African dishes and everyday meals.

I firmly believe that to be a truly brilliant cook is a gift, but to cook well is simply a matter of picking good recipes and following them. I take pleasure in seeing how competent my own children are in the kitchen as they reproduce many family favourites.

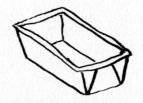

GLORIA JACOBSON PINK

In Saint John, Canada, where I grew up, there was no kosher butcher, baker or caterer so everybody cooked, baked and entertained from scratch. When it came time for a wedding, Bar Mitzvah or any other *simcha* all the women gathered in the *shule* kitchen and prepared everything. It was the best of times, with very strong communal friendships. To this day people talk about 'the great Saint John cooks'.

My mother was a fantastic cook and made everything seem very easy. When she wrote down her recipe for *gefilte* fish it came with a tip that I use constantly: 'Take your time, read the recipe carefully and use your own judgment as to taste.' To me, that is what cooking is all about.

I remember her making the dough for *puter kuchen* (cinnamon buns) on Saturday night. It was left to rise in the fridge overnight and then we woke to the aroma of freshly baked buns on Sunday morning. It has now become one of our favourite dishes to break the fast after Yom Kippur.

My husband and I moved to Halifax, Nova Scotia, soon after marrying, having met at Jewish summer camp. I now became one of the women who cooked, baked and entertained. When my daughter got married, we created a magnificent buffet of homemade cakes and desserts, all made with love by my friends and me. My mum had already passed away by then, but her friend from Saint John brought a huge box full of squares and cookies, which she made from Mum's recipes. What a thrill to have a reminder of her with us.

Fast forward many years and I continue to entertain for family and friends. It might be a *yom tov* dinner for 25, brunch for 75 at home to celebrate a *simcha* or a dinner party just for fun. Sharing recipes with my children and grandchildren, baking and cooking, the tradition goes on.

GLORIA'S RECIPES

We were looking for a good pecan pie recipe (one of my favourite pies!) to include in our collection and just weren't having any luck with the ones we tried. So I just love this take on the classic. It's great there's no blind-baking of the pastry, which makes the whole thing a little easier to make.

~*Lynn, MMCC*

See Elana's story on page 246

Elana Jacobs

Walnut Honey Tart

Pastry

150 g (1 cup/5½ oz) plain (all-purpose) flour
50 g (scant ¼ cup/1¾ oz) caster (superfine) sugar
90 g (3¼ oz) unsalted butter, at room temperature
1 egg, lightly beaten

Filling

300 g (2½ cups) walnut pieces
150 g (⅔ cup) caster (superfine) sugar
2 tablespoons water
150 g (⅓ cup) honey
100 g (3½ oz) butter
1 teaspoon vanilla extract

You will need a 23 cm (9 inch) tart tin with a removable base.

To make the pastry, combine the flour and sugar in a bowl. With your fingertips, rub in the butter until the mixture resembles coarse breadcrumbs. Make a well in the centre of the flour mixture and pour in the egg, then mix with a wooden spoon until it comes together . Remove from the bowl and knead lightly on the benchtop for a minute or so. Shape into a disc, wrap in plastic wrap and refrigerate for 1 hour.

Preheat the oven to 180°C (350°F/Gas 4).

To make the filling, roughly chop the walnuts and set aside. Place the sugar and water in a saucepan over medium heat and stir until the sugar is dissolved. Reduce the heat to low–medium and, very slowly, without stirring, bring it to the boil, then continue to simmer for 10 minutes or until it turns a deep caramel colour. Remove the caramel from the heat and carefully add the honey and the butter, stirring to combine. Return to low–medium heat and boil for a few minutes until it thickens a little. Remove from the heat and stir in the walnuts and vanilla. Allow to cool slightly.

To assemble the tart, remove the pastry from the fridge. Roll out the pastry on a floured benchtop until slightly larger than the tin. With floured fingers, press the pastry into the base and up the side of tin, using the rolling pin to even out the top edge. Pour in the filling, smoothing the top so it is even.

Bake the tart for 35 minutes or until the top is a deep golden brown.

Serves 10

We understand why this is Gloria's grandchildren's favourite cake. And why they love the egg sauce almost more than the cake! We had never heard of egg sauce, but once we tasted it, we were sold. Gloria's original recipe calls for molasses instead of golden syrup. Over many conversations with her, we established that Australian molasses (dark treacle) is too strong for this cake. When we tried it with a cup of golden syrup instead, it was perfect. And we'll have double egg sauce thanks, just like her grandchildren. ～ *MMCC*

See Gloria's story on page 247

Gloria Jacobson Pink

Hot Gingerbread Cake with Egg Sauce

115 g (4 oz/1 stick) unsalted butter, at room temperature
90 g (½ cup, loosely packed/3¼ oz) brown sugar
1 egg
350 g (1 cup) golden syrup (light treacle)
375 g (2½ cups/13¼ oz) plain (all-purpose) flour
2 teaspoon bicarbonate of soda (baking soda)
1 teaspoon ground ginger
1 teaspoon ground cinnamon
½ teaspoon ground cloves
¼ teaspoon sea salt
250 ml (1 cup) boiling water

Egg sauce

3 eggs, at room temperature
115 g (½ cup) caster (superfine) sugar
1 teaspoon vanilla extract

Preheat the oven to 175°C (345°F/Gas 4). Line a 23 cm (9 inch) square or 26 × 20 cm (10¼ × 8 inch) rectangular cake tin.

In an electric mixer, cream the butter and sugar. Add the egg, beating well, then the golden syrup. Beat to combine.

In a bowl, sift together the flour, bicarbonate of soda, ginger, cinnamon, cloves and salt. Add the sifted ingredients to the mixing bowl, alternating with the hot water, and mix until smooth. Pour into the prepared tin.

Bake for 40 minutes or until a skewer inserted into the cake comes out clean.

To make the egg sauce, in an electric mixer, whisk together the eggs, sugar and vanilla for about 5 minutes until light, fluffy and thick. This sauce is best made just before serving.

Serve the cake warm or at room temperature, cut into squares and topped with the egg sauce.

Serves 10

See Gloria's story on page 247

Gloria Jacobson Pink

Blueberry Tart

Pastry

185 g (1¼ cups/6½ oz) plain (all-purpose) flour

40 g (3 tablespoons) icing (confectioners') sugar

¼ teaspoon sea salt

150 g (5½ oz) cold unsalted butter, chopped

Filling

170 g (¾ cup) caster (superfine) sugar

20 g (2 tablespoons) cornflour (cornstarch)

pinch of sea salt

2 tablespoons cold water

2 tablespoons lemon juice

15 g (3 teaspoons) unsalted butter

1 kg (6 cups/2 lbs 4 oz) fresh blueberries

whipped cream, to serve

Preheat the oven to 180°C (350°F/Gas 4). Grease a 25 cm (10 inch) tart tin with a removable base.

To make the pastry, in a food processor, combine the flour, icing sugar and salt and process for 5 seconds. Add the butter and pulse until clumps begin to form. Gather into a ball. With your hands, press the pastry over the base and side of the tin. Prick all over with a fork. Bake for 25 minutes or until the pastry is golden; the pastry will shrink a little in the tin. Allow to cool completely.

For the filling, whisk the sugar, cornflour and salt in a large heavy-based saucepan to blend. Gradually add the cold water and lemon juice, whisking until smooth. Add the 2 cups of the blueberries and mash coarsely with a potato masher.

Add the butter and cook over medium heat for about 10 minutes or until the mixture thickens, boils and becomes jammy, stirring occasionally. Remove from the heat and fold in the remaining blueberries.

Tip the filling into the prepared crust and refrigerate until cold, at least 1 hour.

Serve with whipped cream.

Serves 10–12

SYLVIA STRICKER

I'm one of a handful of children born in the Ferramonti concentration camp near the small town of Cosenza in Calabria, Southern Italy. In the late 1930s, my parents lived in Berlin where my father owned a stamp shop. It was a very difficult time and the shop was destroyed during Kristallnacht. My parents were captured in Berlin and went to separate prisons; they were later reunited and sent to Ferramonti in 1940.

Fortunately for us, the Italians were not like the Germans and while we spent four years in the camp we never starved nor feared for our lives. It was not until we moved to Palestine in 1945 that we actually felt hunger, as the conditions were so difficult in those early years of Israel's life. My sad introduction to baking was when my mother, after a long time collecting ration cards, was finally able to secure all the ingredients to make her very special German torte. When baked, she placed it on a special glass stand and it looked absolutely delicious! I was only eight years old and I can still remember the feeling as I picked up the whole torte and it slipped through my hands, crashing onto a pile of dirt that my mother had just swept up. I can still feel the pain as I watched my beloved mother crying as she tried to salvage what was left.

In 1950 we moved to Sydney and I remember the four-day trip vividly, especially the huge basket of apples being offered by the air hostess. I took the biggest, reddest apple I had ever seen, a real treat. I learnt to cook as my father loved his sweets and I wanted to re-create the cakes of his childhood. I watched my mother as she cooked, but all her recipes were in German. She would put a 'bit of this' and a 'bit of that' in her cakes and I would madly write it all down.

Nowadays, Friday nights are an important celebration for my extended family and we rarely miss the opportunity to share a meal and listen to everyone's stories. It is still a pleasure for me to always make the desserts; it is this ritual that brings us together week after week.

SYLVIA'S RECIPE

Fladen: page 256

A layered continental slice from the old world – we looked at the recipe, handwritten on a piece of lined foolscap paper, and wondered how on earth we were going to re-create it. We took a deep breath, followed Sylvia's recipe step by step, phoned Sylvia and her good friend Ziggy with a few questions, then literally high-fived around the kitchen when we got it right. This is a great recipe to start a day before serving as all the fillings and the pastry can be made ahead. ∼*MMCC*

See Sylvia's story on page 254

Sylvia Stricker

Fladen

80 g (¼ cup) apricot jam (jelly)
icing (confectioners') sugar

Pastry

375 g (1½ cups/13½ oz) plain
    (all-purpose) flour
75 g (⅓ cup/2¾ oz) caster (superfine)
    sugar
¾ teaspoon baking powder
190 g (6¾ oz) unsalted butter, at room
    temperature
2 egg yolks
2 tablespoons brandy

Apple layer

4 granny smith apples
80 g (½ cup) sultanas (golden raisins)
115 g (½ cup) caster (superfine) sugar
juice of 2 oranges
1 cinnamon stick

To make the pastry, combine the flour, sugar, baking powder, butter, egg yolks and brandy in a bowl and mix with a wooden spoon. Turn onto a lightly flour benchtop and knead lightly until smooth. (Alternatively, place all the ingredients in a food processor and process until a ball forms.) Divide into 4 balls, flatten each one slightly, wrap in plastic wrap and refrigerate for 30 minutes.

To make the apple layer, peel, core and thinly slice the apples. Place with the sultanas, caster sugar, orange juice and cinnamon stick in a large heavy-based saucepan and simmer over low–medium heat for 30 minutes or until the apple is soft and translucent. Drain to remove any excess juice and allow to cool.

To make the poppy seed layer, place the poppy seeds, milk, vanilla and caster sugar in a heavy-based saucepan and bring to the boil over medium heat. Simmer for about 15 minutes or until all the liquid has disappeared, stirring from time to time. Tip the mixture into a bowl and allow to cool.

To make the walnut layer, in a bowl, mix together the walnuts, caster sugar, milk, vanilla and lemon zest.

Poppy seed layer

150 g (5½ oz) freshly ground poppy seed
250 ml (1 cup) milk
2 teaspoons vanilla extract
115 g (½ cup) caster (superfine) sugar

Walnut layer

175 g (6 oz) ground walnuts
55 g (¼ cup) caster (superfine) sugar
60 ml (¼ cup) milk
2 teaspoons vanilla extract
finely grated zest of 1 lemon

Preheat the oven to 180°C (350°F/Gas 4). Line a 20 cm (8 inch) square cake tin with two rectangles of baking paper with enough overhang to hold when lifting the cake out.

Roll out the first ball of pastry between 2 pieces of baking paper to fit the cake tin. Carefully lay it in the bottom of the tin, patching with excess bits to fill in any holes. Spread the pastry with half of the apricot jam. Spread the poppy seed mixture over the jam to form an even layer.

Roll out the second ball of pastry as above and carefully lay it on top of the poppy seed layer. Spread the apple mixture on top to form an even layer.

Roll out the third ball of pastry as above and carefully lay it on top of the apple layer. Spread the remaining apricot jam and then the walnut mixture to form an even layer. Roll out the final ball of pastry as described above and carefully lay it on top. This layer of pastry will be the top of the cake, so take care to ensure it has no holes or cracks. Prick with a fork all over and bake for 1 hour or until golden brown.

Allow to cool in the tin. Carefully lift the fladen out and dust with the icing sugar to serve.

Serves 12

Photo on page 255

We kept saying 'We just don't need another chocolate cake. We have Lyndi's chocolate chiffon, Carol's flourless, Elza's celebration cake' ... But Natty simply insisted. And then we tasted it. This is not an ordinary chocolate cake – this torta gianduja is an Italian Baci chocolate in the guise of a cake and it is a necessity. And don't forget the shiny chocolate ganache (like we did in the photo)! ~ *MMCC*

See Garry's story on page 260

Garry Enston

Flourless Chocolate Hazelnut Cake

230 g (8¼ oz) best-quality dark chocolate (70%)
200 g (7 oz) butter, chopped
250 g (9 oz) ground roasted or raw hazelnuts
6 eggs, separated
200 g (1 scant cup/7 oz) caster (superfine) sugar
60 ml (¼ cup) hazelnut or almond liqueur
whipped cream, to serve

MMCC's chocolate ganache

125 ml (½ cup) pure cream (35% fat)
250 g (9 oz) best-quality dark chocolate (70%)
½ teaspoon lemon juice
whole roasted hazelnuts, to decorate

Preheat the oven to 180°C (350°F/Gas 4). Line a 23 cm (9 inch) spring-form cake tin.

To make the cake, break the chocolate into pieces. In a heatproof bowl over a saucepan of simmering water, melt the chocolate and butter. Stir in the hazelnut meal then stir in the liqueur.

In an electric mixer, beat the egg yolks and sugar together until pale and creamy, then beat in the chocolate mixture until thoroughly combined.

In a separate bowl, whisk the egg whites until stiff peaks form.

Place a couple of spoons of the egg white in the chocolate mixture and stir to thoroughly combine, then, with a large metal spoon or spatula, gently fold in the remaining egg white.

Spoon the mixture into the prepared tin and bake in the centre of the oven for 40 minutes or until a skewer inserted into the cake comes out clean.

Remove from the oven, undo the latch on the cake tin and allow the cake to cool completely in the tin on a wire rack.

Meanwhile, to make the ganache, roughly chop the chocolate. In a small heavy-based saucepan over medium heat, heat the cream until it is just starting to boil. Remove from the heat and add the chocolate, stirring until the chocolate has melted and the mixture is smooth. Stir in the lemon juice. Allow the ganache to cool a little and thicken before spreading over the top of the cooled cake.

When the cake is cool, remove it from the tin, cover with the chocolate ganache and decorate with whole roasted hazelnuts. Serve with whipped cream on the side.

Serves 8–10

GARRY ENSTON

My love of food is definitely genetic. In 1903 my grandmother's cousin was the first woman to ever publish a traditional Czech cookbook. I have a copy in German, which I presume contains some fantastic recipes, if only I could translate them.

As Europe fell under Nazi occupation in 1939, my parents left Prague to start a new life in Perth, Australia. I remember how much my mum, Edith, loved good food and to entertain, even though she was not a passionate cook herself. She was very particular about what food was served and how it was presented, and luckily we had a wonderful Hungarian house-keeper who prepared delicious continental food. My father was a consummate continental gentleman who always complimented the dish as it was served to him, but they were most heartfelt when it was the nostalgic foods he remembered from his mother's kitchen.

My mother had a number of wonderful cake recipes from her mother, and also her uncle, who was the pastry chef at the Palace Hotel in Prague. She entered one of them, chocolate poppyseed cake, into a cooking competition in the *West Australian* newspaper. Perth was not familiar with continental cakes or how delicious they were. Dad sent in the recipe, copied out

in Czech, and naturally this tweaked the curiosity of the judges who then had to translate it. The cake was so unusual and delicious that it won first prize and my mother won a trip for two to Europe with $500 spending money!

In 1980 I married Fay, who is Macedonian with Greek heritage. It was exciting to be introduced to her delicious Mediterranean cuisine, which is quite different from my Eastern European background. Fay's Aunt Lilly bought her an electric hand beater for her twelfth birthday and ignited a passion for baking that continues to this day.

I have been very spoilt with all my favourite foods as Fay continues both our culinary traditions, cooking both continental and Greek Macedonian dishes. She also makes my favourite birthday cake for me every year, dobos torte, a true labour of love, as this was the cake our Hungarian housekeeper made for me when I was young.

We love the traditions of our cultures as expressed by food. It gives our family a strong sense of identity as well as keeping the customs alive. As Fay's family says, 'We live to eat whereas everyone else eats to live!'

GARRY'S RECIPES

Flourless Chocolate Hazelnut Cake: page 258
Edith's Plum Cake: page 263

Part of what we do in the MMCC kitchen is to try out the different recipes we receive for the same dish, often from all over the world. We ended up with nine (yes, nine) plum cakes to try and we tasted them all in one day. Apart from the sugar coma we slumped into in the afternoon, it was one of the most interesting mornings we've had. Who would think that differences in tin shape, plum size and way of mixing would have such an impact on the finished product? All the cakes were really good, but this one definitely and unanimously stole our hearts. ∼ *MMCC*

See Garry's story on page 260

Garry Enston

Edith's Plum Cake

180 g (6½ oz) unsalted butter, at room temperature

345 g (1½ cups/12¼ oz) caster (superfine) sugar

4 eggs

1 teaspoon vanilla extract

finely grated zest of 1 lemon

300 g (2 cups/10½ oz) self-raising (self-rising) flour

25 sugar plums or 12 medium plums, halved and pitted

icing (confectioners') sugar, for dusting

double cream, to serve

Preheat the oven to 180°C (350°F/ Gas 4). Line a 33 × 23 cm (13 × 9 inches) rectangular baking tin, leaving an overhang up the sides to make lifting the cake out easier.

In an electric mixer, cream the butter and sugar until light and fluffy. Add the eggs, one at a time, beating well after each addition. Add the vanilla extract and lemon zest. Fold in the flour until just combined.

Spoon the batter into the prepared tin and spread evenly. Lay the plums cut side up in rows on top of the batter, without pressing them into the mixture.

Bake for 1 hour or until a skewer inserted into the centre of the cake comes out clean.

Allow the cake to cool in the tin and lift out using the baking paper.

Dust with icing sugar and serve warm or at room temperature with cream.

Serves 16–20

The marmalade syrup with this cake is like a gift with purchase. You get a superb, flourless citrus cake topped with shiny, sticky peel and a jar of the BEST mandarin marmalade to go with it. Don't forget to use the leftovers on hot buttered toast. ~ *Jacqui, MMCC*

See Kathy's story on page 266

Kathy Miller

Mandarin Cake with Marmalade Syrup

4 thin-skinned mandarins
    (about 480 g/1 lb 1 oz in total)
1 lemon
6 eggs
300 g (1⅓ cups/10½ oz) caster
    (superfine) sugar
300 g (3 cups/10½ oz) ground almonds
    (almond meal)
1 tablespoon baking powder
whipped cream, to serve

Marmalade syrup

3 mandarins
2 limes
1.5 litres (6 cups) water
690 g (3 cups) caster (superfine) sugar
1 tablespoon brandy

Line a 22 cm (8½ inch) spring-form cake tin.

Wash all the fruit very well; do not peel.

To make the fruit purée for the cake, put the 4 mandarins and 1 lemon into a saucepan and cover with water. Bring to the boil, cover and simmer over low–medium heat for 1 hour or until the fruit is soft. Drain and allow to cool. Cut the fruit in half and remove all the seeds. In a food processor or blender, purée the fruit (with the skin) and set aside.

While the fruit is cooking, make the marmalade syrup. Thinly slice the mandarins and limes, remove and discard any seeds and place in a heavy-based medium saucepan. Add the water and bring to the boil, then reduce the heat to low and simmer, for 1 hour or until the fruit is soft. Add the sugar and simmer for at least 1 hour or until a rich syrup forms. The syrup should reduce to 2 cups. Strain off ½ cup of the syrup into a heatproof jug, add the brandy to the strained syrup and set aside.

Preheat the oven to 180°C (350°F/Gas 4).

In an electric mixer, whisk the eggs until creamy and light. Add the sugar and continue to whisk for a few minutes. Add the ground almonds and baking powder and whisk for a minute or two to combine. Fold in the fruit purée and pour into the prepared tin.

Bake for 1 hour 10 minutes or until a skewer inserted in the centre of the cake comes out clean.

Remove the cake from the oven and prick the top all over with a wooden skewer. Pour the strained syrup over the top of the cake. Decorate the cake with the peel from the marmalade syrup. Allow to cool in the tin.

Serve warm or at room temperature with extra marmalade syrup on the side and whipped cream.

Serves 10–12

KATHY MILLER

My English mother would cook a delicious, heart-warming hot roast beef lunch with Yorkshire pudding every Sunday for our family. Along with the blancmange and strawberry trifle for dessert, it was an unusually British tradition for a Jewish family living in Johannesburg. My mother's sister used to serve a fancy afternoon tea from a trolley with dainty biscuits every Sunday afternoon. I think these little treats encouraged me to bake cakes just like hers. My mother was also quite practical – I remember she used to take a big baking dish down to the local Italian restaurant to be filled with a delicious traditional lasagne.

My husband and I left South Africa some 30 years ago, as we were not happy with the deteriorating political situation and didn't want our teenage boys to join the South African Army and uphold apartheid. We have lived in Sydney ever since and have made a wonderful life here.

My mother-in-law had a great influence on my baking. I remember with such fondness watching her bake old-fashioned sawa cookies – shortbread biscuits made with a cookie press, decorated with cherries and chocolate sprinkles. Nowadays I have embraced healthy modern cooking which ties in with my passion for teaching pilates. I love to *patchke* (fuss) in the kitchen, starting every dish from scratch.

KATHY'S RECIPE

Mandarin Cake with Marmalade Syrup: page 264

SUSAN BAROCAS

If you look closely at the official photos from the past two White House Seders, you can see them. There, sitting on silver serving dishes on the beautifully set table, are my charoset balls!

I still get a jolt of surprise and pleasure when I think back to my three years serving as the guest chef for the Obamas' Seder. I remember after the first year, someone remarked that I could check that off my bucket list. Really? I gotta tell you that cooking at the White House was never on any list of mine. Who could have imagined it for this self-taught cook, teacher, caterer and writer?

Each year, standing in the compact White House kitchen, cooking all day with the other chefs, the anticipatory nervousness quickly disappeared as the joy of where I was and what I was doing took over. After the first year, I was able to add a few Sephardic items to the menu, including those charoset balls, which have become one of my trademark dishes over the past twenty years. And each year, as I ground the fruit and nuts mixture, then rolled the balls in uniform sizes, I truly felt that, somehow, my parents, grandparents and even unknown ancestors were there with me, smiling and sharing this most unexpected and amazing experience.

I've been cooking since I was a young child and still have my first cookbook from 1959 when I was seven: *Betty Crocker's Cook Book for Boys and Girls*. While I started cooking because I liked it and it was fun, by the time I was eleven, family circumstances meant it became my job to fix dinner nearly every weeknight for my parents and three siblings. When this kind of responsibility is thrust on you as a kid, I think eventually you face a choice as I did: resent that responsibility, rejecting it as soon as possible, or embrace it and make it your own. I was fortunate because cooking remained mostly enjoyable for me, becoming a positive piece of my identity growing up ... and this was way before Food Network!

To this day, I find the kitchen a place of unending creativity and self-expression. It is also where I connect strongly with my family history and my Jewish heritage, both the Sephardic and Ashkenazic sides, as well as with my now 20-year-old son, both while he was growing up and still today.

SUSAN'S RECIPE

Charoset Balls: page 272

FAY FILLER

I hold my heritage close to my heart. I can still smell my mother's delicious cooking when I sit at the *Shabbos* or *yom tov* table with my precious children, grandchildren and great-grandchildren. It takes me back to my childhood and reminds me of special times that we spent together as a family – sitting, eating, talking and laughing.

I was born in a small town in Poland, Tarnogrod, and was only seven years old when Germany and Russia invaded in 1939. I recall the night we had to flee, hiding in our barn when we heard shooting and bombs nearby. My father was taken aside by some of the Russians who warned him that my family should escape to Russia immediately. My parents took me, together with six of my siblings, and we grabbed the first train we could. One of my brothers stayed behind to look after my grandparents. Once in Russia, we were sent to a Siberian labour camp, where we lived under harsh and cruel conditions. I'll never forget stealing a potato for my mother from the commander's garden. From there we went to Kazakhstan, where we lived until the war ended.

My family decided it was best to move as far away from Europe as possible after the war. I came to Sydney because my sister's sister-in-law, who was already living here, was able to sponsor five of us to start a new life. The rest of my family followed a short time later; sadly, my brother and grandparents who stayed behind in 1939 did not survive. My father made it to Australia, but died six weeks later.

Now, being the last surviving member of eight children, it makes me sad to think that I have none of my siblings to turn to and discuss the years gone by. We shared so many wonderful times – it was always our love for each other and a table of food that brought us together. I miss it so much.

I am, however, the proud matriarch of my own family with three sons, nine grandchildren and three great-grandchildren. I get so much *nachas* when my family stand side by side with me in the kitchen so I can teach the recipes I learnt from my mother and grandmother.

FAY'S RECIPE

Polish Apple Strudel: page 270

For many years, I had heard Fay's extended family rave about this special cake-like strudel. We spent many hours trying to replicate what Fay has been making for over 60 years (and could probably whip up blindfolded). We watched her, she supervised us, we practised and practised some more until we were able to write the recipe for her strudel that was exactly the same as her lucky family had been enjoying for so long. Fay always makes this recipe well ahead of serving as it is at its best after sitting in the fridge for a few days. ～ *Natanya, MMCC*

See Fay's story on page 268

Fay Filler

Polish Apple Strudel

2 tablespoons vegetable oil, for greasing and baking
¼ cup sugar, for sprinkling

Dough

400 g (2⅔ cups/14 oz) plain (all-purpose) flour, plus extra
125 g (1 scant cup/4½ oz) self-raising (self-rising) flour
125 g (heaped ½ cup/4½ oz) sugar
80 ml (⅓ cup) vegetable oil
1 teaspoon bicarbonate of soda (baking soda)
1 tablespoon white vinegar
220 ml (1 scant cup/7¾ fl oz) warm water

Start this recipe at least a day before serving.

Grease a baking tin or roasting pan (32 × 24 cm/13 × 9½ inches) with 1 tablespoon of the oil.

To make the dough, in a large bowl, mix together the flours. Make a well in the flour and add the sugar, vegetable oil and the bicarbonate of soda. Immediately pour the vinegar on top of the bicarbonate of soda and wait a few seconds for the mixture to froth. With your hands, start to mix the liquid in the well, slowly adding the water and bringing in the flour bit by bit to form a rough dough.

Tip the dough onto a lightly floured benchtop and bang it down on the benchtop a few times, then knead lightly for 2–3 minutes or until it becomes smooth.

Divide the dough into 2 equal pieces for the 2 rolls of the strudel. Starting with 1 piece, knead lightly for about 2 minutes, adding a sprinkle of the extra flour from time to time, until you have a smooth ball. Repeat with the remaining piece. Leave the dough, covered with a tea towel (dish cloth), to rest on the benchtop for at least 1 hour.

Filling (for both rolls)

8 large granny smith apples
125 ml (½ cup) vegetable oil
500 g (1½ cups) apricot or strawberry
    jam (jelly)
110 g (½ cup) sugar
160 g (1 cup) sultanas (golden raisins)
4 teaspoons ground cinnamon

Preheat the oven to 180°C (350°F/Gas 4). To prepare the filling, peel and grate the apples into a bowl.

Take 1 piece of the dough and, with a rolling pin, roll it out on a lightly floured benchtop into a circle, turning it over from time and time and re-flouring the benchtop if needed, until the dough becomes as thin as possible (almost transparent), around 60 cm (24 inch) in diameter.

With your hand, spread half the oil and then half the jam all over the dough. Take handfuls of half the apple and spread out on top of the jam. Sprinkle half the sugar on the apple, followed by half the sultanas. Sprinkle with half the cinnamon.

To roll the strudel, with floured hands, start at the edge closest to you and start to roll it up. Stretch and pull the rolled part towards you each time before you roll it over and continue until you reach the other side. Fold over the ends of the roll to seal. Coil the roll along the inside perimeter of the greased pan, seam-side down.

Repeat with the remaining dough and filling and place inside the other roll so it is coiled in the centre of the pan. Flatten the coils a little with your hands, and spread both rolls evenly with the remaining tablespoon of oil, then sprinkle with the sugar, using the sugar to fill in any holes in the dough. Using the back of a knife, press indentations all along the rolls about 4 cm (1½ inches) apart, as if you were marking slices, being careful not to pierce the dough.

Bake for 1½ hours or until dark golden. Allow to cool completely. Cover with plastic wrap and refrigerate for at least 1 day before serving. Serve at room temperature.

Serves 20

Photo on page 269

These had us at the get-go. Just call them Jewish bliss balls. ~ *MMCC*

See Susan's story on page 267

Susan Barocas

Charoset Balls

240 g (2 cups) pitted dried dates
100 g (about 7) dried figs
160 g (1 cup) raisins or sultanas
  (golden raisins)
60 g (about 12) dried apricot halves
120 g (1 cup) roughly chopped walnuts
½ teaspoon ground cinnamon, or to taste
2 pinches ground allspice
1½ tablespoons sweet red wine or
  grape juice
80 g (½ cup) raw or toasted almonds,
  ground

Line a baking tray and set aside.

Using a food processor, pulse and grind the dates, figs, raisins (or sultanas) and apricots coarsely. Add the walnuts, cinnamon, allspice and wine or grape juice and pulse until the mixture is well chopped but with pieces still visible and starting to stick together. Pulse it a few more times until the mixture forms a large ball, taking care not to over-process.

With slightly damp hands, gently roll the mixture into large-marble sized balls and roll each ball in the ground almonds. Place the balls in a single layer on the prepared tray and refrigerate until firm, about 3 hours. The charoset balls can then be layered in a container and stored in the refrigerator for up to 3 weeks.

Makes about 36

The first time I came across these Sephardi biscuits was at a *minyan*, a prayer ceremony after a funeral, in Sydney. The women of the community brought bags of freshly baked *kakas* (caraway biscuits) on each day of the seven days of mourning. Perhaps the circular shape represents ongoing life. The next time they appeared was when Rachel sent us her recipe. Her Sephardi community – who settled in India from Baghdad – made them at various Jewish festivals throughout the year. We think it's really great to have a recipe for one dough that makes both a savoury and sweet biscuit. ~ *Natanya, MMCC*

See Rachel's story on page 101

Rachel Dingoor

Kakas and Babas

Dough

300 g (2 cups/10½ oz) self-raising (self-rising) flour

150 g (1 cup/5½ oz) plain (all-purpose) flour

50 g (1¾ oz) caster (superfine) sugar

¼ teaspoon sea salt

85 g (3 oz) unsalted butter, at room temperature

160 ml (⅔ cup) tepid water

50 ml (2½ tablespoons) vegetable oil

½ teaspoon vanilla extract

1 egg, beaten, for eggwash

For kakas (caraway biscuits)

½ teaspoon caraway seeds

For babas (date biscuits)

250 g (1⅔ cups) pitted dried dates

3 teaspoons vegetable oil

60 ml (¼ cup) water

sesame seeds, to garnish

Preheat the oven to 200°C (400°F/Gas 6). Line 2 large baking trays.

To make the dough, in an electric mixer, slowly beat together the flour, sugar, salt and butter until it resembles crumbs. Combine the water, oil and vanilla, add to the flour mixture and gently mix until it comes together. Separate the dough into 2 equal balls and wrap each in plastic wrap. Refrigerate for 30 minutes.

To make the *kakas*, take out a ball of dough. Add the caraway seeds to it and knead a couple of times to evenly distribute. Divide the dough into small walnut-sized balls. With your hands, roll each ball into a thin strand and form a ring, sealing the ends together. Place on a prepared tray. Brush with the eggwash and bake for 15 minutes or until lightly golden. Allow to cool on a wire rack.

To make the *babas*, place the dates, oil and half of the water in a heavy-based saucepan. Cover and cook over low heat for 5 minutes. Add the remaining water and continue to cook, covered, for 15 minutes or until the dates soften and have a jam-like consistency, squashing them with a wooden spoon to break them up. Set aside and allow to cool slightly.

Take out the other ball of dough and divide into large walnut-sized balls. Take one and flatten it in the palm of your hand to form a 6 cm (2½ inch) disc. Spread one teaspoon of the date filling in the centre. Mould the disc around the filling, seal it at the top and reshape it into a ball, making sure all the filling is covered. Pat the filled ball down to flatten it into a thin disc. Brush with the eggwash, sprinkle with the sesame seeds and prick the tops several times with a fork.

Place on the other prepared tray and bake for 15 minutes or until lightly golden. Allow to cool on a wire rack.

Store the biscuits in an airtight container for up to 2 weeks.

Makes 30 *kakas* and 20 *babas*

This is an American recipe so 'scone' rhymes with 'stone'. It is different from an English or Australian 'scone', which rhymes with 'Ron'. American scones are slightly flatter and more dense with a crusty outside, mostly triangular or wedge shaped and perfect for holding a big dollop of cream.

~ MMCC

See Eydie's story on page 192

Eydie Desser

Buttermilk Scone

300 g (2 cups/10½ oz) plain (all-purpose) flour, plus extra
75 g (⅓ cup/2¾ oz) caster (superfine) sugar
1½ teaspoons baking powder
½ teaspoon bicarbonate of soda (baking soda)
¼ teaspoon sea salt
90 g (3¼ oz) cold unsalted butter
125 ml (½ cup) buttermilk
1 egg
½ teaspoon vanilla extract
75 g (½ cup) currants or raisins
butter and honey or jam (jelly) and cream, to serve

Preheat the oven to 190°C (375°F/Gas 5). You will need an ungreased baking tray.

In a large bowl, sift together the flour, sugar, baking powder, bicarbonate of soda and salt. Cut the butter into 1 cm (½ inch) cubes and distribute over the flour mixture.

With a pastry cutter or a knife, cut in the butter until the mixture resembles coarse crumbs.

In a small bowl, mix together the buttermilk, egg and vanilla. Add this to the flour mixture and stir to combine, then knead lightly until a dough is formed. Add the currants or raisins.

With lightly floured hands, put the dough onto the baking tray and pat into a 20 cm (8 inch) diameter circle. With a serrated knife, cut the circle into 8 wedges, almost all the way through.

Bake for 20 minutes or until the top is lightly browned and a skewer inserted into the scone comes out clean.

Remove from the oven and, using a slide, transfer the scone to a wire rack to cool.

Serve warm or cool completely. Best eaten the same day. Serve with butter and honey or jam (jelly) and cream.

Serves 8

The girls tried my nana's nut loaf for the first time on our working retreat in Byron Bay. We spent four days locked away from all distraction, madly finishing the testing of recipes for this book. A lot of heated debates were had, and one afternoon's tension was relieved when we all sat down with a good strong cuppa and a thickly buttered slice of nut loaf. Disagreements were resolved, frustrations were calmed and all was good in the MMCC house.

~ Jacqui, MMCC

Jacqui Israel

Nana's Date Nut Loaf

250 ml (1 cup) boiling water
1 (black tea) tea bag
115 g (¾ cup) pitted dried dates
140 g (¾ cup, lightly packed) brown sugar
60 g (2 oz) unsalted butter
180 g (6½ oz) plain (all-purpose) flour
1½ teaspoons ground cinnamon
1 teaspoon baking powder
½ teaspoon bicarbonate of soda (baking soda)
pinch of sea salt
60 g (½ cup) chopped walnuts

Preheat the oven to 160°C (325°F/Gas 3). Grease a loaf tin.

Steep the tea bag in the boiling water for 30 seconds, then discard the tea bag.

Roughly chop the dates and put in a saucepan with the tea, sugar and butter over medium–high heat. Bring to the boil and simmer for 1 minute. Set aside to cool.

Sift the flour, cinnamon, baking powder, baking soda and salt into a bowl. Add the walnuts and mix through. Pour the cooled date mixture onto the dry ingredients and mix well with a wooden spoon. Tip into the prepared tin.

Bake for 35 minutes or until cooked through. Serve with butter and/or cheese.

Makes 1 loaf

ZOLI ROMER

My parents escaped from communist Budapest together with my adored grandmother in 1956 and headed for Adelaide, a relatively quiet city where my great uncle lived.

Though a multicultural city, Adelaide had only two continental cake shops at the time. My dad, Zoli – who loved baking – got himself a bicycle and rode many kilometres into the city centre each day to work different shifts at Adelaide's iconic Aussie cake shop, Balfours. As none of the locals could pronounce 'Zoli', he became known as John. After a couple of years, my parents took a huge risk and opened their own cake shop in the busy seaside suburb of Glenelg: the Susie Cake Shop.

Though the continental cakes were spectacular, the locals weren't used to them, so Dad started to cater to the masses with cupcakes, lamingtons and other Aussie classics. The shop became a massive success. I still remember Dad having to go to Adelaide Airport to dispatch his cargo of 'Susie Cheese Pockets' to an interstate function. There was even a political party called 'The Susie Cheesecake Party', though their success didn't equal Dad's!

I became an object of curiosity at school among my peers, as not only was I from a European family, my parents owned a cake shop. I was constantly asked: 'Were you named after the shop, or the shop after you?'

Dad was the only pastry cook in Adelaide making *challah*, and even the locals loved to buy them. Every September he would start making his *beigli* to be ready for *yom tov* and would continue until Christmastime when they were still being collected by the boxful.

The shop was open seven days a week and my parents worked long hours. After a rare trip to the USA, Dad returned with great inspiration and developed a new yeast bun, named 'American Beauty'. It became one of his best sellers and people travelled from all over Adelaide for this new delicacy. He was also renowned for his delicious jam ring biscuits, which still remain a favourite of mine today. Dad is now 98 and is more than happy to share his recipes with me and others who ask, as they often do.

– *Susie Owen, daughter*

ZOLI'S RECIPE

Jam Ring Biscuits: opposite page

It is so satisfying to find a recipe from many decades ago and enable its continued life. When Zoli's daughter Susie got in touch with us, we were thrilled to hear her dad's story and be able to re-create some of his treats. And the jam rings remind us all of our childhood. ~ *MMCC*

Zoli Romer

Jam Ring Biscuits

300 g (2 cups/10½ oz) plain (all-purpose) flour, plus extra

300 g (2 cups/10½ oz) self-raising (self-rising) flour

400 g (14 oz) unsalted butter, at room temperature

200 g (1¼ cups/7 oz) icing (confectioners') sugar

2 eggs, lightly beaten

1 tablespoon vanilla sugar (see note)

110 g (⅓ cup) strawberry or apricot jam (jelly)

icing (confectioners') sugar, extra

Preheat the oven to 180°C (350°F/Gas 4). Line a large baking tray.

In an electric mixer, beat together the flours, butter, icing sugar, egg and vanilla sugar until a dough is formed. Roll the dough into a disc, wrap in plastic wrap and refrigerate for 30 minutes.

On a lightly floured benchtop, roll out the dough to a thickness of 2–3 mm (⅛ inch). Using a 7 cm (2¾ inch) round cookie cutter, cut out 40 circles. Half will be for the base of the biscuits and half will be for the top ring.

Using a 4 cm (1½ inch) round cookie cutter, cut out the centre of 20 of the circles to form a ring. To re-use the centre circles that are not needed, join them together, knead lightly, cover with plastic wrap and refrigerate for at least 10 minutes; you will then be able to roll out some extra biscuits.

Place the large circles and rings on the prepared baking tray.

Bake for 15 minutes or until pale golden, then allow to cool on the tray. When cool, spread ¾ teaspoon of jam across each large circle. Place the ring on top of each base. Sprinkle with the extra icing sugar if desired.

Store in an airtight container for up to 1 week.

Note – To make vanilla sugar, store a split vanilla bean in 1 kg (2 lb 4 oz) caster (superfine) sugar in an airtight container. Shake vigorously and allow the vanilla flavour to permeate for at least 1 week before using. Seal the container until ready to use. Lasts for months.

Makes 36

Photo overleaf

Part of our *nachas* is seeing the joy our cooks' families get from being part of our project. Martin is so happy that his late mother Eve's recipe is in our book; it is a beautiful legacy for his family. Her story will now be told across many generations, in many places around the world, as people make and savour her delightful biscuits. And how can we not love a biscuit that is named (and looks like) a toy we all grew up with? ~ *MMCC*

See Eve's story on page 284

Eve Winecier

Yoyos

175 g (6 oz) unsalted butter, at room temperature
40 g (¼ cup/1½ oz) icing (confectioners') sugar, sifted
¼ teaspoon vanilla extract
225 g (1½ cups/8 oz) plain (all-purpose) flour, sifted
40 g (¼ cup/1½ oz) custard powder, sifted

Filling

50 g (1¾ oz) butter, softened
80 g (½ cup/3 oz) icing (confectioners') sugar, sifted
25 g (2 tablespoons/1 oz) custard powder, sifted

Preheat the oven to 180°C (350°F/Gas 4). Line a baking tray.

In an electric mixer, cream together the butter and icing sugar until light and fluffy. Add the vanilla extract, the flour and custard powder and mix gently until a dough forms. Roll teaspoonfuls of the dough into walnut-sized balls and place on the prepared tray. Flatten the top of each with a fork. This will make about 32 biscuits.

Bake for 12 minutes or until just golden underneath. Allow to cool on a wire rack.

To make the filling, in an electric mixer, beat the butter, icing sugar and custard powder together until smooth.

Once the biscuits are completely cool, place ½ teaspoon of the filling on the flat side of one biscuit and press the flat side of another on top to form a sandwich.

Makes 16. Store in an airtight container for up to 1 week.

EVE WINECIER

I remember the pleasure my mother had in baking enormous *challahs* that held centre stage on many *simcha* head tables, including the weddings of my three sisters.

My mother, Eve Winecier, was born in Biala Poldowski, Poland, but grew up and spent most of her life in the small coastal town of Hastings, New Zealand. Our grandparents had immigrated to New Zealand in 1919 and were part of the foundations of an isolated but observant Jewish community that thrived for many years.

As a young woman, Eve moved to Wellington where she met my father, Sam, a Holocaust survivor, and they married. They moved back to Hastings and raised us – four children – in a traditional Jewish home that was always full of laughter and the aromas of Mum's cooking.

Eve's traditional upbringing placed food at the centre of her family life and cooking seemed to be so natural for her. She also knew how to use the amazing produce that New Zealand had to offer. We grew up eating the best of both worlds with *kreplach* and chicken soup competing with epic lamb roasts with all the trimmings. All meals were finished with some of the abundant preserved fruits that filled our cupboards.

It was in baking that Eve really excelled. She worked in bakeries in Hastings and Wellington after leaving school and practised her skills at home making a non-stop array of biscuits, slices and cakes. It was her favourite pastime and she would always produce tins full of fresh biscuits – Kiwi crisps, peanut biscuits, afghans and yoyos. In Mum's opinion there was never a bad time for a yoyo biscuit with a cup of tea or a glass of milk.

Two of my sisters and I moved to Melbourne before our parents joined us in 1981. My last sister arrived in 2009, and we all now live here with our own families. Each of us has inherited Mum's love for cooking, faithfully replicating her favourite recipes and passing them on to our own children.

Mum passed away in 2003 and her ten grandchildren still remember hanging off their nana's apron strings while she effortlessly made them their favourite treats. At the top of their list were her yoyos, which always truly melted in the mouth with every bite.

– *Martin Winecier, Eve's son*

EVE'S RECIPE

Yoyos: page 283

DEVORAH BARNES

I am consumed by wanderlust. Every year I try to visit at least one country I haven't been to before, and at last count I have been to almost 50. As much as I adore travel, I do love coming home to my familiar, comfortable environment, and back to my absolute passion – cooking. For me it's a labour of love, a tangible way to express love for my family and friends.

My travels and diverse heritage have fuelled an obsession for collecting recipes from all over the world. My Libyan-born father grew up in Israel with Italian and Spanish parents and my mom is second-generation South African from Russian stock. I have enjoyed years living in London and parts of the USA, and now I am happy to call Johannesburg home.

When I was little, I couldn't wait to lick the bowl whenever my mother made a chocolate cake. Even now I love to cook anything sweet; my specialty is baking and decorating birthday cakes for my nieces and nephews. These laughter-filled escapades are always spent with my sister, Tanya, after the children go to bed. They are an opportunity for us to spend quality time together and to create memories that will last forever.

DEVORAH'S RECIPE

Muesli Rusks: page 286

South African rusks go as far back as the Anglo Boer war, when soldiers travelled across the country with 'twice-baked' biscuits, called rusks, as they lasted the journey and didn't spoil. They dunked the rusks into their hot coffee (yum!), which is what we all grew up doing. I'd searched for years for the best recipe and, when my friend Devorah shared hers with me, I finally found my perfect rusk. ～ *Lynn, MMCC*

See Devorah's story on page 285

Devorah Barnes

Muesli Rusks

450 g (3 cups/1 lb) wholemeal (whole-wheat) flour

125 g (1 cup/4½ oz) natural muesli with dried fruit

100 g (1 cup/3⅓ oz) oat bran

95 g (½ cup, lightly packed/3¼ oz) brown sugar

1½ teaspoons baking powder

¾ teaspoon bicarbonate of soda (baking soda)

½ teaspoon cream of tartar

½ teaspoon sea salt

250 g (9 oz) butter, melted

250 ml (1 cup) buttermilk

Start this recipe a day before serving.

Preheat the oven to 190°C (375°F/Gas 5). Line a large baking tray.

In a bowl, combine the flour, muesli, oat bran, sugar, baking powder, bicarbonate of soda, cream of tartar and salt. Mix well. Add the melted butter and buttermilk and, with a wooden spoon, stir for a few minutes until well combined.

Shape the mixture into ovals using an ice-cream scoop or 2 dessert spoons and place side by side, touching, on the prepared trays. This will make about 35 ovals. Bake for 45 minutes or until golden. The rusks will join together while baking.

Remove from the oven and allow to cool for at least 30 minutes.

Reduce the temperature to 100°C (210°F). Separate and space out the baked rusks on the tray and bake for a further 6 hours or until golden and dry.

Store in an airtight container for up to 1 month.

Makes 35

I grew up around the corner from Helen and her family and I remember the early Kez's Kitchen's days and their iconic (and super-thin) almond bread biscuit. I loved it way back then, and I'm so excited we finally have Helen's heirloom recipe for *mandelbrot* (Yiddish for almond bread) to share with the world. ~ *Lisa, MMCC*

See Helen's story on page 290

Helen Carp

Almond Bread

250 g (1½ cups) raw almonds
6 egg whites, at room temperature
230 g (1 cup/8¼ oz) caster (superfine) sugar
300 g (2 cups/10½ oz) plain (all-purpose) flour

Preheat the oven to 165°C (330°F/Gas 3). To toast the almonds, place them on a baking tray and cook for 20 minutes. Allow to cool slightly.

Lightly grease a small loaf tin.

In an electric mixer, whisk the egg whites until soft peaks form, then gradually add the sugar, whisking until thick and glossy. Mix in the flour, beating slowly. Using a spatula, gently fold in the almonds.

Pour the mixture into the prepared tin and bake for 1 hour or until a skewer inserted in the middle comes out clean. Remove from the tin and allow to cool. If not slicing immediately, wrap in plastic wrap and refrigerate for up to 2 days or freeze until ready to slice and bake.

Line 2 large baking trays. Remove the loaf and slice with a sharp serrated knife into 3 mm (⅛ inch) slices, then place the slices flat on the prepared trays.

Bake for 25 minutes or until light golden brown. Place on a wire rack to cool completely.

Store in an airtight container for up to 2 weeks.

Makes 50

HELEN CARP

How I loved going to my buba's for fried liver and onions on a Saturday evening to see out Shabbat. Now, my grandchildren and I adore cooking together. We have spent many wonderful days devising TV show-inspired cooking competitions and setting up our own production lines to make biscuits such as our favourite melting moments. Over the years, I've also visited their schools to teach the students baking.

I live in Melbourne, a proud third-generation Australian. My father's family came to Australia from Warsaw, Poland, in the 1920s, thankfully before the war. Incredibly, when my first grandson was born, there were five generations of the family living in Australia.

My Polish buba was a traditional European cook, who never seemed to use a recipe, but put together the most delectable meals every Friday night. My Australian nana would make afternoon tea every Friday, which became a family tradition. They both welcomed us with an abundance of food and love.

My own cooking started at school in domestic science class. My mother worked and arranged for someone else to prepare quite plain meals. This inspired me to make sure my own family always had wonderful food on the table and a freshly baked cake or a batch of biscuits ready and waiting. This led to the creation of Kez's Kitchen, which my daughter Keren and I started in 1991. I am still involved some 25 years later and the company is going strong, baking biscuits and selling them around the world.

I value the traditions that surround so many of our dishes; the love that goes into making labour-intensive *kneidlach* and *gefilte* fish, and the smell of slow-cooking *cholent* wafting through the house remind me of my childhood and the festivals that bring unique flavours and foods.

HELEN'S RECIPES

Frangipani Cake: page 243
Almond Bread: page 289

MARSHA SHALVI

Forty-five years ago, I moved from Southend-on-Sea in Essex, England, to Israel for the sheer love of this country and all it stands for. I now live with my husband along the sandy beach coast of Netanya, Israel. I love the freedom of being a secular Jew in a country where I don't have to think twice about who I am. I admire the strength of the Jewish heritage, including the wonderful Yiddish language, and all the recipes that have survived through endless generations, hurdles and heartache.

I love how our traditional foods can make us feel like part of one big happy family, wherever we are in the world. My first Friday dinner at the home of an Israeli family featured chopped liver, chicken soup and roast chicken. My first Friday dinner at the home of an Australian family also included chopped liver, chicken soup and roast chicken. These traditional dishes cross borders and bring the Jewish people together.

I love to cook what my grandchildren love – meatballs and chicken schnitzels. I have become well known for my halva cookies and it is especially heart-warming that my daughter-in-law and granddaughter in Australia bake the cookies with me – all on Skype or FaceTime.

MARSHA'S RECIPE

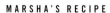

Halva Biscuits: page 292

HUGUETTE ADES

I have such wonderful memories of life in Egypt, living in both Alexandria and Cairo, especially coming home after school and eating a most delicious rice pudding with cinnamon on top. Sadly my life changed at age ten when I lost my mother. It was time to start looking after myself and, thanks to my older sister, I learnt the basics of cooking.

I married at age 22 and later moved with my husband to Adelaide, where he had family. I was blessed with the most wonderful sister-in-law, Renée, an exceptional cook who taught me so much, including one of my favourite recipes, *menenas*. Hers looked like lace and were always perfect – every single one was exactly the same size.

We loved to entertain, often holding parties and cooking for many people. I'd serve food that was influenced by my early life in Egypt, which was a very cosmopolitan country with a strong French, Italian, Spanish and Greek influence. Those memories still make me smile. My husband was vegetarian, so I adapted my cooking and he told me we should always eat at home – he much preferred my cooking to any restaurant. I told him that wasn't quite fair!

Things are a little bit quieter now. My favourite time is baking *biscuits doux* (sweet biscuits) with my three granddaughters in Australia. Until recently, I even posted boxes of them to two of my granddaughters when they were living in the USA, by airmail!

HUGUETTE'S RECIPES

Syrian Pita Bread (Pain Shami): page 47
Menenas: page 294

We're always excited by recipe recommendations from family members. Dora Hechtman from Sydney sent us this recipe from her daughter's mother-in-law, Marsha, from Israel. If you love halva or tahini, as we do, you will adore these. Say no more. As an option, you can replace the tahini with peanut butter. ~ *MMCC*

See Marsha's story on page 291

Marsha Shalvi

Halva Biscuits

100 g (3½ oz) unsalted butter,
   at room temperature
110 g (½ cup/4 oz) caster
   (superfine) sugar
1 teaspoon vanilla extract
135 g (½ cup/4¾ oz) tahini
   (raw sesame paste)
180 g (1 cup plus 2 tablespoons/6½ oz)
   plain (all-purpose) flour
½ teaspoon baking powder
40 blanched almonds

Preheat the oven to 160°C (325°F/Gas 3). Line a large baking tray.

In an electric mixer, beat the butter and sugar until creamy. Add the vanilla and tahini and mix.

Sift the flour and baking powder together and fold into the mixture with a wooden spoon. With your hands, gently roll small walnut-sized balls of dough and place on the prepared tray. Press an almond on top of each ball.

Bake for 20 minutes or until golden underneath. Remove from the oven and allow to cool completely on the tray.

Store in an airtight container for up to 1 week.

Makes 40

We had the pleasure of the company of the charming Huguette in the MMCC kitchen, making these extraordinary shortbread pastries. Videoing her every move, we watched so we could replicate the way she kneaded each piece of dough in her hand, flattened it in her palm and then shaped it around the sticky date filling. Using her pastry pincher – a little device that looks like wide tweezers with tiny prongs on the end – we learnt to delicately mark a pattern along both sides of the pastry, meeting at the top. So pretty. These lovely date pastries bring a bit of the old world into our modern times.

~ MMCC

See Huguette's story on page 291

Huguette Ades

Menenas

500 g (3⅓ cups) pitted dried dates
250 ml (1 cup) water
½ teaspoon vanilla sugar
   (see note page 281)
⅛ teaspoon ground cinnamon
200 g (1⅓ cups/7 oz) plain
   (all-purpose) flour
300 g (2 cups/10½ oz) self-raising
   (self-rising) flour
300 g (10½ oz) unsalted butter, melted
2 tablespoons water
icing (confectioners') sugar, for dusting

In a glass bowl, place the dates with the water. Microwave on high for 3 minutes. Drain the water and transfer the dates to a food processor, then process until it is a thick paste. Allow the mixture to cool completely and set aside. Add the vanilla sugar and cinnamon. Set aside.

Preheat the oven to 160°C (325°F/Gas 2). Line a baking tray.

To make the dough, sift the flours together into a bowl. Add the melted butter and water and mix with a wooden spoon or by hand until you have a soft dough.

Measure 30 g (1 oz) pieces of the dough and knead each one a little in your hand until it is smooth. Form a disc of about 8 cm (3 inches) in your flattened palm.

Put a teaspoon of the date mixture in the centre of the disc and bring the dough up and around to seal. With your hands, shape it into a torpedo with slightly pointed ends, turning the menena over so the seam is at the bottom.

Using a pastry pincher or a fork, gently mark the pastry in a 'V' shape from one end to the other along the top ridge. Repeat with the remaining dough and date mixture.

Place the *menenas* on the prepared tray and bake for 20 minutes or until golden underneath. Allow to cool completely, then dust with icing sugar. Store in an airtight container at room temperature for up to 1 week.

Makes 36

We Australian girls had our first taste of *teiglach* in Sydney thanks to the huge South African community here. So popular, and essential at Jewish New Year, we found these ring biscuits soaked in very dark sweet syrup quite unusual. We never imagined that, in 2015, Karyn and her daughter Robyn would come to our kitchen and lead us on our own journey into the magical world of *teigels*. We watched, took notes and learnt. It took us a couple of tries in the MMCC kitchen and then we succeeded! We are delighted to share this recipe – which we now love – to help carry on the old Lithuanian tradition of *teiglach* and bring them into the 21st century. ~ *M M C C*

See Karyn's story on page 300

Karyn Moskow

Teiglach

6 eggs, less 1 white
2 tablespoons sunflower oil
2 tablespoons brandy
1 teaspoon caster (superfine) sugar
1 teaspoon ground ginger
½ teaspoon baking powder
finely grated zest of 1 large orange
3 cups (450 g/1 lb) plain (all-purpose) flour, plus extra

Line a large baking tray and sprinkle with flour.

To make the *teigel*, in a large bowl of an electric mixer, whisk the eggs for about 5 minutes or until light and fluffy. Change to the beater attachment and, with the motor running, add the oil, brandy, sugar, ginger, baking powder and zest.

Add 2 cups of the flour and mix gently. Slowly add the remaining flour, a little at a time, until a sticky dough is formed that is easy to handle. Tip the dough onto a floured benchtop. Remove a walnut-sized piece of dough and, with floured hands, roll into a small sausage. Fold the sausage over so the ends are on top of each other, then roll out once again to form a sausage. Make the *teigel* by wrapping the sausage around 2 fingers to form a ring, then press lightly to join the ends. Place the *teigel* on the prepared tray. Repeat until all the dough has been used.

Put the tray outside (covered with an insect net if needed) in the sun until they are hard, for at least 1 hour (and up to 2 hours), turning halfway through.

Syrup

2 kg (4½ lb) golden syrup
  (light treacle) (see note)
440 g (2 cups) sugar
500 ml (2 cups) water
2 tablespoons ground ginger
500 ml (2 cups) boiling water

To cook the *teigel*, place the golden syrup, sugar and water in an extra-large stockpot (preferably 20 litre/20 quarts, stainless steel) and bring to the boil over high heat. Tie a clean tea towel (dish cloth) around the lid to prevent moisture dripping into the pot while boiling. Once the syrup is boiling, slip in the *teigels* and cover with the lid. Give it a shake and wait to see the steam coming out of the top. Once this happens, reduce the heat to medium and boil gently for 20 minutes. Remove the lid and very gently stir to coat all the *teigels* in syrup; do this quickly, then replace the lid. Ensure that the syrup continues to boil steadily, not too fast. Lift the lid and stir every 10 minutes or so until the *teigels* sound hollow and hard when tapped with a wooden spoon. This will take around 35–45 minutes. Watch carefully towards the end that the syrup doesn't burn; it needs to be dark, thick and frothy but not burnt.

Once the *teigels* sound hollow, add the ginger and stir again. Turn off he heat and very carefully add the boiling water. Stir gently and, using a slotted spoon, remove the *teigels* one by one and place on baking paper on the benchtop.

Store in an airtight container for up to 2 weeks. Freeze for up to 2 months.

Note – Karyn uses 'Lyle's' brand golden syrup and always re-uses the syrup from cooking the *teigels* for baking or desserts. If making another batch of *teigels*, combine up to two tins of the 'used' syrup with three tins of new syrup.

Makes 35–40

Photo overleaf

KARYN MOSKOW

I was taught to cook almost everything from scratch, thanks to my mother, Ray Kibur, who always believed in cooking and eating homemade and healthy food.

I was born and grew up in Bloemfontein, the judicial capital of South Africa, and moved to Sydney some thirty years ago. My grandparents came to South Africa in search of a better life from Lithuania, Russia and Ireland, bringing their Jewish traditions with them. My mother's grandparents stayed behind in Lithuania and Mum remembers them sending tins of *teiglach*, sweet syrup biscuits baked from an heirloom family recipe, all the way to South Africa. It must have taken months for them to arrive by sea post. She still remembers the aroma as she popped a tin open and ate the syrup straight out with a spoon.

My mother and I would cook all the traditional Jewish foods for the festivals and family celebrations at our home but it was the *teiglach* that she struggled to re-create with the same taste as her grandmother's and took years to get it right. She then taught me to make *teiglach* and years later showed my young daughters how to make them. We all relish the sheer joy of eating them, now that we have perfected the recipe. I keep a huge pot especially to make *teiglach* and always enjoy spending the day making an enormous batch. It's wonderful to share them with my family and friends for special *simchas*.

Cooking is a labour of love for me. Now that my children are adults, I realise how important traditional foods are. I love cooking with my two daughters, and they are now teaching me a thing or two. Nothing makes me happier than hearing my grandchildren's excitement as they smell the chicken soup cooking on my stove and they truly love our other traditional foods like *perogen* for Rosh Hashanah and *kneidlach* for Passover. Now we have four generations connected to our heritage through the food we make.

KARYN'S RECIPES

Poached Peaches with Seekhund: page 216
Teiglach: page 296

EVE GRAF

My mother, Eve Graf, was the proud wife of the first rabbi of the Cardiff Reform Synagogue in Wales. She was born in Berlin, Germany, in 1918, and was brought up by her widowed mother. Eve met and married my father, a rabbi, in Berlin when she was only 19, and as newlyweds they were forced to flee from their home with his parents. My father was very brave and outspoken against the Nazi regime and after Kristallnacht it was no longer safe for them. That was the spring of 1939, a mere six months before the outbreak of World War II.

Thankfully my parents were sponsored for immigration by relatives living in Manchester and so they headed to Britain. My father found a post as a rabbi in the Reform Synagogue in Bradford, where my brother and I were born. From here we moved to the Welsh capital, Cardiff, to set up the newly formed reform community; it is still the only one in Wales. My father was the first rabbi in 1948 when the Cardiff New Synagogue opened, later to be called the Cardiff Reform Synagogue. He was a ground-breaking rabbi, involving women in the service, using music to add Passover spirituality and encouraging the *cheder* (religious school) children to run their own services. Often after the service when everybody had left, he would change out of his gown and play the organ, sometimes improvising his own music.

Eve was beautiful, elegant and had a quiet dignity. She was ever so capable and was an all-round excellent, inventive cook, renowned for her superb baking. Many recipes were learnt from her mother, who sadly perished in the camps, and her sister-in-law who thankfully had moved to South Africa before the war. Eve was very thoughtful and helpful to everybody; we regularly had people joining us for a meal after synagogue services or for afternoon tea. She was in every way a traditional *rebbetzin*: chair of the synagogue Catering Committee, an active member of the Ladies' Guild, and she served on the *Chevra Kadisha*.

My mother passed away in 1992. No one will ever make almond slices as light and melt-in-the-mouth as hers.

– *Barbara Graf, daughter*

EVE'S RECIPE

Passover Almond Slices and Jam Cookies: see overleaf

These are the most exciting Passover cookies we have seen in a long time. This wonderful recipe from last century and the other side of the world will now start its new journey in Australia. Back in the 1950s, Eve encouraged the many refugees to enliven the synagogue's social events with their baking skills. Diana Soffa, who shared Eve's recipe with us, says that the almond slices are the only reason her own family survives Passover. The dough ingredients make enough for one tray of slices and one batch of cookies. ~ *MMCC*

See Eve's story on page 301

Dough

115 g (⅔ cup/4 oz) potato flour, plus extra
115 g (heaped ¾ cup/4 oz) superfine matzo meal (cake meal)
75 g (⅓ cup/2¾ oz) caster (superfine) sugar
60 g (½ cup, packed/2 oz) ground almonds or hazelnuts
140 g (5 oz) unsalted butter, at room temperature
finely grated zest of ½ lemon
1 egg, beaten

Slices Topping

80 g (¼ cup) tart apricot jam (jelly)
115 g (4 oz/1 stick) butter, at room temperature
115 g (½ cup) caster (superfine) sugar
120 g (1 cup, packed) ground almonds or hazelnuts
2 eggs
3 teaspoons superfine matzo meal (cake meal)
1 tablespoon vanilla sugar (see note on page 281)
70 g (½ cup) slivered almonds

Jam Cookies

2 tablespoons tart apricot jam (jelly)

Eve Graf

Passover Almond Slices and Jam Cookies

Preheat the oven to 180°C (350°F/Gas 4). Line a 28 × 18 cm (11 × 7 inch) slice tin.

To make the dough, in a large bowl, mix the flour, matzo meal, sugar and ground nuts together with a wooden spoon. Rub in the butter with your fingertips until you have crumbs, then add the lemon zest and egg and mix until a dough is formed. (Alternatively, this can be done in the food processor.)

Divide the dough into 2 pieces. Set 1 aside. On a lightly potato-floured benchtop, roll out 1 piece to fit the tin and lay the dough on the base. Spread the jam all over the dough.

For the topping, in an electric mixer, combine the butter, sugar, nuts, eggs, matzo meal and vanilla sugar and beat until smooth and creamy. Spread the topping over the jam and scatter with the slivered almonds. Bake for 45 minutes or until golden brown. Allow to cool, then cut into small squares.

While they are baking, start the cookies. You will need a lined baking tray. Using the remaining dough, form smooth small walnut-sized balls. This will make about 24 balls. Place on the prepared tray and, using the top of your thumb, make an indent in the top of each cookie and flatten slightly. Spoon a little jam into each indentation. Bake for 20 minutes or until golden underneath.

Store in airtight containers for up to 1 week.

Makes 21 almond slices and 24 jam cookies

Being a self-confessed brownie addict, I am happy to report we have chosen a winner out of the many brownies we have tasted over the years and tested in our kitchen. Just after we launched our first book in LA, I sampled these at Joan's on Third. Lucky for all of us, Joan has agreed to share her recipe. Take care to not overcook – the centre should be slightly gooey.

~ *Jacqui, MMCC*

See Joan's foreword on page 6

Joan McNamara

Joan's on Third Chocolate Brownies

115 g (4 oz) best-quality dark chocolate (90%)

225 g (8 oz) best-quality dark chocolate (70%)

225 g (8 oz/2 sticks) unsalted butter

460 g (2 cups) caster (superfine) sugar

4 eggs

1 teaspoon vanilla extract

½ teaspoon sea salt

75 g (½ cup/2¾ oz) plain (all-purpose) flour

Preheat the oven to 160°C (325°F/Gas 3). Generously grease a 33 × 23 cm (13 × 9 inch) baking tin and line the base, greasing the paper as well.

Break the chocolate into pieces. Over a double boiler, melt the chocolate and butter. Pour the melted mixture into a mixing bowl or bowl of an electric mixer. Add the sugar and beat until smooth. Add the eggs, vanilla extract and salt and beat well. Gently fold in the flour, just until no lumps remain.

Pour the batter into the prepared tin and smooth the top with a spatula. Bake for 40 minutes or until the sides begin to pull away from the tin. Allow to cool in the tin before cutting.

Makes 12

Thanks

We are so grateful to the generous-spirited and most supportive Catherine Milne, our publisher at HarperCollins Publishers Australia for her understanding of, and commitment to, our project. She got us from the beginning. Thanks to project editor Belinda Yuille and Madeleine James for perfecting all our imperfections in the kindest way possible.

We are thrilled to have a super-talented creative team behind this book. We adore photographer Alan Benson for his brilliant photographs, amazing use of light and his big-heartedness, humour and all-day coffee service. Food stylist David Morgan transforms even the most simple to spectacular, like a magician, with unlimited patience for the five women buzzing around him. We are ecstatic to have book designer Daniel New on board with his inspiring ideas and fabulous designs.

We couldn't do what we do without our incredible behind-the-scenes team. Thanks to Rachel Quintana for her hard work in our test kitchen and studio; she is an essential and much-loved part of the team. We are indebted to Debbie Swibel for taking on the enormous job of recipe filing and office admin. Huge thanks to Michele Brooks, who came on board to draft all the biographies in the book. All have worked with such great efficiency and care, easing our workload so we had time to write this book.

We thank the following who have supported us so generously by donating amazing produce and ingredients:

Excellent chooks and ducks with equally excellent service from the Biboudis family from Birds Galore in Rose Bay North.

Fabulous pasture-raised and grass-fed beef, veal and lamb from our very own MMCC Paula Horwitz's Field to Fork in Bondi, a super-stylish butchery and home-style meal provedore.

An incredible range of every spice we could desire (and more) from herb and spice merchants Gewürzhaus (in those gorgeous little glass jars!) available at their fairy-tale stores in Sydney and Melbourne and online.

The very best fresh fruit, veggies and herbs, as well as a magnificent range of dairy and deli products from our local one-stop-shop, Parisi's Food Hall, Rose Bay.

Thanks to our solicitors Arnold Bloch Leibler, our accountants and auditors MBP Advisory and our accountant Meilea McClelland of Dakota Corporation for doing all the things needed to run a business that we *still* have no idea how to do. And for doing it all *pro bono*.

To Peter Ricci from Yakadanda, for ongoing website assistance, and Selina Power and Madeline Johnston from Super Power Digital, for our social media guidance, all being there pretty much 24/7. To Marnie Perlstein (Personal Fashion Stylist), Garry Siutz (Hair and Makeup) and Samantha Robinson (those beautiful aprons!), thanks for helping us look our best.

To our longstanding MMCC friends – thank you from the bottom of our hearts for your support and guidance: Shannon Blanchard from The Cru Media, Linda Mottram (former host Mornings on ABC 702 Sydney), Sue Jenkins from Accoutrement Cooking School, Dana Cowin (former Editor-in-Chief *Food & Wine*), Vic Alhadeff (CEO, NSW Jewish Board of Deputies), food writer Jill Warren Lucas, food writer and cooking teacher Nancie McDermott, writer Caroline Baum, film-maker Eva Orner and, of course, Joan McNamara, creator of LA foodie institution Joan's on Third.

We welcome our new MMCC friends to the family, with many thanks for helping us in our recipe-collecting endeavours: Karen Berman (worldatmytable.wordpress.com), Paul Entis (Jewish Food Experience), journalist Alex Galbinski, Pat Tanumihardja (ediblewords.com) and Tami Weiser (theweiserkitchen.com).

To the following wonderful cooks who gave us extra guidance in the kitchen: Huguette Ades, Lainie Cadry, Amos Cohen, Rachel Dingoor, Fay Filler, Candy Gold, Nava Levy, Karyn Moskow, Naomi Scesny and Anita Zweig. And an extra shout-out to Lainie, Rachel, Fay and Karyn for making and baking for our photo shoot.

Monday Morning Cooking Club is a not-for-profit company and 100 per cent of all our profits from sales of this book (and all books before) go to charity. We appreciate our ongoing relationship with WIZO NSW and WIZO Australia. Visit our website, mondaymorningcookingclub.com.au, for a full list of charities we support.

Last but not least, it's thanks to the never-ending encouragement and love from our wonderful families, and all their understanding of our many absences and distractions, that the MMCC project is even possible.

~ The MMCC girls xxx

Glossary

Ashkenazi Jews of Eastern European descent.

Bat Mitzvah A girl's coming of age when she turns 12.

beigli A Hungarian pastry roll usually filled with either walnuts or poppy seeds.

Buba / Bubba Grandmother.

bulkas A traditional yeast bun; can be scrolled, pulled apart, and stuffed with chocolate, cinnamon or jam. Popular in South Africa for breaking the fast.

Chabad Also known as Lubavitch, a Hasidic religious movement, well known for its outreach. So when your child is wandering and hungry in Nepal, you know there's always a bowl of chicken soup and a Shabbat meal.

chagim Jewish religious festivals. A really good excuse to gather the extended family together and overindulge in traditional foods.

challah (pronounced HAH-lah) A traditional Jewish plaited yeast bread (often enriched with egg) prepared for Sabbath and festivals; served in pairs.

Chanukah The festival celebrating the 'miracle of the oil' from when the first temple in Jerusalem was destroyed over 2000 years ago. A great excuse to eat fried foods.

charoset / haroset A delicious combination of fresh and/or dried fruits, nuts and wine eaten at the Passover feast to represent the mortar (cement) used by the Jewish people when they were slaves in Egypt. Ingredients vary depending on local products and cuisines. The most common version from Eastern Europe uses apple, walnuts, cinnamon and wine. Excellent on top of matzo.

Chevra Kadisha A Jewish organisation that ensures the bodies of deceased Jews are prepared for burial in the Jewish tradition.

cholent A traditional Jewish dish of (usually) meat, potatoes, beans and barley, which is made before Shabbat begins on a Friday, then slowly cooks all night and is served for Sabbath lunch on Saturday.

couscoussier Double-chambered food steamer to cook couscous. The broth is cooked in the bottom and the couscous is steamed on the top.

fressing Eating with joy and abandon.

gefilte fish A traditional Jewish dish of minced and well-seasoned fish, which is then made into patties and boiled in stock. Traditionally served with a slice of carrot on top and horseradish (*chrain*) on the side.

gribenes Crisp chicken skin and onions fried in rendered chicken fat.

hamantashen Triangular pastry usually stuffed with jam, poppy seeds or cream cheese, eaten on the festival of Purim.

kneidlach Also known as matzo balls, these traditional Jewish dumplings (made from matzo meal, eggs and schmaltz) are served in chicken soup at the Passover feast.

kosher If you keep kosher, you follow the Jewish dietary laws of kashrut; for example, not eating meat and milk products at the same meal, and not eating shellfish, pig products and certain other fish and animals.

kreplach Pasta dumplings filled with meat to eat in chicken soup, like a Jewish ravioli.

Kristallnacht Also referred to as the Night of Broken Glass, a pogrom against Jews throughout Nazi Germany on 9–10 November 1938. Jewish homes, hospitals, businesses and schools were ransacked throughout Germany and Austria.

latkes Shallow-fried potato pancakes, traditional at Chanukah, and delicious anytime, doubles up as a canape with *crème fraîche* and smoked salmon on top.

lokshen kugel Traditional Ashkenazi baked pudding, mostly made from egg noodles.

lubavitcher A member of the Hasidic community. See Chabad. Named after a town in White Russia where the movement was based for 100 years.

mandelbrot Almond bread, aka Jewish biscotti. Twice cooked biscuits, perfect to fress with a cup of tea, especially when you can't fit another thing in.

matzo / matzo meal (matzah) An unleavened bread, like a large square water cracker, eaten at Passover. Matzo meal is ground matzo and is available in coarse, fine or superfine varieties.

matzo kugel Like lokshen kugel but made with matzo instead of noodles.

mazel / mazal Luck, as in 'in life you need a bit of mazel'.

minyan A quorum of ten men (over the age of 13) required for traditional Jewish prayer. Also refers to the prayer gathering after a funeral.

nachas The inexplicable joy one gets from something, often one's children or one's dog.

pareve / parev As part of a kosher diet, neither a meat nor a milk product; can be eaten with anything at any time, includes fruit and vegetables, and interestingly, fish.

Passover See Pesach.

Pesach The eight-day festival of Passover where no bread is eaten to remember the days the Jews were slaves in Egypt, and when our challenge is to cook and eat well without letting bread, flour or leavened products pass our lips.

rebbe Yiddish for rabbi, often used in the Hasidic world.

rebbetzin The wife of a rabbi, often heavily involved in the synagogue community.

Rosh Hashanah The Jewish New Year, celebrated with prayers and much feasting, particularly apples dipped in honey (for a sweet year) and lots of honey cake.

schmaltz The direct translation is 'fat'. In cooking, it is the rendered fat of a chicken; on your body, some say it is the result of too much schmaltz in your cooking.

Seder The customary feast held at Passover time where we sit for hours, drinking too much wine, eating too much food and re-telling the Passover story.

Sephardi / Sephardic In essence, Jews of the Iberian Peninsula (now Spain and Portugal) descent, but nowadays it has a wider meaning and includes Jews who are not Ashkenazi, for example of Iraqi, Indian and North African origin.

Shabbat / Shabbos The Sabbath, a day of complete rest. Begins at sunset on Friday and ends at sunset on Saturday; no work, much prayer and abundant eating.

shmeared / schmeared Our technical term for spreading, e.g. I shmeared butter on my toast.

shtetl A small Jewish village in Eastern Europe. Think *Fiddler on the Roof.*

shul / shule Synagogue, the Jewish house of prayer.

simcha A celebration which pretty much always involves a huge amount of food.

sufganiyot Round fried doughnuts stuffed with jam (jelly). Often eaten at Chanukah to symbolise the oil used in the Temple.

Yehudim Hebrew for Jewish people.

Yeshivah An orthodox Jewish college or seminary.

Yiddish The old spoken language of many Ashkenazi Jews; a mix between German, Hebrew and other languages. Now it is mainly used by parents who don't want their children to understand what they are saying, and for those words that have no direct translation in English.

yiddishkeit The Jewish way of life, customs and practices.

Yom Kippur The Day of Atonement, when the Jewish people atone for their sins. It is a solemn day of fasting, which ends with the blowing of the Shofar (a ram's horn) and yet another feast.

yom tov / yom tovim Jewish festivals and holy days, also a really good excuse to gather the family around the table and eat traditional food. See chagim.

Permissions

Bialys (page 26) adapted and reprinted with permission of the author, from *Meatballs and Matzah Balls: Recipes and Reflections from a Jewish and Italian Life* by Marcia A. Friedman, published by Elsa Jacob Publishing, 2013.

Corn Torte (page 38) adapted and reprinted with permission of the author, from *Pati's Mexican Table: The Secrets of Real Mexican Home Cooking* by Pati Jinich, published by Rux Martin/Houghton Mifflin Harcourt, 2013.

Mufleta (page 56) originally published on theweiserkitchen.com, adapted and reprinted with permission from the author and *The Weiser Kitchen.*

Gazpacho (page 68) reproduced with permission of the author and publisher, from *Absolutely Delicious* by Sharon Glass, published by ATV CC, 2005.

Fish Cakes (page 98) adapted and reprinted with permission of the publisher, from *Ramsay's Best Menus*, by Gordon Ramsay, published by Quadrille (an imprint of Hardie Grant), 2010.

Kale Salad with Gouda (page 86) recipe adapted and printed with permission of the chef from Five Leaves restaurant in Brooklyn NY.

Baked Mustard–Herb Chicken Legs (page 131) from *The New York Times*, 2004-07-14 © 2004 *The New York Times*. All rights reserved. Used by permission and protected by the Copyright Laws of the United States. The printing, copying, redistribution, or retransmission of this Content without express written permission is prohibited.

Roast Chicken with Herbs, Garlic and Shallots (page 128) by Abigail Johnson Dodge, adapted and reprinted with permission from the May 2000 issue of *Fine Cooking* magazine, © 2000, by The Taunton Press Inc. (finecooking.com)

Roman Lamb (page 149) adapted and reprinted with permission of the author, from *Cooking with Myrna Rosen*, published by Howard B. Timmins (Pty) Ltd, 1978.

Standing Rib Roast with Horseradish Crust (page 166) recipe adapted and reprinted from the recipe for 'Roast prime rib of beef with horseradish crust and wild mushrooms' from *Tyler Florence's Real Kitchen: An Indispensable Guide for Anyone who Likes to Cook* by Tyler Florence, copyright © 2003 by Tyler Florence. Used by permission of Clarkson Potter/Publishers, an imprint of the Crown Publishing Group, a division of Penguin Random House LLC. All rights reserved. Any third party use of this material, outside of this publication, is prohibited. Interested parties must apply directly to Penguin Random House LLC for permission.

Olive Oil Chocolate Mousse (page 230) adapted and reprinted with permission of the author, from *Let's Cook Spanish: A Family Cookbook*, by Madrid-based chef and food writer Gabriela Llamas, published by Quarry Books, Quarto Publishing Group USA Inc. (lahuertadelemperador.com)

Warm Date Cake with Pecan Caramel Sauce (page 232) original recipe from (the late) Gretta Anna Teplitzky, adapted and printed with permission of her son, Martin Teplitzky.

Strawberry Rhubarb Cobbler (page 239) adapted and reprinted with permission of the author, from *The Summertime Anytime Cookbook: Recipes from Shutters on the Beach* by Dana Slatkin, published by Clarkson Potter, 2008.

Kitchen Notes

We have tested, retested and tested again to ensure these recipes can be replicated in your kitchen.

MEASUREMENTS

We use standard Australian metric measurements in our test kitchen.

1 cup = 250 ml = 9 fl oz
1 tablespoon = 20 ml = ¾ fl oz
1 teaspoon = 5 ml
1 oz = 28 g

If you are using a 15 ml tablespoon, add an extra teaspoon for each tablespoon specified.

For cake, biscuit and pastry recipes, precision is essential and we recommend weighing ingredients using a digital scale.

OVENS

Our recipes are tested in a domestic oven on conventional heat settings. Oven temperatures can vary and you may need to adjust the cooking time or temperature according to your oven.

SALT

We use two types of salt: fine-grained best-quality salt for most cooking and baking needs, and flaky salt for seasoning during and after cooking.

Kosher salt is not readily available in Australia, however it is interchangeable with either of these.

LANGUAGE

Our books use standard English spelling and grammar, irrespective of where the recipe or contributor originates.

IMPORTANT BITS

1 lemon, juiced = 50 ml (2½ tablespoons) juice
1 stick butter = 113.5 g = 8 (US) tablespoons = 4 oz
   (we have rounded 113.5 g to 115 g in the recipes)
1 sachet (envelope) dried yeast = 7 g = 2¼ teaspoons
Crushed garlic = minced garlic
Shallots/spring onions = green onions = scallions
All herbs are fresh, unless stated otherwise

To make self-raising (self-rising) flour, sift 2 teaspoons baking powder with 150 g (1 cup/6 oz) plain (all-purpose) flour

Eggs are free-range, minimum weight 67 g (2⅓ oz)

For recipes that contain raw eggs, please consult your doctor before eating if you are at risk of the effect of salmonella poisoning.

Index

Kritzer, Amy 85
kugel, pecan-glazed noodle 240

lamb
    and eggplant, Persian 144
    and pea soup 76
    Roman 149
    tagine with dates 146
    Yemenite Rosh Hashanah 150
lavosh 25
lentils and poached chicken 123
Levy, Fela 19
Levy, Nava 54
Levy Redzepi, Nadine 112
Libyan beef with beans 175
lime ice cream 223
liptauer dip (körözött) 34
lithri plaki (fish with ouzo) 110
loaf, Nana's date nut 278
lubia polow 182

malabi, coconut rose 224
malawach 50
mandarin cake with marmalade
    syrup 264
mandelbrot (almond bread) 289
marinated fish 120
marmalade syrup 264
McNamara, Joan 6
meatball tagine with chickpeas 164
menenas 294
Miller, Kathy 266
Monday Morning Cooking Club 7
    chocolate ganache 258
    essential tomato sauce 189
Moroccan carrot and chard salad 170
Moskow, Karyn 300
mousse, olive oil chocolate 230
muesli rusks 286
mufleta 56

Nacamulli, Silvia 198
Nana's date nut loaf 278
New York deli coleslaw 90
Niselow, Lynn 13
Norwegian herring salad 21

oat and seed bread 32
olive oil chocolate mousse 230
olive and pistachio chicken 132
onion, pickled red 120

pain shami (Syrian pita bread) 47
pancakes (mufleta) 56
pangrattato 66
paprika chicken livers 44
parsley, garlic and chilli sauce (zhoug) 51
parsnips and carrots, chermoula-
    spiced 204
passionfruit ice cream 222
Passover almond slices and jam
    cookies 302
pasta alla Norma 200
pasta e patate soup 75
pâté, smoked fish 24
pea and lamb soup 76
peaches, poached, with seekhund 216
pecan
    candied 81
    caramel 240
    caramel sauce 232
    glazed noodle kugel 240
Penny, Naomi 143
Persian chicken soup with gondi 72
Persian cucumber salad 191
Persian lamb and eggplant 144
pickled red onion 120
pie, sweet potato 244
pilaf, Israeli rice 212
pita bread 47
plum cake, Edith's 263
poached chicken with lentils 123
poached peaches with seekhund 216
Polish apple strudel 270
potato
    baked, with horseradish cream 203
    salad, German 202
poussin, fried (backhendl) 124
pudding (savoury), egg strata 192
pudding (sweet), crystallised ginger 236
pumpkin, roasted, and sweet corn salad 94

quinoa herb salad 118

Rabin, Annie 19
rack of veal with herbs 156
red onion, pickled 120
rhubarb strawberry cobbler 239
rice
    with cauliflower, Bengali 210
    lubia polow 182
    pilaf, Israeli 212
    pudding (risalamande) 228

risalamande 228
Ritz, Laurelle 186
roast chicken with herbs, garlic and
    shallots 128
roasted beetroot dip 46
roasted cauliflower 66
    and pear salad 78
roasted pumpkin and sweet corn salad 94
Robbaz, Ronit 106
Roman lamb 149
Romer, Zoli 280
Rosen, Myrna 220
Rosengren, Sissel 20
rusks, muesli 286

Safta Fela's borekas 43
salad
    beetroot and walnut 91
    coriander and chickpea 104
    dressing see dressing; sauce (savoury)
    German potato 202
    grilled capsicum (salade cuite) 170
    heirloom tomato with feta dressing 82
    Israeli farro 89
    kale with gouda 86
    Moroccan carrot and chard 170
    Persian cucumber 191
    quinoa herb 118
    roasted cauliflower and pear 78
    roasted pumpkin and sweet corn 94
    wilted spinach 81
salade cuite (grilled capsicum salad) 170
salmon
    barbecued, with quinoa herb salad 118
    citrus and fennel roasted 117
sambal goreng, chicken 137
Sassoon, Solomon 162
satay
    sauce 160
    beef and chicken 160
sauce (savoury)
    Baja cream 120
    cherry for roast duck 140
    Grandma's super ketchup 35
    horseradish cream 203
    MMCC's essential tomato 189
    satay 160
    tahina 91, 94
    tahini–yoghurt 118
    zhoug 51
    see also dressing